# Get Start
# German

## Rosi McNab

Advisory editor
Paul Coggle

C000182452

For UK order enquiries: please contact Bookpoint Ltd,
130 Milton Park, Abingdon, Oxon OX14 4SB.
*Telephone:* +44 (0) 1235 827720. *Fax:* +44 (0) 1235 400454.
Lines are open 09.00–17.00, Monday to Saturday, with a 24-hour
message answering service. Details about our titles and how to
order are available at www.teachyourself.com

For USA order enquiries: please contact McGraw-Hill Customer
Services, PO Box 545, Blacklick, OH 43004-0545, USA.
*Telephone:* 1-800-722-4726. *Fax:* 1-614-755-5645.

For Canada order enquiries: please contact McGraw-Hill Ryerson
Ltd, 300 Water St, Whitby, Ontario L1N 9B6, Canada.
*Telephone:* 905 430 5000. *Fax:* 905 430 5020.

Long renowned as the authoritative source for self-guided learning –
with more than 50 million copies sold worldwide – the *Teach Yourself*
series includes over 500 titles in the fields of languages, crafts,
hobbies, business, computing and education.

British Library Cataloguing in Publication Data: a catalogue record
for this title is available from the British Library.

Library of Congress Catalog Card Number: on file.

First published in UK 1992 as *Teach Yourself Beginner's German*
by Hodder Education, part of Hachette UK, 338 Euston Road,
London NW1 3BH.

First published in US 1992 by The McGraw-Hill Companies, Inc.

This edition published 2010.

The *Teach Yourself* name is a registered trade mark of
Hodder Headline.

Typeset by MPS Limited, A Macmillan Company.

Illustrated by Barking Dog Art, Sally Elford, Oxford Designers and
Illustrators Ltd.

Printed in Great Britain for Hodder Education, an Hachette UK
Company, 338 Euston Road, London NW1 3BH?

The publisher has used its best endeavours to ensure that the URLs
for external websites referred to in this book are correct and active
at the time of going to press. However, the publisher and the author
have no responsibility for the websites and can make no guarantee
that a site will remain live or that the content will remain relevant,
decent or appropriate.

Hachette UK's policy is to use papers that are natural, renewable
and recyclable products and made from wood grown in sustainable
forests. The logging and manufacturing processes are expected to
conform to the environmental regulations of the country of origin.

Impression number    10 9 8 7 6 5 4 3 2

Year                          2014 2013 2012 2011

# Contents

# Credits

# Meet the author

Rosi McNab is a very experienced language teacher and author. Her ground-breaking language training materials, books, videos, audio and interactive CDs are in use in schools, colleges and homes all over the world.

She attributes her success to the fact that she always approaches language training from the learner's perspective. Her favourite quotation is 'you cannot teach a language, you can only create the situation in which it can be learned' (Wilhelm von Humboldt, German philosopher and linguist 1767–1836). She has spent most of her working life trying to create situations to help people of all abilities and from all walks of life to learn other languages. One of the biggest barriers to language learning is lack of confidence in one's own ability. As a school pupil herself she was led to believe that she was 'no good' at languages, but later she found the difference between being taught and being helped to learn. For this reason she is guided by what a learner can learn rather than what a book or teacher can teach. In books for beginners she avoids complicated grammatical terminology and explains structures in layman's language and by example, and suggests ways to help you to remember new words and phrases more easily.

# *Only got a minute?*

As Europe's largest economy Germany is a key member of the EU and German is one of the three working languages of the EU. It is spoken by about 105 million native speakers and another 80 million non-native speakers. It is the official language in Germany, Austria, Liechtenstein, Luxembourg and part of Switzerland and a recognized official language in the Czech Republic, Denmark, Hungary, Namibia, Romania and Slovakia.

English and German share a common Anglo-Saxon heritage and many of the most common English words have Germanic roots. The meaning of some words is obvious: **Winter** – *winter*; **Sommer** – *summer*; **Butter** – *butter*; **Wind** – *wind*; **Hand** – *hand*; **Arm** – *arm*.

Some are a little less obvious but if you say them aloud their meaning becomes clear: **Wasser** – *water*; **Tee** – *tea*; **Milch** – *milk*; **Zucker** – *sugar*; **Regen** – *rain*; **Sonne** – *sun*; **Willkommen** – *welcome*.

Most names of countries are the same or easy to understand: **England** – *England*; **Schottland** – *Scotland*; **Amerika** – *America*; **Spanien** – *Spain*; **Frankreich** – *France*; **Afrika** – *Africa*.

Some words have taken slightly different meanings in English: **Flasche** – *flask* = *bottle*; **Schweinefleisch** – *swine flesh* = *pork*; **Hund** – *hound* = *dog*.

And some everyday words are quite obvious: **ein Glas Wein** – *a glass of wine*; **eine Flasche Bier** – *a bottle of beer*; **ein Kännchen Kaffee** – *a can (pot) of coffee*: **Telefon** – *telephone*; **Foto** – *photo*; **Computer** – *computer*!

However, you may have noticed one difference … in German all nouns begin with a capital letter!

Language is much more than the study of vocabulary or grammar. This course will focus on your needs as a beginner and on what you want to achieve through the medium of German. The aim is to help you interact with German-speaking people.

# 5 Only got five minutes?

**Guten Morgen!** – *Good morning!*
A lot of English words sound similar to German words. Listen out for them! The context will also help you to understand them.

**1 Bitte** means *Please*.
Be polite: Use it when you stop someone to ask for help.
**Entschuldige** means *Excuse me*.
**Entschuldigen Sie bitte** means *Excuse me please* but you can just say '**bitte**' for short!
If someone thanks you:
You should reply '**bitte**' – *(please) don't mention it.*

**2 Danke** means *Thank you*.
People often use the full expression **Danke schön**.
The two dots symbol over the letter ö is called an **Umlaut** and means you 'squash' the sound of the letter. Try pouting your lips as you say [schurn].
**Vielen Dank** [feelen dank] means *Many thanks* (**v** is pronounced [f])
A lot of words are related to English words.
Look for similarities to help you remember new words. A word which begins with t or th in English will often begin with a **d** sound in German: *this* – **dies** [dees]; *that* – **dass**

**3 Sprechen Sie Englisch?** – *Do you speak English?*
**Sprechen** is like the English word *speak*.
*Speak you English?*
In German you start the question with the main verb:
*Speak you English?*
*Go you to town?* – **Gehen Sie in die Stadt?**
*Must you go?* – **Müssen Sie gehen?**
When you are asking a question the word for *you* is **Sie**.

**4** Ja [ya] means yes and **nein** [nine] means *no*!

**5** Talking about yourself
The word for *I* is **ich**.
**ich habe** – *I have*
**ich bin** – *I am*
It isn't written with a capital i – **ich**.
After **ich** the verb usually ends with **-e**.
**Ich habe** – *I have*; **Ich gehe** – *I go*.

**6** Saying you don't understand
**Ich verstehe nicht** – *I don't understand*. **v** sounds [f]
**verstehe** is pronounced [fairshtayer].
**Ich verstehe nicht.** – lit. *I understand not.*
**v** and **w**
In German **w** is pronounced [v]
Think of the name of the car manufacturer **Volkswagen**.
It sounds: [Folksvaagen] or [fow vay] (VW) for short.
A lot of German question words begin with the letter **w**.
**Wie?** [vee] – *How?*; **Was?** [vas] – *What?*; **Wann?** [van] – *When?*;
**Wo?** [vo] – *Where?*

**7** Watch out for **Wer?** [vair]
It sounds as if it ought to mean *Where?* but it means *Who?*
**Wer kommt?** – *Who is coming?*

**8** Ask to have something repeated:
**Wie bitte?** – *Pardon?* [lit. *How, please?*]

**9** When you see the combined letters **ei** or **ie** you pronounce the
SECOND one as it sounds in English:
**ei** is pronounced [eye]; **ie** is pronounced [ee]
Remember: **ein Glas Bier** – [eye'n glass beer]!

**10** Saying goodbye
**Auf Wiedersehen** means *Goodbye* but other expressions commonly
used include **Tschüss** – *'Bye*.
To make the sound purse your lips and say [tchews] but better still
listen to the recording and imitate it.
**Tschüss** is a widely used and less formal way of saying *Goodbye*.

# 10 Only got ten minutes?

**Twenty starters**

**1** *Hello! Good day!* – **Guten Tag!**

**Gut** means *good* and **Tag** means *day*. A lot of English words sound similar to German words because they come from the same Anglo-Saxon roots as the German language. (Saxony is a part of Germany.) Listen out for the Anglo/Germanic words, like **Bus** and **Butter!**

**2** *Goodbye* – **Auf Wiedersehen**

The letter **w** is pronounced like the English letter *v* so **wiedersehen** sounds [veedersayun] and means *to see again*, and, of course, **Volkswagen** is pronounced [Folks-vaagen]! The letter **v** is pronounced like the English letter *f*.

**3** *I don't understand* – **Ich verstehe nicht**

**Ich** means *I*, **verstehe** means *understand* and **nicht** means *not*.

*I understand not.* There is no need to translate *don't* or *doesn't* into German, just say what you want to say and add *not*. Don't worry, it's easy!

**4** *Please* – **Bitte**

Be polite! **Bitte** means *Please*, but you can use **Bitte** as *Excuse me.* You could say **Entschuldigen Sie bitte** – *Excuse me please*, but **Bitte** will do just as well!

**5** *Thank you* – **Danke schön**

The two dots on the **ö** is called an Umlaut and 'squashes' the sound of the **o** so **schön** sounds like [shurn]. You could also just say **Danke** – *Thanks*.

If someone says **Danke schön** to you you should reply **'bitte'** (*please, don't mention it*).

**6** *Sorry!* – **Entschuldige.**

In the UK we say 'sorry' a lot whether we mean it or not. **Entschuldige** really means *Excuse me*. If someone bumps into you they will probably not say anything but if you bump into someone and want to say 'sorry' this is the best thing to say.

**7** *How are you?* – **Wie geht's?**

This sounds like [vee gates] (V Gates not Bill Gates) so it is easy to remember. It is the informal greeting and it means *How goes it?* and it does not expect you to recite your medical history. The full phrase is: **Wie geht es Ihnen?** but **Wie geht's?** [vee gates] will do just fine.

**8** *Fine, thanks* – **Gut danke**

**Gut** is our word *good* but you pronounce it [goot], and you already know **danke** so that's easy. It is the normal reply to **Wie geht's?**

**9** *I am sorry about that* – **Tut mir Leid**

If you have said: **Wie geht's?** and your respondent has obviously said something that implies they are 'not fine' the best thing to say is **Tut mir Leid** [toot meer light]. It will make you sound properly sympathetic.

### 10 *Yes and no* – **Ja und nein**

*Yes* is easy, it is just **Ja** [yah]... *No* – **Nein** is pronounced [nine].
If you are being offered something it is as well to say: **Ja bitte**, or
**Nein danke**. If it is a nice refreshing glass of white wine on a hot
day and you say **danke**, they will think you mean **Nein danke** and
assume you don't want it. It is a mistake you only make once.

### 11 *What are you called?* – **Wie heißen Sie?**

**Wie,** which is pronounced [vee] means *How: How (are you called?).*
The funny letter in **heißen** is a double **ss**, and whenever you have
the combined vowels **ei** or **ie** you pronounce them like the second
of the two letters: **ei** is pronounced like the English letter *i* or [aye]
and **ie** is pronounced like the letter *e* or [ee], so in that simple
phrase you have four main rules of pronunciation! **w** is *v*, **ei** is *i* and
**ie** is *e* and **ß** is pronounced *ss*. **Sie** means *you.*

**12** *My name is …* – **Ich heiße …**

**Ich** means *I* and **heiße** means *am called*. You could also say: **Mein Name ist …** but the phrase **Ich heiße** also teaches you that after **ich** the verb ends in **-e. Ich heiße**. The **ch** sounds like the *ch* in the Scottish word *loch* as in Loch Lomond.

**13** *I have* – **Ich habe**

You have just learned that after **ich** (*I*) the verb ends in **-e**. The infinitive, the part you find in the dictionary, ends in **-en** so when you say 'I do something' in German you take the **n** off the infinitive. **Haben** means *to have*, so take off the **n** to make **habe: ich habe** – *I have*.

**14** *I am* – **Ich bin**

Of course just when you have learned one rule you come across the exception: the verb *to be* is irregular in most languages and so it is in German, too. This is because it is the most used verb so it has got worn out through over-usage. Look at the English verb *I am, you are, he is …* – the infinitive is *to be*! In German the infinitive is **sein** but the bit you want just now is **ich bin …** .

**15** *I would like* – **Ich möchte.**

You know the Umlaut 'squashes' the sound of the *o* so it sounds a bit like **'ich murchte'** but listen to the recording to hear it properly. **Ich möchte** doesn't sound as if you were saying you would like something but that is what it means and it is one of the most useful phrases you will learn.

**16** *I would like a glass of beer* – **Ich möchte ein Glas Bier**

A good example of German being like the English! **Glas** and **Bier** are both pronounced in the English way. Now all you have to do is substitute the **ein Glas Bier** with whatever you need and you can ask for anything you would like: **ein Glas Wein, eine Tasse Kaffee, eine Pizza, eine Dose Cola ...**

Did you notice that all the nouns like **Glas** (*glass*), Tasse (*cup*), **Dose** (*can*) are written with a capital letter? And of course **Wein** (*wine*) sounds like vine, which is where it comes from.

**17** *Red wine or white wine?* – **Rotwein oder Weißwein?**

**Rot** is *red* and **weiß** is *white*. Remember your rules of pronunciation ... **weiß** is pronounced [vice]. German likes putting two (or sometimes more) words together to make a new word so *red wine* is **Rotwein** and *white wine* is **Weißwein**. [vice vine]. **Rot** is pronounced [rote], not 'rot' as in rotten.

**18** *Where is ...?* – **Wo ist ...?**

The German word for *Where?* is **Wo?**, which you remember is pronounced [vo].

**19** *Where is the hotel?* – **Wo ist das Hotel?**

The word for hotel isn't going to present much problem, but in German all nouns are either masculine, feminine or neuter words and **Hotel** is a neuter word so you say **das Hotel**.

The word for *station* is a masculine or **der** word: **der Bahnhof**, and the word for *town* is a feminine or **die** word: **die Stadt**.

**Der** sounds [dare] and **die** of course sounds [dee]!

The tip is to try to learn the **der/die** or **das** together with a new word as try to commit it to memory – after all, German children have to – but don't worry about it too much if you do get it wrong, because it's the word that follows which is important and if you get that right you will still be understood.

## 20 *The station* – **Der Bahnhof**

Once you have learned one word you can usually recognize (and use) bits of it in other places. **Bahn** is the word for *way* as in **Autobahn** (*way for cars* or *motorway*), **Eisenbahn** or *'iron way'* (*railway*)! **Deutsche Bahn** or **DB** is *German Rail*, the sign you will see on trains and stations, **Straßenbahn** or *'streetway'* is the *tram* and **Untergrundbahn** is the *underground railway*. **Hof** means *palace, large building, court* or *courtyard*, so you can take your pick, but **Bahnhof** just means *railway station*.

# Introduction

The guidelines given in this introduction are intended to provide some useful advice on studying alone and on how to make the most of the course.

If you have the recording, make sure you have your CD player nearby when you are working as you should use it to listen to the dialogues and the exercises. If you don't have a CD player, use the **Pronunciation notes** to help you pronounce the words properly. You should always read the words and the dialogues out loud. This will give you confidence to use them when called upon to do so in a real situation.

People learn in different ways: some like to learn rules, a very few find it easy to learn by heart, some like to learn by writing things down and others prefer to learn by association. Try different methods until you find which works best for you.

---

## How the units work

Within each unit you will find the following components:

### DIALOGUES

As you get more confident you should try taking one or other part in the dialogue. All the dialogues are on the recording. You should practise saying them with the recording.

## VOCABULARY BOXES

These contain **keywords** – words (and phrases) which will help you to understand the text. Practise saying them out loud. Try different ways to help you remember their meaning. Here are some ways you might find helpful:

**1** Cover up the English and see if you can remember what the words mean.
**2** Cover up the German and see if you can remember the German words. You will find this much more difficult.
**3** Write down the first letter of each word and see how many you can remember.
**4** Choose five new words or expressions and try to learn them.
**5** Count how many words there are and see how many you can recall. See if you can think of English words which sound similar, e.g.

**Hund** – (*hound*) *dog*;
**Blume** – (*bloom*) *flower*

### EXERCISES

The various exercises provide practice in the German that you have learned in each unit. It is important to make good use of them so that you can be sure of understanding and remembering the language in one unit before you go on to the next.

The answers to the exercises are given at the back of the book.

### LISTENING EXERCISES

You will need to use the recording for these.

## PRONUNCIATION NOTES

These notes will help you with the pronunciation of new words. However, don't forget to also make good use of the full **Pronunciation guide** given later in this **Introduction**.

In the early units a phonetic version of the sound of words is given in square brackets for new words in the word lists.

### LEARNING TIPS

Suggested strategies for helping you to learn and memorize what you are learning.

### INSIGHT BOXES

These are author's tips, notes about the language, useful expressions and hints about when to use them.

### WORD PATTERNS

All languages behave according to certain patterns and rules. This section helps you by providing models of the patterns of the language. When you have got used to one pattern you can often make lots of new expressions simply by changing a word or part of a word.

### TEST YOURSELF

At the end of each of Units 1–10 there is a 'test yourself' section.

There is also a consolidation test after every five units.

### NOTE ON UNIT 11

Unit 11 is a reference unit on German verbs and does not work like the other units. Although it includes some exercises, there are no dialogues. It is not necessary to learn all the material in Unit 11 at once, but it includes information to which you will need to refer as you continue with the second half of the course.

## SYMBOLS

◄◗ This indicates that the recording is needed for the following section.

This indicates a section giving information about the customs and way of life of the German-speaking countries.

---

## Pronunciation guide

A few tips to help you acquire an authentic accent:

**1** Always say everything out loud, preferably as if you were talking to someone on the other side of the room!
**2** Whenever possible get someone to say the dialogues with you. Listen carefully to the recording, or if possible ask a native speaker to read some of the words for you.
**3** Record your voice and compare it with the recording.
**4** Ask a native speaker to listen to your pronunciation and tell you how to improve it.
**5** Make a list of words that give you trouble and practise them.

And now practise saying these place names:

◄◗ **CD1, TR 1**

Köln Bonn Berlin München Wien Zürich Düsseldorf Frankfurt Hamburg Hannover Leipzig Halle Freiburg Basel

[curl-n] [bon] [bairleen] [m*in-chen] [veen] [ts*irich] [d*isseldoorf] [frank-furt] [ham-burg] [hano-fer] [l-eye-pt-sich] [hal-uh] [fry-boorg] [bah-zel]

* ü sounds as if you were trying to say **u** but actually say **i**!

## German sounds

Most English speakers have little difficulty in pronouncing the German sounds because the two languages share some of their linguistic roots and they both belong to the same family of languages. Many German words are spoken aloud as they are spelt.

### THE CONSONANTS

◆ **CD1, TR 1, 01:16**

Most of these sounds are the same as in English spoken in the south of England. The ones which are not have asterisks:

| | | |
|---|---|---|
| b | as in *bath* | Bad |
| c | as in *camping* | Campingplatz |
| d | as in *dark* | dunkel |
| f | as in *free* | frei |
| g | as in *garden* | Garten |
| h | as in *hard* | hart |
| *j | as *y* in *yes* | ja |
| k | as in *climb* | klettern |
| l | as in *last* | letzte |
| m | as in *man* | Mann |
| n | as in *night* | Nacht |
| p | as in *place* | Platz |
| *qu | as *kv* in *Kvetch* | Qualität *(quality)* |
| r | produced at the back of the throat | rot |
| *s | as *z* in *zone* | Sohn (son) |
| t | as in *tea* | Tee |
| *v | as *f* in *follow* | Volkswagen (**folksvaagen**) |
| *w | as *v* in *van* | Wecker *(alarm clock)* |
| x | as in *fax* | Fax |
| y | as *y* in *yen* | Yen |
| *z | as *ts* in *tsetse* | Zeitung *(newspaper)* |

[In southern Germany, the 'r' is trilled.]

## THE VOWELS

◀) CD1, TR 1, 02:47

The vowels have a long and short form.

The short form is normally used when followed by two or more consonants and the long form when followed by one consonant, or h + one consonant.

The short form is given first:

| a as *a* | in *cat* | Katze |
|----------|----------|-------|
| | *father* | Vater |
| e as *e* | in *bed* | Bett |
| *ay* | *day* | Tee *(tea)* |
| i as *i* | in *pit* | mit *(with)* |
| | *kilo* | Kilo |
| o as *o* | in *not* | noch *(yet)* |
| | *home* | ohne *(without)* |
| u as *u* | in *butcher* | Bus |
| *oe* | in *shoe* | Schuh |
| | | Guten Tag! *(good day)* |

## SPECIAL LETTERS AND SOUNDS

◀) CD1, TR 1, 03:29

**1** It is difficult to represent these sounds in English. If possible you should listen to the recording and practise them after it:

ä ö ü

¨ is called an 'Umlaut' and is used on an a, o or u. It changes the sound of the word.

The short form is given first:

| ä sounds | *eh* | Mädchen (*girl*) |
| | *ay* | spät (*late*) |
| ö sounds | *uh* | wöchentlich (*weekly*) |
| | *er* | schön (*pretty*) |
| ü sounds | *i* | fünf (*five*) |
| | *u* | Bücher (*books*), Tür (*door*) |

**2** ß represents 'ss' and is used after a long vowel:
Straße (*street*), Fuß (*foot*)

**3** ch is pronounced as *ch* in the Scottish word *loch*
ich (*I*) Buch (*book*)

**4** au is pronounced *ow* as in *owl* Frau (*Mrs*)
Auf Wiedersehen! (*goodbye*)
äu is pronounced *oy* as in *coy* Fräulein (*Miss*)

**5** At the end of a word:

| b | is pronounced *p* | halb (*half*) |
| d | is pronounced *t* | Hund (*dog*) |
| g | is pronounced *k* | Tag (*day*) |
| ig | is pronounced *'ch* | fertig (*ready*) |
| s | is pronounced *s* (not *z*) | Haus (*house*) |

**6** ei is pronounced *eye* drei (three),   Wein (*wine*)
ie is pronounced *ee* vier (four),   Bier (*beer*)

**7** sch is pronounced *sh* as in Schuh (*shoe*)
sp is pronounced *shp* as in spät (*late*)
st is pronounced *sht* as in Stadt (*town*)

**8** e at the end of a word is pronounced *-uh:*
Bitte (*please*) Danke (*thank you*)

# 1

# Grüßen und Begrüßung
## Greetings

In this unit you will learn how to
- *Say 'hello' and 'goodbye'*
- *Greet and address someone*
- *Ask to speak to someone*
- *Say you don't understand*
- *Ask if anyone speaks English*

## Before you start

Read the introduction to the course which gives some useful advice on studying alone and on how to make the most of the course.

If you have the recording, make sure you have it handy as you'll be using it when you work with the **Dialogues** and the **Pronunciation notes**. If you don't have the recording, use the **Pronunciation guide** in the introduction to help you with the pronunciation of new words and phrases.

## LEARNING TIPS

To help yourself to use this course as effectively as possible, follow this study guide (and adapt it to suit your own learning patterns as you go along, if you wish):

**1** Listen to or read the **Dialogues** once or twice (listen without the book first of all, if you have the recording).
**2** Go over each one bit by bit in conjunction with the **Key words**. Do the same for each of the **Key words** that has no accompanying dialogue.
**3** Use the **Learning tips** to help you remember the **Key words**.
**4** Study the **Language notes** and **Word patterns** as these give you information that you will use over and over again later.
**5** Do the **Exercises** and the **Test yourself exercise** if there is one at the end of the unit; check your answers in the **Key to the exercises** at the end of the book.

### Insight

Don't try to do too much at once! Most people find they learn better if they study for short periods e.g. 20 minutes or take frequent breaks. After your break try to recall what you learned last! It will help to 'fix' it in your long-term memory.

**Guten Tag, Herr Braun!** *Good day, Mr Brown!*

◄) CD1, TR 2

| | |
|---|---|
| **Herr** [hair] | *Mr* |
| **Frau** [fr-ow] | *Mrs* |
| **gut** [goot] | *good/well* |
| **danke** [dankuh] | *thanks* |
| **guten Tag** [gooten tahk] | *good day* |
| **Wie geht es Ihnen?** [vee gate es ee-nen] | *How are you?* |
| **Es geht mir gut.** [es gate meer goot] | *I am well. (lit. It goes to me well)* |
| **auf Wiedersehen** [ow-uf veeder-say-un] | *goodbye* |
| **auch** [ow-uch] | *also* |

**Hallo** and **hi** are both used as informal greetings.

### LEARNING TIPS

**1** If you have the recording listen to the words and repeat them after the recording.

**2** To help you learn the new words and phrases cover up the meaning and see how many you can remember. Listen again and think of what the words mean as you hear them. Then cover up the German words and see if you can remember them.

### DIALOGUE 1

CD1, TR 3

| | |
|---|---|
| **Frau Taylor** | Guten Tag, Herr Braun. [gooten tahk hair brown] |
| **Herr Braun** | Guten Tag, Frau Taylor. |
| **Frau Taylor** | Wie geht es Ihnen? [vee gate es ee-nen?] |
| **Herr Braun** | Danke, es geht mir gut, und Ihnen? [dankuh, es gate meer goot, unt ee-nen?] |
| **Frau Taylor** | Auch gut, danke. [ow-uch goot dankuh] Auf Wiedersehen, Herr Braun! [ow-uf veeder-say-un] |
| **Herr Braun** | Auf Wiedersehen, Frau Taylor! |

## LEARNING TIPS

**1** Imagine that you are Mrs Taylor. Greet Herr Braun, answer his question and complete the conversation.
**2** Now practise Herr Braun's part of the conversation.

## Insight

To give you confidence and improve your pronunciation you should read the words and expressions out loud.

Exercise 1
How do you say the following?

**a** good day
**b** also
**c** Mr

**d** goodbye
**e** well
**f** I'm well

**g** thank you
**h** how are you?
**i** and

---

## Guten Tag, Frau Meyer! *Good day, Mrs Meyer!*

◆ **CD1, TR 4**

In the first dialogue you were talking to a man. In this dialogue you learn how to address a woman.

<table>
<tr><td>QUICK VOCAB</td><td>Guten Morgen! [gooten more-ghen]</td><td>Good morning!</td></tr>
<tr><td></td><td>Tschüs or Tschüss [tshewss]</td><td>bye</td></tr>
<tr><td></td><td>Guten Abend! [gooten ah-bend]</td><td>Good evening!</td></tr>
<tr><td></td><td>Gute Nacht! [gootuh nacht]</td><td>Good night!</td></tr>
<tr><td></td><td>ich bin [ich bin]</td><td>I am</td></tr>
<tr><td></td><td>nicht so gut [nicht so goot]</td><td>not so well</td></tr>
<tr><td></td><td>Das tut mir Leid. [das toot meer lite]</td><td>I'm sorry.</td></tr>
</table>

**Angenehm!** [anger-name]

*Pleased to meet you!*
*(lit. pleasant/nice)*

**Ich habe Kopfschmerzen.**
[ich habuh kopf-schmairtsen]

*I have a headache.*

### PRONUNCIATION TIP

Remember **ch** as in **loch**.

### LEARNING TIPS

**1** Most learners find it helpful to practise saying the words (after the recording if you have it). Try covering up the English words and see if you can remember what the German words mean. Then cover up the German words and see if you can remember them.

Germans use 'Frau' when addressing a young woman of about 18 or more whether she is married or not. They tend to be formal and will usually shake hands when meeting you or saying goodbye and add your name to the greeting:

As a general rule you use:

**Guten Morgen** *first thing in the morning,*
**Guten Tag** *after about 10 am,*
**Guten Abend** *after 5 pm and*
**Gute Nacht** *when you are going to bed.*
**Tschüss, Tschüssi** *'bye* are widely used in informal situations.
**Servus, Ade** *'bye* are both used informally in southern Germany.

## Insight

Did you notice? All nouns in German are written with a capital letter.

Not sure if a word is a noun or not? If it is a noun you can say 'a', 'the' or 'my' in front of it!

## DIALOGUE 2

**CD1, TR 5**

| | |
|---|---|
| **Mr Smith** | Guten Tag, Frau Meyer! Ich bin Martin Smith. |
| **Frau Meyer** | Guten Tag, Herr Smith! Angenehm. Wie geht es Ihnen? |
| **Mr Smith** | Danke, gut, und Ihnen? |
| **Frau Meyer** | Nicht so gut. Ich habe Kopfschmerzen. |
| **Mr Smith** | Das tut mir Leid. Auf Wiedersehen, Frau Meyer. |
| **Frau Meyer** | Auf Wiedersehen, Herr Smith. |

Practise the same dialogue for use: **a** early in the morning; and **b** in the evening.

Exercise 2
Welches Wort fehlt? *Which word is missing?*

a   Es ... mir gut.
b   Ich ... Martin Smith.
c   Das tut ... Leid.
d   Auf .............., Frau Meyer.

Listening exercise 1
**CD1, TR 6**

Listen to these people and work out what time of day it is:

  i   *early morning*
 ii   *later morning*
iii   *late afternoon*
 iv   *night time*

Now listen again and add if they are addressing (a) a man, (b) a woman or (c) a young woman.

In southern Germany and Austria people often say:

**Grüß Gott!** [grewss got]   *Good day!* (lit. *greet God*)

6

## Verzeihung *Excuse me, please*

🔊 **CD1, TR 7**

You have learned how to greet someone
you know or to whom you have been
introduced. The next dialogue teaches
you how to ask for someone and say you
don't understand.

| | |
|---|---|
| **Verzeihung.** [fair-tseye-hoong] | *Pardon/Excuse me, please.* |
| **Sind Sie …?** [zindt zee …?] | *Are you …?* |
| **Mein Name ist …** [mine nahm-uh ist …] | *My name is …* |
| **Wie bitte?** [vee bittuh?] | *Pardon?* |
| **Ich heiße …** [ich high-suh …] | *I am called …* |
| **Wie heißen Sie?** [vee high-sen zee?] | *What is your name?* |
| **Ich verstehe nicht.** | *I don't understand.* |
|   [ich fair-shtayuh nicht] | |
| **Er ist nicht da.** [air ist nicht daa] | *He is not here.* |
| **heute** [hoy-tuh] | *today* |
| **Sprechen Sie Englisch?** | *Do you speak English?* |
|   [shprech-un zee ehng-lish?] | |
| **Ich verstehe ein bisschen.** | *I understand a bit.* |
|   [ich fairshtay-uh 'ine biss-schun] | |
| **Wann kann ich ihn sehen?** | *When can I see him?* |
|   [van can ich een zay-un?] | |
| **morgen** [more-gun] | *tomorrow* |
| **Vielen Dank.** [feel-un dank] | *Many thanks.* |

**QUICK VOCAB**

### PRONUNCIATION TIPS

**ei** sounds **aye**   **ie** sounds **ee**

**v** sounds **f** – remember **Volkswagen** is pronounced 'folksvaagen'.

## LEARNING TIP

Useful techniques for learning!

**1** Read the words/phrases out loud and concentrate on the pronunciation. Then read or *listen* again and think of the meaning. Finally cover up the German words and see how many you can remember.

### DIALOGUE 3

| | |
|---|---|
| **Mr Smith** | Verzeihung, sind Sie Herr Schulz? |
| **Herr Kryschinski** | Nein. Mein Name ist Kryschinski. |
| **Mr Smith** | Wie bitte? |
| **Herr Kryschinski** | Ich heiße Kryschinski. Wie heißen Sie? |
| **Mr Smith** | Smith. |
| **Herr Kryschinski** | Angenehm. Herr Schulz ist heute nicht da. |
| **Mr Smith** | Ich verstehe nicht. |
| **Herr Kryschinski** | Herr Schulz ist nicht da. |
| **Mr Smith** | Sprechen Sie Englisch? |
| **Herr Kryschinski** | Ich verstehe ein bisschen. Mr Schulz is not here. |
| **Mr Smith** | Wann kann ich ihn sehen? |
| **Herr Kryschinski** | Morgen. |
| **Mr Smith** | Vielen Dank. Auf Wiedersehen. |
| **Herr Kryschinski** | Auf Wiedersehen, Herr Smith. |

## Insight

Reading the dialogue out loud and then practising each part in turn and seeing how much you can remember helps to fix the new phrases in your long-term memory.

### Exercise 3

Wie sagt man das auf Deutsch? *How do you say it in German?*

**a** *What is your name?*
**b** *I don't understand*
**c** *I am called …*
**d** *Excuse me, please.*
**e** *tomorrow*

**f** *Herr Schulz is not here.*
**g** *goodbye*
**h** *Pardon?*
**i** *a bit*

## TEST YOURSELF

**1** What greeting would you use at these times?

a         b         c         d

**2** Imagine you are staying in a hotel in Germany and Frau Hoffmann calls for you at 6pm. What would you say to her?
- **a** Guten Morgen
- **b** Guten Tag
- **c** Guten Abend
- **d** Gute Nacht

**3** During the evening she says:

**Es geht mir nicht gut.** What would you say?
- **a** Vielen Dank
- **b** Auf Wiedersehen
- **c** Das tut mir Leid

**4** How do you pronounce these words and phrases?
- **i** Wie geht es Ihnen?
- **ii** und
- **iii** Danke
- **iv** Herr
- **v** Frau
- **vi** auch
- **vii** Auf Wiedersehen

**5** Welches Wort fehlt? Which word is missing?
- **a** Sind ... Herr Braun?
- **b** Wie ......?
- **c** Ich ........ nicht.
- **d** Ich ..... Fred.
- **e** Wie ...... Sie?
- **f** Er ist ..... da.
- **g** ............ Wiedersehen.
- **h** Ich verstehe ein ........

**6** Welche Antwort passt? *Which is the right answer?*
- **a** Wie heißen Sie?
- **b** Sprechen Sie Englisch?
- **c** Wie geht es Ihnen?
- **d** Sind Sie Herr Brown?
- **i** Ja, ein bisschen.
- **ii** Mein Name ist Schulz
- **iii** Nein, ich bin Herr Taylor
- **iv** Gut, danke und Ihnen?

Check you can understand which is the right answer: i, ii or iii?

a The speaker says i good morning ii good day iii good evening.
b S/he is called i Fräulein Schmidt ii Herr Schmidt iii Frau Schmidt.
c S/he i speaks English ii speaks some English iii doesn't speak English.
d S/he i says s/he is not well ii says s/he is very well iii asks if you are well.

## Sign language

How many of the signs do you know already?

Congratulations! You have now completed the first unit.

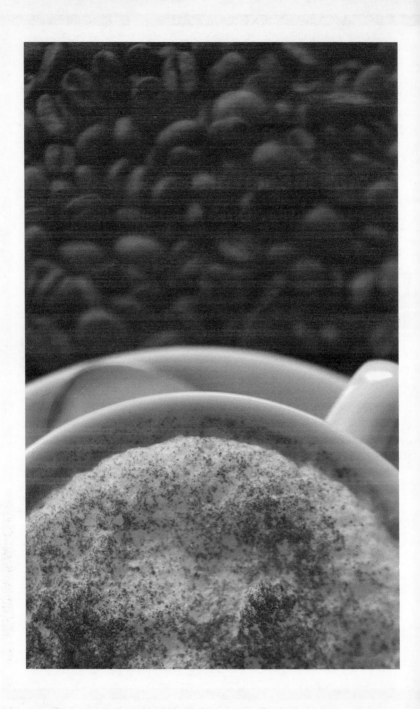

# 2

# Trinken Sie eine Tasse Kaffee?
## Would you like a cup of coffee?

In this unit you will learn how to
- *Say 'please' and 'thank you'*
- *Say what you would like to drink*
- *Ask someone what they would like to drink*
- *Ask for a drink at a café*
- *Ask for the bill*

---

## Kaffee und Kuchen *Coffee and cakes*

◀) **CD1, TR 10**

This box includes the words you need for the first dialogue:

| | |
|---|---|
| **Trinken Sie ...?** [trink-en zee] | *Would you like (to drink) ...? (lit. drink you ...?)* |
| **eine Tasse Kaffee** [eye-nuh tass-uh café] | *a cup of coffee* |
| **Ja, gerne.** [yah, gair-nuh] | *Yes, I would like to. (lit. yes, willingly)* |
| **mit** [mitt] | *with* |
| **ohne** [oh-nuh] | *without* |
| **Milch und Zucker** [milch unt tsook-uh] | *milk and sugar* |

| German | Pronunciation | English |
|---|---|---|
| **ein Stück Kuchen** | ['ine shtewk coo-chen] | *a piece of cake* |
| **bitte schön** | [bitt-uh shurn] | *here you are* |
| **bitte** | [bitt-uh] | *please* |
| **Danke/Danke schön.** | [dank-uh/dank-uh-shurn] | *Thank you.* |
| **Ich trinke keinen Kaffee.** | [ich trink-uh kine-uhn café] | *I don't drink coffee.* |

### LEARNING TIPS

**1** Say the words out loud (after the recording), concentrating on the pronunciation.
**2** Cover up the English and see if you can remember what all the German words and phrases mean.
**3** Cover up the German and see if you can remember it.

### SAYING 'PLEASE' AND 'THANK YOU'

If you thank someone in German they will reply **bitte**, which usually means please but in this case it means *don't mention it*.

If someone offers you something and you say **danke** they will take it to mean *no thank you*. If you want it, say **bitte** instead. This is a mistake you are likely to make only once!

> **Insight**
> If someone says **danke** to you don't forget to reply **bitte**!

### COFFEE

Germans tend to drink a lot of coffee, and they drink quite strong 'real' coffee in preference to instant coffee. It is usually served with cold milk or **Kaffeesahne** (cream for coffee – like evaporated milk) and white sugar (**Zucker**) or **Kandis** (crystallized sugar lumps).

If you want decaffeinated coffee you ask for **koffeinfrei** [coffaynfry], i.e. free of caffeine, or **entkoffeinierten Kaffee** (decaffeinated coffee). If you want artificial sweetener you ask for **Süßstoff**.

## DIALOGUE 4

You are visiting Herr Braun and are offered coffee and cakes after your journey.

♦ CD1, TR 11

| | |
|---|---|
| **Sie (you)** | Guten Tag, Herr Braun. Wie geht es Ihnen? |
| **Herr Braun** | Gut, danke und Ihnen? |
| **Sie (you)** | Auch gut, danke. |
| **Herr Braun** | Trinken Sie eine Tasse Kaffee? |
| **Sie (you)** | Ja, gerne. |
| **Herr Braun** | Mit Milch und Zucker? |
| **Sie (you)** | Ohne Zucker. |
| **Herr Braun** | Ein Stück Kuchen? |
| **Sie (you)** | Ja, bitte. |
| **Herr Braun** | Bitte schön. |
| **Sie (you)** | Danke. |
| **Herr Braun** | Bitte. |

### LEARNING TIPS

**1** Read the dialogue out loud.
**2** On the recording, play Herr Braun's part and see if you can say your part.
**3** Now imagine you are Herr Braun. Play your part on the recording and see if you can say his part.

Wie trinken Sie Kaffee? *How do you like your coffee?*

**a** mit Milch
**b** mit Milch und Zucker
**c** mit Milch und ohne Zucker
**d** mit Zucker und ohne Milch
**e** Ich trinke keinen Kaffee.

## Ich trinke lieber Tee *I prefer tea*

🔊 **CD1, TR 12**

In the first dialogue of this unit you were in Germany, now Herr Braun is visiting you. What are you going to offer him?

| | |
|---|---|
| **Wie war die Reise?** [vee var dee rye-zuh?] | *How was the journey?* |
| **Ich bin müde.** [ich bin mew-duh] | *I am tired.* |
| **Ich trinke lieber ...** [ich trink-uh lee-buh] | *I would prefer ... (lit. I drink rather ...)* |
| **Tee** [tay] | *tea* |
| **oder** [ode-uh] | *or* |
| **Zitrone** [tsit-rone-uh] | *lemon* |
| **keinen Zucker** [kine-en tsuckuh] | *no sugar* |
| **Schokoladenkuchen** [shock-o-lahd-uhn-koochen] | *chocolate cake* |
| **Apfelsaft** [app-fell-zaft] | *apple juice* |
| **Orangensaft** [or-ahnge-enn-zaft] | *orange juice* (**Orangensaft** is commonly shortened to **O-Saft**.) |
| **Tomatensaft** [toe-marten-zaft] | *tomato juice* |
| **eine Dose** [doze-uh] | *a can* |
| **eine Flasche** [flash-uh] | *a bottle* |

### LANGUAGE NOTES

In German new words are often made by adding two (or more) words together. When you meet one of these long words look for the place where it divides and work out what the different parts mean, e.g.

| | | |
|---|---|---|
| **Apfelkuchen** | = | Apfel + Kuchen |
| | = | *apple cake* |
| **Biergarten** | = | Bier + Garten |
| | = | *beer garden* |

## LEARNING TIPS

**1** Say the words out loud (after the recording).
**2** Cover up the English and check you know what they mean.
**3** Now cover the German and see if you can say the German words.

Exercise 1
Was trinken Sie? *What are you drinking?*

**Alkoholfreie Getränke** *Non-alcoholic drinks*

## DIALOGUE 5

| | |
|---|---|
| **Sie** | Hallo, Herr Braun. Wie geht es Ihnen? |
| **Herr Braun** | Gut, danke und Ihnen? |
| **Sie** | Wie war die Reise? |
| **Herr Braun** | Nicht so gut, ich bin müde. |
| **Sie** | Trinken Sie eine Tasse Kaffee? |
| **Herr Braun** | Ich trinke lieber Tee. |
| **Sie** | Mit Milch oder mit Zitrone? |
| **Herr Braun** | Mit Milch. |
| **Sie** | Und Zucker? |
| **Herr Braun** | Nein. Kein' Zucker.* |
| **Sie** | Ein Stück Schokoladenkuchen? |

*(Contd)*

| Herr Braun | Gerne. |
|---|---|
| Sie | Bitte schön. |
| Herr Braun | Danke. |
| Sie | Bitte. |

*The correct form is **keinen Zucker** but most people miss off the -en when they are speaking.

### LEARNING TIPS

1 Practise both sides of the conversation.
2 Think about what the words and phrases mean as you say them.
3 Remember to say them out loud!

Exercise 2
What do these mean? Use the breakdown process explained under **Language notes** to work out what they are:

a **Reisebüro**
b **Reiseschecks**
c **Reisekosten**
d **Zitronentee**

---

## Im Café *In the café*

◄) CD1, TR 14

QUICK VOCAB

| | |
|---|---|
| **Was darf es sein?** [vas darf es zine?] | *What can I get you?* (lit. *What may it be?*) |
| **Ich möchte …** [ich merch-tuh] | *I would like …* |
| **Haben Sie …?** [hah-bun zee?] | *Have you …?* |
| **zu süß** [tsoo zew-ss] | *too sweet* |
| **zu trocken** [tsoo trock-en] | *too dry* |
| **halbtrocken** [halp-trock-en] | *medium* (lit. *half-dry*) |
| **ein Glas Wein** ['ine glass vine] | *a glass of wine* |
| **zwei Gläser Wein** [tsv-eye glazer vine] | *two glasses of wine* |

18

| | |
|---|---|
| **ein Glas Bier** ['ine glass beer] | *a glass of beer* |
| **Zahlen, bitte.** [tsah-len] | *The bill, please. (lit. to pay)* |
| **rot/weiß** [rote/vice] | *red/white* |
| **Das macht 5.** (fünf) euro. [das macht finf ow-ro] | *That is 5 euros.* *(lit. That makes 5 euros)* |
| **Ich trinke keinen Alkohol.** [al-coe-holl] | *I don't drink alcohol.* |

Most German wine is white.

The best known are probably the Rhine wines (**Rheinwein**) such as:

**Liebfraumilch** – sold in a brown bottle.

**Moselwein** – from the vineyards on the banks of the river Moselle/ or Mosel – sold in a green bottle.

**Frankenwein** – which comes from **Franken** or Franconia (a region in northern Bavaria) – sold in a green bottle shaped like a bulb.

Terms of reference:

**Tafelwein** – is table wine.

**Landwein** – is a local wine, from the 'Land' or 'region'.

**Qualitätswein** – is a quality wine.

**Qualitätswein mit Prädikat** – is a quality wine that has no added sugar. Quality wines can be:

    **Kabinett** – (the grapes are picked early and the wine is drier);

    **Spätlese** – (the grapes are picked late and are probably sweeter);

    **Auslese, Beerenauslese** and **Trockenbeerenauslese** – (sweeter wines).

| | |
|---|---|
| **Zum Wohl!** [ts-oom vole] | *Cheers!* |
| **Prost!** [proost] | *Cheers!* |

## DIALOGUE 6

| | |
|---|---|
| **Kellner (waiter)** | Was darf es sein? |
| **Sie (you)** | Ich möchte ein Glas Wein, ein Glas Bier und eine Tasse Kaffee. |
| **Kellner (waiter)** | Rotwein oder Weißwein? |
| **Sie (you)** | Weißwein. |
| **Kellner (waiter)** | Süß oder trocken? |
| **Sie (you)** | Halbtrocken. |
| **Kellner (waiter)** | Bitte schön. |
| **Sie (you)** | Danke. |
| **Kellner (waiter)** | Bitte. |
| **Sie (you)** | Zahlen, bitte! |
| **Kellner (waiter)** | Das macht 5 (fünf) Euro. |

## LEARNING TIPS

1 Read both parts of the dialogue out loud.
2 Cover up the right-hand side and practise ordering drinks.

Exercise 3
What would you say if you wanted to order the following?

20

# TEST YOURSELF

1 Imagine Herr Braun has come to see you.
   How would you ask him:
   a  what the journey was like?
   b  if he would like something to drink?
   c  if he would like milk and sugar in his coffee?
   d  if he would like a piece of cake?

2  Now you are visiting Herr und Frau Braun in Germany.
   Pair up the following questions and answers.
   a  Wie geht es Ihnen?           i    Gerne.
   b  Trinken Sie ein Glas Wein?   ii   Ja, bitte.
   c  Rotwein oder Weißwein?       iii  Weißwein.
   d  Süß oder trocken?            iv   Gut, danke.
   e  Noch ein Glas? ...!          v    Halbtrocken.

Listening exercise 3
◀⑨ CD1, TR 16

What have they ordered?
   a  The man orders a glass of i red wine ii white wine iii beer.
   b  The woman orders a cup of i tea ii coffee iii hot chocolate.
   c  The boy orders a glass of i coke ii lemonade iii milk.
   d  The girl orders a glass of i orange ii tomato iii apple juice.

Listening exercise 4
◀⑨ CD1, TR 17

Which is the right answer?
   a  The speaker says i good morning ii good day iii good evening.
   b  She offers you i tea ii coffee iii wine.
   c  She offers you i a biscuit ii a piece of lemon cake iii a piece of
      chocolate cake.

## Sign language

**1** What drinks can you get here?

| Heiße Getränke | |
| --- | ---: |
| Tasse Kaffee | €2,80 |
| Kännchen Kaffee | €5,60 |
| Tasse Kaffee koffeinfrei | €2,80 |
| Kännchen Kaffee koffeinfrei | €5,60 |
| Tasse ½ Schoc + ½ Kaffee | €3,00 |
| Kännchen ½ Schoc + ½ Kaffee | €6,00 |
| Tasse Schokolade | €2,80 |
| Kännchen Schokolade mit Sahne | €5,60 |
| Kännchen Tee | €5,60 |
| Tasse Tee mit Rum | €4,50 |
| Glas Kamillentee | €2,80 |
| Glas Pfefferminztee | €2,80 |

**Imbiss** snack
**Sahne** cream
**Kännchen** pot

**2** How would you order these for your friends?

And what would you order for yourself?

# 3

# Was kostet es?
## What does it cost?

In this unit you will learn how to
- *Say the numbers to 100*
- *Understand German numbers when you hear them*
- *Use German money*
- *Recognize German prices and telephone numbers*

---

## Die Zahlen von 1 bis 20 *The numbers from 1 to 20*

🔊 **CD1, TR 18**

| | | |
|---|---|---|
| 0 **null** | 5 **fünf** [finf] | 9 **neun** [(an)noyn] |
| 1 **eins** [(H)eins] | 6 **sechs** [zex] | 10 **zehn** [tsayn] |
| 2 **zwei** [tsv-eye] | 7 **sieben** [zeebun] | 11 **elf** |
| 3 **drei** [dry] | 8 **acht** | 12 **zwölf** [tsvulf] |
| 4 **vier** [fear] | | |

## LANGUAGE NOTES

German numbers are easy to learn. You only have to learn the
numbers 1–12 and then you can make up all the numbers to 20.
For the 'teens' just add 'three', 'four' etc. to 'ten', ie.

| | |
|---|---|
| Thirteen is 'three + ten' | **dreizehn** |
| Fourteen is 'four + ten' | **vierzehn** |
| Fifteen is 'five + ten' | **fünfzehn** |
| For sixteen, **sechs** loses its last '**s**': | **sechzehn** |
| For seventeen, **sieben** loses its '**en**': | **siebzehn** |
| Eighteen is 'eight + ten' | **achtzehn** |
| Nineteen is 'nine + ten' | **neunzehn** |
| Twenty is | **zwanzig** |

## LEARNING TIPS

**1** Read all the numbers out loud or listen to the recording and say
the numbers after it.
**2** Try to say the first six numbers without looking. Now try the
numbers six to 12.
**3** Now make up the numbers 13–20 and say them out loud.
Remember that 16 and 17 need special treatment.

# Wo wohnen Sie? *Where do you live?*

🔊 **CD1, TR 19**

| | |
|---|---|
| **Wie ist Ihre Adresse?** | *What is your address?* |
| [vee ist ear-uh adress-uh?] | |
| **ich wohne** [ich vone-uh] | *I live* |
| **er wohnt** [air vone-t] | *he lives* |
| **sie wohnt** [see vone-t] | *she lives* |
| **die Adresse** [dee adress-uh] | *address* |
| **die Straße** [dee shtrah-suh] | *street* |
| **die Allee** [dee al-lay] | *avenue* |

## DIALOGUE 7

🔊 CD1, TR 20

| | |
|---|---|
| Wo wohnen Sie? | In Berlin. |
| Wie ist Ihre Adresse? | Friedrichstraße 17. |
| Und wo wohnt | |
| Frau Zimmermann? | Sie wohnt Mozartstraße, Nummer 16. |
| Und Fritz Sievers? | Er wohnt Bonner Allee 9. |
| Und Helmut Grün? | Unter den Linden 14. |
| Und Boris Fischer? | Das weiß ich nicht. |

### LEARNING TIPS

**1** Practise saying both sides of the dialogue.
**2** Now how would you tell Herr Fischer where these people live?

Note that German addresses have the house number after rather than before the street name.

| | |
|---|---|
| Silke Taraks | Beethovenstraße 18 |
| Jörg Quecke | Lindenstraße 14 |
| Sandra Müller | Bonner Allee 2 |
| Christian Schulz | Auf dem Hang 7 |

## Exercise 1

Put these numbers in the right order:
sechs fünfzehn zehn neunzehn fünf siebzehn sieben
vier dreizehn eins acht zwanzig elf sechzehn
zwei vierzehn neun achtzehn zwölf drei

## Exercise 2

What are these numbers? Write them out in full and say them out loud.

## More practice with numbers

◀) **CD1, TR 21**

QUICK VOCAB

| | |
|---|---|
| **Wie viel?** [vee feel] **Wie viele?** [vee feel-uh] | *How many?* |
| **Wie viele Flaschen Wein?** | *How many bottles of wine?* |
| **Wie viele Tassen Tee?** | *... cups of tea?* |
| **Wie viele Eisportionen?** | *... ice creams?* |
| **Wie viel Stück Kuchen?** | *How many pieces of cake?* |

26

| **Was möchten Sie?** [vas murch-tun zee] | *What would you like?* |
|---|---|
| **Ich möchte ...** [ich murch-tuh] | *I would like ...* |
| **Bringen Sie mir ...** [bring-en zee mere] | *Please bring me ...* |
| **der Kellner** [dare kell-nuh] | *the waiter* |
| **Sonst noch etwas?** [zonst noch etvas] | *Anything else?* |
| **Noch was?** [noch vas] | *Anything else?* |
| **Ist das alles?** [ist das al-us] | *Is that all?* |

Exercise 3

**a** *Wie viel Flaschen Wein?*

**b** *Wie viel Glas Bier?*

**c** *Wie viel Eisportionen?*

**d** *Wie viel Stück Apfelstrudel?*

**e** *Wie viel Stück Kuchen?*

**f** *Wie viele Tassen Tee?*

Apfelstrudel is a dessert made with apple, cinnamon and raisins wrapped in a thin envelope of filo or flaky pastry cooked and served with a dusting of *icing sugar* **Puderzucker** and *cream* **Sahne** or *custard* **Vanillesoße**.

## Ich möchte *I would like*

### DIALOGUE 8

CD1, TR 22

| | |
|---|---|
| **Kellner** | Was möchten Sie? |
| **Sie** | Ich möchte vier Gläser Wein. |
| **Kellner** | Rotwein oder Weißwein? |
| **Sie** | Drei Gläser Weißwein und ein Glas Rotwein. |
| **Kellner** | Noch was? |
| **Sie** | Zwei Gläser Limonade, und zwei Tassen Kaffee. |
| **Kellner** | Noch was? |
| **Sie** | Ja. Acht Stück Apfelstrudel. |
| **Kellner** | Ist das alles? |
| **Sie** | Ja, danke. |

### LEARNING TIP

**1** Practise your part of the dialogue.

Exercise 4
Now see if you can ask for these:

28

Listening exercise 5
🔊 **CD1, TR 23**

Schreiben Sie die Nummern auf! *Listen and write down the numbers.*

---

## Die Zahlen von 20 bis 100 *The numbers from 20 to 100*

🔊 **CD1, TR 24**

### WORD PATTERNS: NUMBERS

You have seen that German numbers 1–20 are very easy to learn. If you know the numbers to 12 and the number for 20 you can make all the other numbers. From **zwanzig** *twenty* you can see that the equivalent of the English ending *-ty* is **-zig**. To create the other 'tens', 'three', 'four', 'five' etc. are placed before **-zig**.

| | |
|---|---|
| **zwanzig** | 20 |
| **dreißig** | 30 |
| **vierzig** | 40 |
| **fünfzig** | 50 |
| **sechzig** | 60 |
| **siebzig** | 70 |
| **achtzig** | 80 |
| **neunzig** | 90 |
| **(ein)hundert** | 100 |

Note the following:

| | |
|---|---|
| **dreißig** | ß instead of z |
| **sechzig** | **sech(s)zig: sechs** loses its -s |
| **siebzig** | **sieb(en)zig:** sieben loses its -en |

Now look at the numbers from 21 to 29:

| | |
|---|---|
| 21 | **einundzwanzig** |
| 22 | **zweiundzwanzig** |
| 23 | **dreiundzwanzig** |
| 24 | **vierundzwanzig** |
| 25 | **fünfundzwanzig** |
| 26 | **sechsundzwanzig** |
| 27 | **siebenundzwanzig** |
| 28 | **achtundzwanzig** |
| 29 | **neunundzwanzig** |

When you say a two-digit number such as 21 you say the unit (or right-hand digit) first.

## Insight

Always remember that in German they say the units before the tens. They used to do it in old English too! "Four and twenty blackbirds baked in a pie."

To complete your knowledge of German numbers, here are the words for a hundred, a thousand and a million:

| | |
|---|---|
| 100 | **(ein)hundert** |
| 1,000 | **(ein)tausend** |
| 1,000,000 | **eine Million** |

## Was macht das? *How much is it?*

QUICK VOCAB

| | |
|---|---|
| **Was darf es sein?** [vas darf es zine?] | *What can I get you? (lit. what may it be?)* |
| **Was kostet das?** | *How much does it cost?* |
| **Wie teuer ist das?** [vee toy-er ist das?] | *How much is it? (lit. how dear is that?)* |

30

## DIALOGUE 9

| | |
|---|---|
| **Kellnerin** | Was möchten Sie? |
| **Sie** | Ich möchte vier Gläser Wein und vier Flaschen Bier. |
| **Kellnerin** | Bitte schön. |
| **Sie** | Was macht das? |
| **Kellnerin** | Das macht €32. |
| | |
| **Kellnerin** | Was darf es sein? |
| **Sie** | Ich möchte vier Tassen Tee und drei Tassen Kaffee. |
| **Kellnerin** | Bitte schön. |
| **Sie** | Was macht das? |
| **Kellnerin** | €19,60. |
| | |
| **Kellnerin** | Was darf es sein? |
| **Sie** | Ich möchte zwei Stück Kuchen und fünf Tassen Kaffee. |
| **Kellnerin** | Bitte schön. |
| **Sie** | Was macht das? |
| **Kellnerin** | €21. |

## LEARNING TIPS

**1** Practise your parts of the dialogues.
**2** Was kostet das? Read the prices out loud.

| | | |
|---|---|---|
| €2,80 | €2,80 | €3,50 |
| *eine Tasse Tee* | *eine Tasse Kaffee* | *ein Stück Torte* |

€7,50 — *ein Glas Rotwein*

€4,50 — *ein Glas Bier*

€3,50 — *eine Flasche Mineralwasser*

€3,50 — *ein Becher Kaffee*

Here is some more practice to help you get used to the sound of the numbers.

### Exercise 5
Look at these numbers and say them in German. Say the digit with the line under it *first*.

**a** 2<u>1</u>  **b** 2<u>5</u>  **c** 3<u>2</u>  **d** 3<u>6</u>  **e** 4<u>3</u>  **f** 4<u>7</u>  **g** 5<u>4</u>  **h** 5<u>8</u>
**i** 6<u>1</u>  **j** 6<u>9</u>  **k** 7<u>2</u>  **l** 7<u>5</u>  **m** 8<u>4</u>  **n** 8<u>8</u>  **o** 9<u>2</u>  **p** 9<u>9</u>

### Listening exercise 6
🔊 **CD1, TR 26**

Now listen and write down which of the above numbers is being said. (If you haven't got the recording, try to get someone to read them to you in a different order.)

Listening exercise 7
🔊 **CD1, TR 27**

Put a ring round the word you hear. (If you haven't got the recording, practise saying both words and listen to the difference or try to get someone to read them to you.)

| | | | | | |
|---|---|---|---|---|---|
| **a** | 24 | 42 | **f** | 67 | 76 |
| **b** | 32 | 23 | **g** | 93 | 39 |
| **c** | 25 | 52 | **h** | 29 | 92 |
| **d** | 46 | 64 | **i** | 48 | 84 |
| **e** | 38 | 83 | **j** | 62 | 26 |

Germans often say their telephone numbers (apart from the code) in twos: e.g. **25 42 89** would be said as **fünfundzwanzig, zweiundvierzig, neunundachtzig.**

The dialling code is called **die Vorwahl** [dee for-vahl].

The international code for England from Germany is **oo 44: null, null, vier, vier.** You then drop the o before your own area code, eg. oo 44(UK) -20 (London) 7743 4163.

Now tell a German friend what number he/she needs to ring you from Germany. Begin with the country code [**Ländervorwahl**] oo44 for the UK.

# TEST YOURSELF

Although it is easy to say the German numbers, it is not so easy to recognize them, especially when they are spoken quickly.

Listening exercise 8
◀) **CD1, TR 28**

How much does it cost? Put a ring round the price you hear. (If you don't have the recording try to get someone to say one number from each pair in German for you.)

| | | | | | | | |
|---|---|---|---|---|---|---|---|
| **a** | €2,50 | or | €5,20 | **f** | €4,75 | or | €4,25 |
| **b** | €12,80 | or | €8,20 | **g** | €14,10 | or | €40,10 |
| **c** | €16,50 | or | €60,50 | **h** | €45,00 | or | €54,00 |
| **d** | €34,60 | or | €43,60 | **i** | €25,00 | or | €52,00 |
| **e** | €50,00 | or | €15,00 | **j** | €72,90 | or | €22,90 |

**1** Now try to order these:

**2** Read the details given about these six people aloud. How old are they and what are their telephone numbers?

**a** Name: Franz Schmidt
Alter: 45
Telefon: 31 53 27

**b** Name: Marion Braun
Alter: 17–
Telefon: 22 95 78

**c** Name: Elisabeth Ant
Alter: 48
Telefon: 87 46 03

**d** Name: Helmut Grün
Alter: 28
Telefon: 48 02 49

**e** Name: Silke Müller
Alter: 32
Telefon: 53 66 31

**f** Name: Paul Schreiber
Alter: 67–
Telefon: 35 64 77–

**3** Can you say how much these cost?

**i** white wine €11,20
**ii** red wine €9,30
**iii** beer €2,10

**iv** ice €1,63
**v** pizza €9,35

# 4

# Das Alphabet
The alphabet

In this unit you will learn how to
- *Say the alphabet*
- *Ask someone to spell their name or where they come from*
- *Spell your own name and address*
- *Spell difficult words*
- *Use the correct form of the word 'you'*

Wie schreibt man das? *How do you spell it?*

**DAS ALPHABET** *THE ALPHABET*

◄» **CD1, TR 29**

| | | | | | | |
|---|---|---|---|---|---|---|
| a – *ah* | b – *bay* | c – *tsay* | d – *day* | e – *ay* | f – *eff* | g – *gay* |
| h – *hah* | i – *ee* | j – *yot* | k – *kah* | l – *ell* | m – *emm* | n – *enn* |
| o – *oh* | p – *pay* | q – *koo* | r – *air* | s – *es* | t – *tay* | u – *ooh* |
| v – *fow* | w – *vay* | x – *icks* | y – *ipsilon* | z – *tset* | | |
| ä – *eh* | äu – *oy* | ö – *er* | ü – *euh* | ß – *ess* | | |

nn = doppel n
ß = *s tset* or scharfes s

## PRONUNCIATION TIP

Letters to watch:

a – ah       v – fow
e – ay       w – vay
i – ee

## LEARNING TIPS

**1** Practise saying the alphabet (after the recording if possible) and check your pronunciation.

**2** Write down the sound of the letters you need to spell your own name and learn them off by heart.

**3** **Wie schreibt man das?** *How do you spell it?* (lit. *how does one write it?*).

**4** Practise spelling these names out loud:

**Peter   Martin   Susanne   Ulrike   Florian**

## Insight

When spelt out 'e' sounds 'ay' and 'i' sounds 'ee'!

## DIALOGUE 10

| | |
|---|---|
| **Sie** | Wie heißen Sie? |
| **Herr Meyer** | Meyer. |
| **Sie** | Wie schreibt man das? |
| **Herr Meyer** | M E Y E R. |
| **Sie** | Und wo wohnen Sie, Herr Meyer? |
| **Herr Meyer** | In Mannheim. |
| **Sie** | Mit doppel 'n'? |
| **Herr Meyer** | Ja. |
| **Sie** | Wo sind Sie geboren? |
| **Herr Meyer** | In Würzburg. |
| **Sie** | Wie schreibt man das? |
| **Herr Meyer** | W Ü R Z B U R G. |
| **Sie** | Vielen Dank. |
| **Herr Meyer** | Nichts zu danken. |

38

## LEARNING TIPS

1 Practise saying both parts of the dialogue.
2 Then answer these questions yourself:
   Wie heißen Sie?              ...
   Wie schreibt man das?       ...
   Und wo wohnen Sie?          ...
   Wie schreibt man das?       ...

3 How would you spell these places in German?
   Chipping Norton   Edinburgh   Conwy   Norfolk
   Stratford   York   Waverley   Oxford

---

## Wie heißen Sie?/Wie heißt du? *What's your name?*

### LANGUAGE NOTES: *SIE* OR *DU?*

Sie – *you*

There are three words for you in German. The most important one to learn is the 'polite' form which you use when addressing people older than yourself and people you don't know very well.

This is the form you have been using so far:

| | |
|---|---|
| **Wie heißen Sie?** | *What is your name?* |
| | *(lit. How are you called?)* |
| **Wo wohnen Sie?** | *Where do you live?* |
| **Haben Sie einen Stadtplan?** | *Have you got a town plan?* |
| **Wie geht es Ihnen?** | *How are you? (lit. How goes it to you?)* |

Du – *you*

This form is used when talking to a child or someone you know well. You would not normally use it to an adult until they invite you to. If you know someone well they may say: **Duzen wir uns.** This means you should use **du** instead of **Sie**.

**Wie heißt du? Wo wohnst du?**
**Wie geht es dir?**

**Hast du einen Stadtplan?**
*How are you? (lit. How goes it to you?)*

If you call each other by your first names you can usually start to use the **du** form.

**Ihr** – *you*

The third form is the plural of **du**. You use it with a group of children or people that you know well.

## Insight
**Du** rhymes with two – when there are just two of you use **du**!

### WORD PATTERNS: *SIE* AND *DU*

When using the **Sie** form the verb ends with **-en**.

When using the **du** form the verb ends with **-st**.

**Kommen Sie mit dem Auto?**
**Kommst du mit dem Auto?**
*Are you coming by car?*

**Spielen Sie Tennis?**
**Spielst du Tennis?**
*Do you play tennis?*

## Exercise 1
**Sie** form or **du** form? Find the right form.

You are talking to Frau Schneider. How would you ask her:

  **a** *How are you?*
  **b** *When are you coming to London?*
  **c** *What are you doing tomorrow?*
  **d** *Do you like playing tennis?*
  **e** *Do you like swimming?*
  **f** *Would you like a cup of coffee?*

## Exercise 2
Now you are talking to Frau Schneider's 13-year-old daughter Melanie. Ask her the same questions, choosing the right ones from those listed below:

  **a** Wie geht es dir?
  **b** Was machst du morgen?
  **c** Wann kommen Sie nach London?
  **d** Schwimmen Sie gern?
  **e** Spielst du gern Tennis?
  **f** Wie geht es dir?
  **g** Was machst du morgen?
  **h** Möchtest du eine Tasse Kaffee?
  **i** Möchten Sie eine Tasse Kaffee?
  **j** Wie geht es Ihnen?
  **k** Was machen Sie morgen?
  **l** Wann kommst du nach London?
  **m** Schwimmst du gern?
  **n** Spielen Sie gern Tennis?
  **o** Was machen Sie morgen?

## Exercise 3
Meet Herr Meyer's 12-year-old daughter. Ask her her name.

  **a** *Which form are you going to use?*
  **b** *Ask her how she is.*
  **c** *Now ask her if she would like a cup of coffee or a glass of orange juice.*

Listening exercise 9
🔊 **CD1, TR 31**

Which form is being used in each of the sentences you hear?

_____

## An der Rezeption *At reception*

🔊 **CD1, TR 32**

| | |
|---|---|
| **Wie schreibt man das?** | *How do you write it?* |
| **Wie buchstabiert man das?** | *How do you spell it?* |
| **Langsamer, bitte.** [lang-zah-muh] | *Slower, please.* |
| **der Name** [dare nah-muh] | *name* |
| **die Postleitzahl** [dee post-lite-tsahl] | *postcode* |
| **die Vorwahl** [dee for-vahl] | *dialling code* |
| **der Vorname** [dare for-nah-muh] | *first name* |
| **der Nachname/Familien-name** [dare nach-nah-muh/ familien-nah-muh] | *surname* |
| **der Bindestrich** | *hyphen* |
| **der Buchstabe** | *letter (character)* |

### DIALOGUE 11

Listen to (or read) these short conversations:

| | |
|---|---|
| Wie heißen Sie? | König. |
| Wie schreibt man das? | K Ö N I G. |
| Und mit Vornamen? | Elke. |
| Wie buchstabiert man das? | E L K E. |

| | |
|---|---|
| Wie heißt du? | Susanne. |
| Wie schreibt man das? | S U S A N N E. |
| Und wie lautet dein Nachname? | Hoffmann. |
| Mit doppel f? | Ja, und doppel n. |

| | |
|---|---|
| Wie heißen Sie? | Fischer. |
| Wie schreibt man das? | F I S C H E R. |
| Und mit Vornamen? | Hans-Peter. |
| Mit Bindestrich? | Ja. |

| | |
|---|---|
| Wie heißen Sie? | Mein Name ist Kistenmacher. |
| Wie schreibt man das? | K I S T E N M A C H E R. |
| Langsamer bitte! | K I S T E N M A C H E R. |

## LEARNING TIP

**1** Practise reading both parts of the dialogues.

Listening exercise 10
◀ **CD1, TR 34**

**Wie heißen Sie?** *What's your name?*

Write the names of the six people.

## DIALOGUE 12

| | |
|---|---|
| **Empfangsdame** | Wie heißen Sie? |
| **Herr Nabockwicz** | Jürgen Nabockwicz. |
| **Empfangsdame** | Wie schreibt man das? |
| **Herr Nabockwicz** | N A B O C K W I C Z. |
| **Empfangsdame** | Wie bitte? |

*(Contd)*

| | |
|---|---|
| **Herr Nabockwicz** | N A B O C K W I C Z. |
| **Empfangsdame** | Woher kommen Sie? |
| **Herr Nabockwicz** | Aus Lodz. |
| **Empfangsdame** | Wie schreibt man das? |
| **Herr Nabockwicz** | L O D Z. |
| **Empfangsdame** | Langsamer, bitte! |
| **Herr Nabockwicz** | L O D Z. |
| **Empfangsdame** | Staatsangehörigkeit? |
| **Herr Nabockwicz** | Polnisch. |
| **Empfangsdame** | Wie ist Ihre Adresse hier in Deutschland? |
| **Herr Nabockwicz** | Eichhornweg 63, Dortmund-Applerbeck. |
| **Empfangsdame** | Schreibt man das mit Bindestrich? |
| **Herr Nabockwicz** | Ja. |
| **Empfangsdame** | Und doppel p? |
| **Herr Nabockwicz** | Ja. |
| **Empfangsdame** | Wie ist die Postleitzahl? |
| **Herr Nabockwicz** | 44267. |
| **Empfangsdame** | Und die Telefonnummer? |
| **Herr Nabockwicz** | 01 23 45. |
| **Empfangsdame** | Und die Vorwahl für Dortmund? |
| **Herr Nabockwicz** | 0230. |
| **Empfangsdame** | Unterschreiben Sie hier. Vielen Dank, auf Wiedersehen. |

## LEARNING TIPS

1 Practise both parts of the conversation.
2 Now give your own answers to the receptionist's questions.

Listening exercise 11
◄) **CD1, TR 36**

Where do these 12 people live? Write down the details they give.

## TEST YOURSELF

**1** **Welcher Buchstabe fehlt?** Which letter is missing?

a Toi.ette
b Ca.é
c B.r
d Restau.ant

e Ho.el
f Ba.nhof
g Stadtzentru.
h Flu.hafen

**2** A little boy is playing with John at the campsite.
How would you ...

a Ask him his name.
b Ask where he is from.
c Ask if he would like a drink of lemonade [Drink you willingly ...?]
d Ask if he likes playing tennis ... [Play you willingly tennis?]

**3** **Sie or du?** Add the correct ending

a Was mach.. du morgen?
b Was mach.. Sie morgen?
c Wann komm.. Sie nach London?
d Wann komm.. du nach London?
e Schwimm.. Sie gern?
f Schwimm.. du gern?

g Spiel.. du gern Tennis?
h Spiel.. Sie gern Tennis?
i Was mach.. du morgen?
j Was mach.. Sie morgen?
k Trink.. du gern eine Tasse Kaffee?
l Trink.. Sie gern eine Tasse Kaffee?

## Sign language

Read the letters on these signs (look back at the alphabet at the beginning of the unit to check the pronunciation of the letters).

**BMW**      VW      **DB**

**WDR**      USA      Pkw

**AG**      GmbH      **EU**

**BRD**

Now see if you can match them up with their meanings.

**Volkswagen** German car manufacturer
**Deutsche Bahn** German railways
**Bayerische Motorenwerke** German car
 manufacturer
**Europäische Union** European Union
**Bundesrepublik Deutschland** Federal
 Republic of Germany
**Gesellschaft mit beschränkter Haftung**
 limited company (ltd)
**Personenkraftwagen** car!
die **Vereinigten Staaten** the United States
**Aktiengesellschaft** public limited
 company (Plc)
**Westdeutscher Rundfunk** German radio
 and TV company

**Quiz**

**1** What would you do with a **Wiener Schnitzel?**
   **a** Wear it   **b** Dance it   **c** Eat it

**2** Who is your **Oma?**
   **a** Your mother   **b** Your grandmother
   **c** Your washing powder

**3** Where would you find the **Kölner Dom?**
   **a** In Munich   **b** In Koblenz   **c** in Cologne

**4** What would you do with a **Schwarzwälder Kirschtorte?**
   **a** Not know how to spell it   **b** Not know how to say it
   **c** Eat it

**5** Your friend invites you to go to a **Kneipe.**
   **a** You say yes   **b** You ask what time the show begins
   **c** You ask if you should take your swimming costume

**6** **Lufthansa** is:
   **a** The German national anthem
   **b** The German national airline
   **c** The highest mountain in Germany

**7** You are going to a party and are asked to bring a **Lederhose.**
   You would:
   **a** Wear it   **b** Eat it   **c** Drink it

**8** What is the English for these towns?
   **a** München   **b** Köln   **c** Stuttgart   **d** Wien

**9** Which of these are rivers and what are they called in English?
   **a** Der Rhein   **b** Die Mosel   **c** Die Donau
   **d** Die Zugspitze

**10** At a party you are offered **Glühwein**. What should you do with it?

    **a** Drink it  **b** Smoke it  **c** Pour it into the nearest plant pot

**11** Tie breaker for the real expert!

There are 16 **Bundesländer** in Germany. Can you pair up the **Bundesländer** with their capitals?

| | |
|---|---|
| Baden-Württemberg | Saarbrücken |
| Bayern | Hannover |
| Berlin | Potsdam |
| Brandenburg | München |
| Bremen | Mainz |
| Hamburg | Wiesbaden |
| Hessen | Bremen |
| Mecklenburg-Vorpommern | Schwerin |
| Niedersachsen | Stuttgart |
| Nordrhein-Westfalen | Hamburg |
| Rheinland-Pfalz | Berlin |
| Saarland | Dresden |
| Sachsen | Magdeburg |
| Sachsen-Anhalt | Kiel |
| Schleswig-Holstein | Erfurt |
| Thüringen | Düsseldorf |

# 5

# An der Rezeption
## At reception

In this unit you will learn how to
- *Give your particulars when booking into a hotel*
- *Ask for and give an address and postcode*
- *Ask for and give a telephone number*
- *Ask for the telephone code*
- *Say where you come from and what nationality you are*
- *Fill in a form*

## Im Hotel *In the hotel*

🔊 **CD1, TR 37**

| | |
|---|---|
| **der Name** [dare nah-muh] | *name* |
| **die Adresse** [dee add-ress-uh] | *address* |
| **die Postleitzahl** [dee post-lite-tsahl] | *postcode* |
| **die Handynummer** [dee handy-numm-uh] | *mobile number* |
| **die Telefonnummer** [dee tele-fone-numm-uh] | *telephone number* |
| **die Vorwahl** [dee for-vahl] | *dialling code* |
| **das Zimmer** [das tsim-mer] | *room* |
| **wählen** [vair-lun] | *to dial* (lit. *to choose*) |
| **besetzt** [buh-zetst] | *engaged* |

QUICK VOCAB

| **frei** [fry] | *free, vacant* |
| **Wie ist ...?** [vee ist] | *What is ...? (lit. how is ...?)* |
| **Sind Sie ...?** [zint zee] | *Are you ...?* |
| **Wie ist Ihre Adresse?** | *What (lit. how) is your address?* |
| **und Ihre Telefonnummer?** | *and your phone number?* |
| **Haben Sie ein Zimmer frei?** | *Have you a room free?* |
| **die Empfangsdame** | *the receptionist* |

## LEARNING TIPS

**1** Practise saying the new words and phrases out loud.
**2** Cover up the English words and see if you can remember what they are in German.
**3** Now cover up the German words and see if you can remember what they mean.

## DIALOGUE 13

CD1, TR 37, 00:58 [SECOND PART OF TRACK]

| | |
|---|---|
| **Herr Braun** | Haben Sie ein Zimmer frei? |
| **Empfangsdame** | Ja. Wie heißen Sie? |
| **Herr Braun** | Braun. |
| **Empfangsdame** | Und mit Vornamen, Herr Braun? |
| **Herr Braun** | Wilfrid. |
| **Empfangsdame** | Und Ihre Adresse? |
| **Herr Braun** | Dortmunder Straße 53, Stuttgart. |
| **Empfangsdame** | Und die Postleitzahl? |
| **Herr Braun** | 70376. |
| **Empfangsdame** | Wie bitte? |
| **Herr Braun** | 70376. |
| **Empfangsdame** | Darf ich Ihre Telefonnummer haben? |
| **Herr Braun** | 53 14 25 74. |
| **Empfangsdame** | Wie ist die Vorwahl für Stuttgart? |
| **Herr Braun** | 0711. |
| **Empfangsdame** | Und die Handynummer? |
| **Herr Braun** | 0170 85 76 32 48 90. |
| **Empfangsdame** | Und haben Sie eine E-Mail- Adresse? |
| **Herr Braun** | Ja: WilfridB123@web.de. |
| **Empfangsdame** | Also, Zimmer 46. Hier ist der Schlüssel. |
| **Herr Braun** | Vielen Dank. |
| **Empfangsdame** | Bitte schön. |

## PRONUNCIATION TIPS

v sounds f and w sounds v
ie sounds ee and ei sounds aye
z sounds ts
ß is ss

## LEARNING TIPS

**1** Read the dialogue out loud and check you understand it.
Take care with the pronunciation.
**2** Cover up the dialogue and listen to the recording. Can you
understand all the numbers?
**3** Listen to the recording again and give your own answers to the
questions.

---

## Woher kommen Sie?
*Where are you from?*

🔊 **CD1, TR 38**

| | |
|---|---|
| **Woher kommen Sie?** [vo-hair common zee?] | *Where are you from?* |
| **Ich bin ...** [ich bin] | *I am ...* |
| **Ich komme aus ...** [ich comme-uh (h)ouse] | *I come from ...* |
| **England** [ehnglant] | *England* |
| **Engländer** [ehng-lenn-duh] | *Englishman* |
| **Engländerin** [ehng-lendur-in] | *Englishwoman* |
| **Deutschland** [doy-tsch-lant] | *Germany* |
| **Österreich** [ur-stir-righ(t)-ch] | *Austria* |

QUICK VOCAB

## WORD PATTERNS: NATIONALITY AND GENDER

In German you sometimes use different forms of a word according to whether it is a man or woman who is speaking.

For instance to say *I am English*, a man would say **Ich bin Engländer**, but a woman would say **Ich bin Engländerin**.

The feminine version of the words is usually made by adding **-in** to the masculine form. For example:

| | |
|---|---|
| Ich bin Brite/Britin. | Ich komme aus Großbritannien. |
| Ich bin Engländer/-in. | Ich komme aus England. |
| Ich bin Schotte/Schottin. | Ich komme aus Schottland. |
| Ich bin Waliser/-in. | Ich komme aus Wales. |
| Ich bin Ire/Irin. | Ich komme aus Irland. |
| Ich bin Australier/-in. | Ich komme aus Australien. |
| Ich bin Neuseeländer/-in. | Ich komme aus Neuseeland. |
| Ich bin Schweizer/-in. | Ich komme aus der Schweiz. |
| Ich bin Amerikaner/-in. | Ich komme aus Amerika or aus den Vereinigten Staaten. |

die Vereinigten Staaten *the United States*
die Schweiz *Switzerland*
Neighbours to Germany may say:
Ich bin Pole/Polin.
Ich bin Belgier/-in.
Ich bin Österreicher/-in.
Ich bin Holländer/-in.
Ich bin Franzose/Französin.
Ich bin Italiener/-in.

### PRONUNCIATION TIPS

**au** sounds **ow** as in **ow**(l)
**ch** is pronounced as in the Scottish word lo**ch**
**i** in Brite and Amerikaner is short, as in *it*, but is long in Ire, as in deep

# EUROPA *EUROPE*

## Exercise 1
What is the German for...?

**a** *Germany* _____
**b** *France* _____
**c** *Italy* _____
**d** *Poland* _____

**e** *Ireland* _____
**f** *Great Britain* _____
**g** *Belgium* _____
**h** *Spain* _____

i  Austria _____        m  Portugal _____
j  England _____        n  Switzerland _____
k  Scotland _____        o  Wales _____
l  Holland _____

**Listening exercise 12**
**◄) CD1, TR 39**

Welche Staatsangehörigkeit haben sie und woher kommen sie?
*What nationality are they and where are they from?* Listen to
the ten people talking about themselves and write down what
they say.

### WORD BUILDING

Look in the list and work out what
**Geburts-** means. You already know
the word for day as in *Good day!*
Now join the two words to form the
word *birthday*: **Geburtstag**.

What does the word **Ort** mean?
(look at **Geburtsort** and **Wohnort**).

## Ortsende

You often see this sign when
leaving a small town or village.
It means you are leaving the
'place' and there will usually
be a speed derestriction sign
beside it.

**Bade-** means bath or bathing; combining it with **Ort** gives us the
German word for a *spa town* or *bathing resort*: **Badeort** [bah-
duh-ort].

## Ein Formular zum Ausfüllen *A form to fill in*

◀) CD1, TR 40

| | |
|---|---|
| **Vorname** [for-nahmuh] | *first name* |
| **Familienname** [familien-nahmuh] | *surname (lit. family name)* |
| **Wohnort** [vone-ort] | *home/domicile* |
| **Anschrift** [an-shrift] | *address* |
| **Staatsangehörigkeit** [shtahts-an-guh-her-ich-kite] | *nationality* |
| **Geburtsort** [geboorts-ort] | *birthplace* |
| **Geburtsdatum** [geboorts-daht-um] | *date of birth* |
| **Familienstand** [familien-shtant] | *family status* |
| **verheiratet** [fair-high-ratet] | *married* |
| **ledig** [lay-dich] | *unmarried* |
| **Ihren Ausweis** [ear-en ows-vice] | *your identity card* |
| **Ihr Pass** [ear pass] | *your passport* |
| **Ihre Kreditkarte** [ear-uh credit cart-uh] | *your credit card* |

QUICK VOCAB

### PRONUNCIATION TIPS

ow as in owl
v sounds f
w sounds v

### LEARNING TIPS

**1** Practise saying the new words out loud.
**2** Look at the German words and see if you can remember what they all mean. Look for ways of remembering new words.

Name: *Fischer*          Vorname: *Helmut*

Geburtsdatum: *22.07–.65*

Anschrift: *Waldstraße 34, Stuttgart*

Postleitzahl: *7–0597*                    Telefonnummer: *12 34 56*

Staatsangehörigkeit: *Österreicher*

Geburtsort: *Salzburg*                    Familienstand: *ledig*

Ausweis/Reisepass: *137–239815*

Unterschrift: *H. Fischer*              Datum: *2004.04.03*
(signature)

## Exercise 2

What do you learn about Herr Fischer from the form above?
Answer the questions below:

- **a** *What is his first name?*
- **b** *What is his address?*
- **c** *What nationality is he?*
- **d** *Is he married or single?*

- **e** *How old is he?*
- **f** *What is his phone number?*
- **g** *Where was he born?*
- **h** *What is his postcode?*

## Listening exercise 13
◄ᴺ **CD1, TR 41**

Listen and see if you can fill in this form.

| Name: | Vorname: |
|---|---|
| Wohnort: | |
| Postleitzahl: | Telefonnummer: |
| Staatsangehörigkeit: | Familienstand: |
| Geburtsort: | Geburtsdatum: |
| Ausweis/Reisepass: | |

Exercise 3
Jetzt sind Sie dran!
*Now it's your turn.*

You are at the Hotel
Stern (star) in Frankfurt.
Practise your part of the
dialogue.

**a** *Ask if they have a room free.*

| | |
|---|---|
| Empfangsdame | Ja. Wie heißen Sie? |
| | Und mit Vornamen? |
| **b** | ................................................................ |
| Empfangsdame | Woher kommen Sie? |
| **c** | ................................................................ |
| Empfangsdame | Staatsangehörigkeit? |
| **d** | ................................................................ |
| Empfangsdame | Und Ihre Adresse? |
| **e** | ................................................................ |
| Empfangsdame | Und die Postleitzahl? |
| **f** | ................................................................ |
| Empfangsdame | Wie bitte? |
| **g** | ................................................................ |
| Empfangsdame | Und Ihre Telefonnummer? |
| **h** | ................................................................ |
| Empfangsdame | Wie ist die Vorwahl? |
| **i** | ................................................................ |
| Empfangsdame | Und Ihre Mobile Nummer? |
| **j** | ................................................................ |
| Empfangsdame | Haben Sie eine E-Mail Adresse? |
| **k** | ................................................................ |
| Empfangsdame | Also, Zimmer 15. |
| | Hier ist der Schlüssel. |
| **l** | ................................................................ |
| Empfangsdame | Bitte schön. |

## Exercise 3

Wie hießen die Fragen? *What were the questions that produced these replies?*

| | | |
|---|---|---|
| a | ...............................? | Schneider. |
| b | ...............................? | Hans. |
| c | ...............................? | Deutsch. |
| d | ...............................? | Dortmund. Am Hang 35. |
| e | ...............................? | 44267 |
| f | ...............................? | 23 54 63 |
| g | ...............................? | 23 54 63 |
| h | ...............................? | 0230 |

# TEST YOURSELF

**Ein Formular zum Ausfüllen** *A form to fill in*

Now fill in this form with your own details:

| | |
|---|---|
| Name: | Vorname: |
| Anschrift: | |
| Postleitzahl: | Telefonnummer: |
| Staatsangehörigkeit: | Familienstand: |
| Geburtsort: | Geburtsdatum: |
| Ausweis/Reisepass: | |
| Unterschrift:<br>(signature) | Datum: |
| E-Mail Adresse: | |

Check you can answer these questions correctly and if not go back and review the unit again.

**Unit 1**

**1** In the morning you should say
  **a** Guten Morgen **b** Guten Abend **c** Gute Nacht

**2** **Das tut mir Leid** means
  **a** I want a light **b** I am sorry **c** I am not well

**Unit 2**

**3** If someone says **Danke** you should respond by saying
  **a** Auf Wiedersehen **b** Danke schön **c** bitte

**4** Ich trinke keine Milch means
  **a** I drink milk **b** I don't drink milk **c** I only drink organic milk

Unit 3

**5** Ich möchte ein Stück Kuchen means
  **a** I can't cook **b** I like sticky cake **c** I would like a piece of cake

**6** Neunzehnhundertvierundneunzig is
  **a** 1940 **b** 1949 **c** 1994

Unit 4

**7** Wie ist die Postleitzahl? means
  **a** What is the postcode? **b** Where is the post office? **c** How is the postman?

**8** When you are talking to one person you know well or a child you use which form of the verb?
  **a** du form which ends in -st **b** the Sie form which ends in -en
  **c** the sie form which ends in -t

Unit 5

**9** If someone says Ich komme aus Österreich it means he/she comes from
  **a** Australia **b** Switzerland **c** Austria

**10** Fill in the gap: __ ist ihre Adresse? The missing word is
  **a** Was **b** Wie **c** Wo

Any problems with questions

1 and 2 go back to Unit 1
3 and 4 Unit 2
5 and 6 Unit 3
7 and 8 Unit 4
9 and 10 Unit 5

# 6

# Im Hotel
## In the hotel

In this unit you will learn how to
- *Book in to a hotel*
- *Ask where things are*
- *Ask when things are*
- *Ask to pay the bill*
- *Say if anything is wrong*
- *Understand how to use the phone*

---

## An der Rezeption *At reception*

◀⬤ CD2, TR 1

| | |
|---|---|
| **Haben Sie …?** | *Have you …?* |
| **ein/das Zimmer** | *a/the room* |
| **Einzelzimmer** | *single room* |
| **Doppelzimmer** | *double room* |
| **Wie lange?** | *How long (for)?* |
| **die Nacht (die Nächte)** | *night (nights)* |
| **das Bad** | *bath* |
| **die Dusche** | *shower* |
| **das Telefon** | *telephone* |
| **Wie viel kostet es?** | *How much does it cost?* |
| **das Frühstück** | *breakfast* |
| **Ist das Frühstück inbegriffen?** | *Is breakfast included?* |

| | |
|---|---|
| Um wie viel Uhr …? | *At what time?* |
| ab … bis | *from … to* |
| im dritten Stock | *on the third floor* |
| der Fahrstuhl | *lift* |
| dort drüben | *over there* |
| bleiben | *to stay or remain* |
| Würden Sie sich bitte eintragen? | *Would you sign in, please?* |

## Insight

Most hotel rooms have an en suite bathroom with a shower, but they are often just called **Zimmer mit Bad**. If you want to specify you want a bath as well as a shower you may need to ask for a room **mit Badewanne und Dusche** – *with bathtub and shower*.

### LEARNING TIPS

**1** Read the German words out loud. How many can you remember?
**2** Decide which it would be useful to learn and which you will only need to recognize. Look for ways to remember the useful phrases.
**3** Cover them up and see how many you can remember.

Exercise 1
How are you going to ask: *Have you a …?*

**a** *single room with shower*
**b** *double room with ensuite bathroom*
**c** *double room with bath and shower*

Exercise 2
Can you remember the word for *where*?

How would you ask:

**a** *Where is the room?*
**b** *Where is the lift?*
**c** *Where is the telephone?*

## DIALOGUE 14

| | |
|---|---|
| **Sie** | Haben Sie ein Zimmer frei? |
| **Empfangsdame** | Einzelzimmer oder Doppelzimmer? |
| **Sie** | Doppelzimmer. |
| **Empfangsdame** | Ja. Wie lange bleiben Sie? |
| **Sie** | Zwei Nächte. |
| **Empfangsdame** | Mit Bad oder mit Dusche? |
| **Sie** | Mit Bad. Wie viel kostet es? |
| **Empfangsdame** | €70. |
| **Sie** | Und was kostet ein Zimmer mit Dusche? |
| **Empfangsdame** | €65. |
| **Sie** | Ist das Frühstück inbegriffen? |
| **Empfangsdame** | Ja. |
| **Sie** | Ich nehme das Zimmer mit Dusche. Um wie viel Uhr ist das Frühstück? |
| **Empfangsdame** | Ab 6.00 Uhr. |
| **Sie** | Bis wann? |
| **Empfangsdame** | Bis 9.00 Uhr. Zimmer 307 im dritten Stock. Der Fahrstuhl ist dort drüben. Würden Sie sich bitte eintragen? Hier ist der Schlüssel. |

### LEARNING TIPS

**1** Make sure you understand all the dialogue.
**2** Read both parts of the dialogue out loud.
**3** Try to answer the receptionist's questions.

Listening exercise 14
🔊 **CD2, TR 3**

Listen to the six customers making their reservations. What sort of rooms do they want? How long are they staying?

## Ich möchte ... *I would like ...*

What other things might you want to ask or say?

Here are some suggestions.

| | |
|---|---|
| **Haben Sie ...** | *Have you ...* |
| **Haben Sie ein Familienzimmer?** | *Have you a family room?* |
| **Haben Sie ein Zimmer ...?** | *Have you got a room ...?* |
| **... mit Doppelbett** | *with a double bed* |
| **... mit Einzelbetten** | *with single beds* |
| **... mit Zusatzbett** | *with an extra bed* |
| **Haben Sie etwas Billigeres?** | *Have you anything cheaper?* |
| **Haben Sie eine Garage?** | *Have you a garage?* |
| **Haben Sie ein Zimmer mit Balkon?** | *Have you a room with a balcony?* |
| **Haben Sie ein Zimmer mit Fernseher?** | *Have you a room with television?* |
| **Haben Sie ein Zimmer mit Telefon?** | *Have you a room with a phone?* |
| **Ich möchte ...** | *I would like to ...* |
| **Ich möchte nach England anrufen.** | *I would like to ring England.* |
| **Ich möchte im Zimmer frühstücken.** | *I would like to have breakfast in my room.* |
| **Ich möchte das Fenster öffnen.** | *I would like to open the window.* |
| **Ich möchte die Heizung ausmachen.** | *I would like to turn off the heating.* |
| **Ich möchte zahlen.** | *I would like to pay.* |
| **Ich möchte eine Quittung.** | *I would like to a receipt.* |
| **Gibt es ...** | *Is there ...* |
| **Gibt es eine Garage?** | *Is there a garage?* |
| **Gibt es eine Tiefgarage?** | *Is there a an underground garage?* |
| **Gibt es einen Parkplatz?** | *Is there a car park?* |
| **Gibt es ein Schwimmbad?** | *Is there a swimming pool?* |
| **Gibt es einen Wellnessbereich?** | *Is there a fitness centre?* |
| **Gibt es eine Bar?** | *Is there a bar?* |
| **Gibt es ein Restaurant?** | *Is there a restaurant?* |

QUICK VOCAB

| **Gibt es ein Telefon im Zimmer?** | *Is there a telephone in the room?* |
| **Ich habe ein Zimmer reserviert.** | *I have booked (reserved) a room.* |
| | *(lit. I have a room booked.)* |
| **Würden Sie mich um ... wecken?** | *Would you wake me at ...?* |
| **Nehmen Sie (Kredit) Karten?** | *Do you take (credit) cards?* |
| **Unterschreiben Sie hier.** | *Sign here.* |

Note that with **der** words **ein** becomes **einen** after **ich möchte ...**, **haben Sie ...?**, **gibt es ...** and many other verbs, e.g.:

Gibt es einen Fitnessraum im Hotel?

(See Unit 8 for more information about **der, die** and **das**.)

**LEARNING TIPS**

**1** Practise reading all the phrases out loud.
**2** If possible find someone to read out phrases to you at random and see if you can recognize the meaning.
**3** Learn the three key phrases:
   **Haben Sie ...?** *Have you [got] a ...?*
   **Ich möchte ...** *I would like ...*
   **Gibt es ...?** *Is there ...?*
**4** See how many of the German phrases you can remember.

Exercise 3
Now you should be ready to complete your part of these dialogues.

| | |
|---|---|
| **a You** | I have booked a room. |
| **Empfangschef** | Ihr Name bitte? |
| **b You** | Give your name. |
| **Empfangschef** | Doppelzimmer mit Bad? |
| **c You** | No. Single with shower. |
| **Empfangschef** | Ach, ja. Zimmernummer 35. |
| **d You** | Pardon? |
| **Empfangschef** | 35. Im dritten Stock. |
| **e You** | Is there a lift? |
| **Empfangschef** | Ja, dort drüben. |
| **f You** | When is breakfast? |
| **Empfangschef** | Ab 6.00 Uhr. |
| **g You** | Can I have a call at 7 o'clock? |
| **Empfangschef** | Ja. Hier ist Ihr Schlüssel. |
| | |
| **h You** | Have you got a room free? |
| **Empfangschef** | Ja. Für wie lange? |
| **i You** | For three nights. |
| **Empfangschef** | Einzelzimmer oder Doppelzimmer? |
| **j You** | Double. |
| **Empfangschef** | Gut. Ein Doppelzimmer mit Bad . |
| **k You** | Is there a telephone in the room? |
| **Empfangschef** | Ja. Und Fernseher. |
| **l You** | How much does it cost? |
| **Empfangschef** | €150 pro Nacht. |
| **m You** | Is breakfast included? |
| **Empfangschef** | Ja. |
| | |
| **n You** | Say you would like your bill. |
| **Empfangschef** | Zimmernummer? |
| **o You** | 811. Do you take credit cards? |
| **Empfangschef** | Ja. Unterschreiben Sie hier, bitte. |
| **p You** | A receipt please. |
| **Empfangschef** | Bitte schön. |
| | |
| **q You** | Ask if you can be woken. |
| **Empfangschef** | Ja, um wie viel Uhr? |
| **r You** | At 7 o'clock. |
| **Empfangschef** | Welche Zimmernummer haben Sie? |
| **s You** | 207. |

## Was ist los? *What's wrong?*

| | |
|---|---|
| **... funktioniert nicht** | *... doesn't work* |
| **die Heizung** | *heating* |
| **die Klimaanlage** | *air conditioning* |
| **das Fenster** | *window* |
| **der Wasserhahn** | *water tap* |
| **das Licht** | *light* |
| **die Glühbirne** | *the light bulb* |
| **der Föhn** | *hairdryer* |
| **der Safe** | *safe* |
| **die Dusche** | *shower* |
| **der Schalter** | *switch* |

| | |
|---|---|
| **Das Zimmer ist ...** | *The room is ...* |
| **Das Zimmer ist zu laut.** | *The room is too noisy.* |
| **Das Zimmer ist zu klein.** | *The room is too small.* |
| **Das Zimmer ist zu kalt.** | *The room is too cold.* |
| **Das Zimmer ist zu heiß.** | *The room is too hot.* |
| **Das Zimmer ist zu teuer.** | *The room is too expensive.* |
| **Es gibt (kein/keine/keinen ...)** | *There's no ...* |
| **Es gibt kein Telefon.** | *There's no telephone.* |
| **Es gibt kein Bad.** | *There's no bath.* |
| **Es gibt keine Bar.** | *There's no bar.* |
| **Es gibt keinen Fernseher.** | *There's no TV.* |
| **Die Heizung funktioniert nicht.** | *The heating doesn't work.* |
| **Das Licht ist kaputt.** | *The light is broken.* |
| **Jemand kommt gleich.** | *Someone will be right with you.* |
| **Welche Zimmernummer haben Sie?** | *What is your room number?* |
| **Wie funktioniert ...?** | *How does ... work?* |
| **Ich nehme es.** | *I'll take it.* |
| **der Zimmerservice** | *room service* |
| **Ich habe meinen Schlüssel verloren.** | *I have lost my key.* |

QUICK VOCAB

**Exercise 4**
Now try these dialogues.

| | |
|---|---|
| **a You** | Excuse me, please. |
| **Empfangsdame** | Bitte? |
| **b You** | My room is too noisy. |
| **Empfangsdame** | Das tut mir Leid. Zimmer 14 ist frei.. |
| **c You** | Is there a shower? |
| **Empfangsdame** | Ja. |
| **d You** | I'll take it. |
| **Empfangsdame** | Hier ist der Schlüssel. Im ersten Stock, links. |
| | |
| **e You** | Excuse me please. |
| **Empfangsdame** | Bitte? |
| **f You** | My room is too hot. How does the heating work? |
| **Empfangsdame** | Es gibt einen Schalter unter dem Fenster. *Am Telefon* |
| **g You** | Room service? |
| **Empfangsdame** | Ja. |
| **h You** | The light is broken. |
| **Empfangsdame** | Jemand kommt gleich. Welche Zimmernummer haben Sie? |
| **i You** | 48. |

| | |
|---|---|
| **j You** | Room service? |
| **Empfangsdame** | Ja. |
| **k You** | Can you wake me at 6.00? |
| **Empfangsdame** | Welche Zimmernummer haben Sie? |
| **l You** | 63. I would like breakfast in my room. |
| **Empfangsdame** | Um wie viel Uhr? |
| **m You** | 7 am. |

---

# Ich möchte nach England anrufen
*I want to make a call to England*

🔊 **CD2, TR 4**

| | |
|---|---|
| **Wie ist die Nummer für die Telefonauskunft?** | *What is the number for directory inquiries?* |
| **Sie wählen ...** | *You dial ...* |
| **11834 für Ausland** | *11834 for abroad* |
| **11833 für Inland** | *11833 for inland* |
| **Polizei 110** | *Police 110* |
| **Feuerwehr 112** | *Fire brigade 112* |
| **Notarzt/Rettungswagen 112** | *Emergency services/ ambulance 112* |
| **Ich suche eine Nummer in Frankfurt.** | *I'm looking for a number in Frankfurt.* |
| **die Vorwahl** | *code* |
| **das Ausland** | *abroad* |
| **das Inland** | *inland* |
| **zuerst** | *first* |
| **und dann** | *and then* |
| **das Ortsgespräch** | *local call* |
| **das Ferngespräch** | *long distance call* |
| **anrufen** | *to call* |
| **drücken** | *to press* |
| **Wiederholen Sie bitte** | *Please repeat* |

QUICK VOCAB

**Ich möchte bitte Herrn
...Frau ...sprechen.**
**Er/Sie ist nicht da.**
**die schwarze Taste**

*I'd like to speak to
Mr.../Mrs... please.*
*He/she isn't here.*
*black key*

## WORD PATTERNS: WORD ORDER

When you say *I want to do something* and use **Ich möchte** the
other verb goes to the end of the sentence.

**Ich möchte** nach Amerika **anrufen.**
**Ich möchte** nach Frankreich **fahren.**
**Ich möchte** Tennis mit Hilda **spielen.**

Exercise 5
Complete the dialogue:

**a** *Say you want to ring England.*
**Sie wählen zuerst 0 und dann
die Vorwahl für England: 00 44.**

**b** *Now say you want to ring room Number 25.*
**Sie wählen die Nummer 25.**

**c** *Ring reception and ask how to make a local call.*
**Sie drücken die schwarze Taste
und wählen die Nummer.**

Tell your German friend how to ring Germany from your home.

(The code for Germany is oo 49.)

Please inform the reception if you are expecting a call and won't be
in your room.

## *TEST YOURSELF*

How would you say the following in German?

**1** There's no
   **a** telephone
   **b** bar
   **c** TV in my room

**2** My room is
   **a** too small
   **b** too hot
   **c** too noisy
   **d** too cold

**3** How would you ask for …
   **a** a double room
   **b** a single room with en suite bathroom
   **c** a family room
   **d** a room with twin beds

**4** And how would you say
   **a** The television is not working.
   **b** How does the air conditioning work?
   **c** Is there a hairdryer?

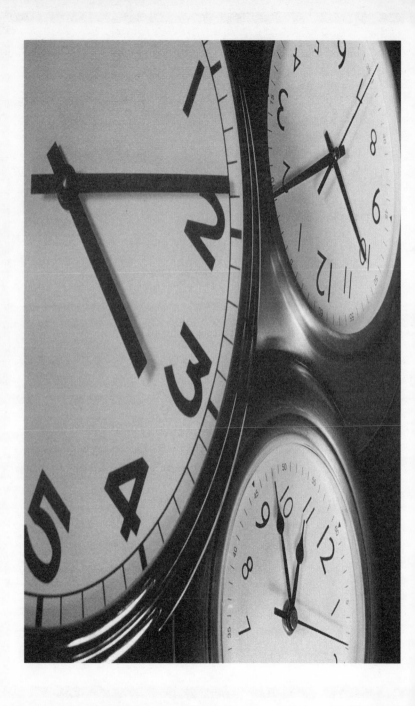

# 7

# Die Uhrzeiten
## Telling the time

In this unit you will learn how to
* *Tell the time in German*
* *Ask what time it is*
* *Recognize the days of the week in German*
* *Make arrangements to meet*

Es ist ...

◀) CD2, TR 5

ein Uhr

acht Uhr

fünf nach eins

Es ist ...

zehn nach zwei

Viertel nach zwei

Viertel nach acht

Es ist …

Viertel vor zwei

fünf vor zwei

zehn nach drei

**Es tut mir Leid.**      *I am sorry.*
**Ich weiß es nicht.**      *I don't know (it).*

### LANGUAGE NOTES

It is easy to remember the word for quarter – **Viertel** – as it is based on **vier** *four*.

In times, **nach** means past and **vor** means *to* (lit. *before*).

The word for o'clock is **Uhr** (lit. *clock*).

### LEARNING TIPS

**1** Read the times out loud.
**2** Cover up the words and see if you can say the times.
**3** Listen to the recording and check your pronunciation.

### DIALOGUE 15

| | |
|---|---|
| **Sie** | Entschuldigen Sie, bitte. Wie spät ist es? |
| **Passant** | Es ist vier Uhr. |
| **Sie** | Danke. |
| **Sie** | Entschuldigen Sie, bitte. Wie viel Uhr ist es? |
| **Passant** | Es ist Viertel nach vier. |
| **Sie** | Danke. |
| **Sie** | Entschuldigen Sie, bitte. Wie spät ist es? |
| **Passant** | Es ist Viertel vor fünf. |
| **Sie** | Danke. |

QV

CD2, TR 6

| Entschuldigen Sie, bitte. | *Excuse me please.* |
|---|---|
| Wie viel Uhr ist es? | *What time is it? (lit. how many o'clock is it?)* |
| Wie spät ist es? | *What time is it? (lit. how late is it?)* |
| Viertel | *quarter* |
| es ist ... | *it is ...* |
| nach | *after/past* |
| vor | *before/to* |
| die Uhr [dee Oo-er] | *clock* |
| die Armbanduhr | *(wrist) watch* |
| Geht die Uhr genau? | *Is the clock/watch right?* |
| Meine Uhr geht nicht. | *My watch has stopped. (lit. is not going.)* |
| Sie ist kaputt. | *It (she) is broken.* |

## LANGUAGE NOTES

There are two ways to ask what time it is.
**Wie spät ist es?** and **Wie viel Uhr ist es?**
The answer is: **Es ist ...**

## LEARNING TIP

**1** Read both parts of the dialogue out loud.

Exercise 1
What would you say for these times?

Es ist ...

## LANGUAGE NOTES

Look at these clocks and the words. Which is the word for *half*?
How can you remember it?

Halb zwei *half past one*

halb zwei          halb drei          halb neun

Now have another look at the words under the clock showing
1.30. Are they what you would expect them to be? What is the
difference? What have you discovered about the way the Germans
say half past the hour?

For 2.30, instead of saying half (*past*) two they say:

half (*to*) three.

## Exercise 2
What would you say for these times? **Es ist ...**

a       b       c       d

## Listening exercise 15
🔊 **CD2, TR 7**

What time is it?

a       b       c       d

## Exercise 3
Jetzt sind Sie dran.

| | |
|---|---|
| **a You** | Ask this gentleman the time. |
| **Passerby** | Es tut mir Leid. Ich weiß es nicht. Meine Uhr ist kaputt. |
| *Bad luck. Try this lady.* | |
| **b You** | What time is it, please? |
| **Passerby** | Viertel nach elf. |
| **c You** | Thank her. |
| **Passerby** | Nichts zu danken. |
| **d You** | Say goodbye. |
| **Passerby** | Auf Wiedersehen. |
| *Now it is your turn to be asked.* | |
| **Herr X** | Entschuldigung! Wie spät ist es? |
| **e You** | Oh dear, you have left your watch in the bathroom. Say you are sorry you don't know. |

## Exercise 4
What would you have said if it had been these times?

8.30    8.45    10.15    14.45    18.30

## Wann treffen wir uns? *When shall we meet?*

◀)) CD2, TR 8

| | |
|---|---|
| die Wochentage | *days of the week* |
| die Woche | *week* |
| am ... | *on ...* |
| am Montag | *on Monday* |
| am Dienstag | *on Tuesday* |
| am Mittwoch | *on Wednesday* |
| am Donnerstag | *on Thursday* |
| am Freitag | *on Friday* |
| am Samstag oder Sonnabend | *on Saturday* |
| am Sonntag | *on Sunday* |

There are two German words for Saturday. **Sonnabend** (lit. *sun eve*) is often used instead of **Samstag** in the north of Germany.

When making arrangements to meet or giving bus or train times Germans usually use the twenty-four hour clock, e.g. 5.00 pm becomes 17.00 Uhr etc.

| | |
|---|---|
| **Wann treffen wir uns?** | *When shall we meet? (lit. when meet we us?)* |
| der Morgen | *morning* |
| der Nachmittag | *afternoon* |
| der Abend | *evening* |
| die Nacht | *night* |
| Mittag | *midday* |

78

| | |
|---|---|
| **Mitternacht** | *midnight* |
| **um** | *at* |
| **um acht Uhr morgens** | *at 8 o'clock in the morning* |
| **um acht Uhr früh** | *at 8 am (lit. at 8 o'clock early)* |
| **um zwei Uhr nachmittags** | *at two in the afternoon* |
| **um sieben Uhr abends** | *at seven in the evening* |
| **Geht das?** | *Is that all right? (lit. goes that?)* |
| **Ich freue mich schon darauf.** | *I am looking forward to it already.* |
| **Bis dann!** | *Till then!* |

### PRONUNCIATION TIPS

ie sounds ee
ei sounds aye
ch as in loch
freue sounds froy-uh

### LEARNING TIP

**1** Practise saying the days of the week aloud.

### Exercise 5

**a** Put these days in the right order, starting with Monday:

| | | | |
|---|---|---|---|
| **Samstag** | **Donnerstag** | **Montag** | **Sonntag** |
| **Mittwoch** | **Dienstag** | **Freitag** | |

**b** Put these times in the right order:

| | | |
|---|---|---|
| **2.00h nachmittags** | **Mittag** | **9.00h früh** |
| **6.00h abends** | **4.00h nachmittags** | **19.00h** |
| **6.00h morgens** | **Mitternacht** | |

### DIALOGUE 16

Mr Taylor is staying at the Hotel Zur Post in Hamburg and rings
Herr Braun to invite him out for a meal.

| | |
|---|---|
| **Herr Braun** | Braun. |
| **Mr Taylor** | Hallo, Herr Braun. Hier Mr Taylor. Ich bin im Hotel Zur Post. Essen Sie heute Abend mit uns? |
| **Herr Braun** | Ja, gerne. Um wie viel Uhr? |
| **Mr Taylor** | Um acht, geht das? |
| **Herr Braun** | Ja. Wann treffen wir uns? |
| **Mr Taylor** | Um halb acht in der Bar im Hotel. |
| **Herr Braun** | Gut. Ich freue mich schon darauf. |
| **Mr Taylor** | Bis dann. *Auf Wiederhören! |
| **Herr Braun** | Auf Wiederhören! |

**\*Auf Wiederhören!** Germans say **auf Wiederhören** (lit. *till I hear you again*), instead of **auf Wiedersehen** (lit. *till I see you again*), when using the phone.

### LEARNING TIP

**1** Practise both parts of the dialogue.

Exercise 6
What would you say to arrange to meet at these times?

**a** *Monday 2.30*      **d** *Tuesday 10.20*      **g** *Friday 8.45*
**b** *Thursday 23.00*   **e** *Sunday 17.45*       **h** *Tuesday midday*
**c** *Saturday 19.00*   **f** *Wednesday 17.30*    **i** *Thursday 18.15*

Exercise 7
Making a phone call. How do you say:

**a** *Goodbye.*
**b** *Is that all right?*
**c** *Till then!*
**d** *I am looking forward to it already.*

# TEST YOURSELF

**1** Wie viel Uhr ist es? Es ist …

**2** Und wann treffen wir uns? Wir treffen uns um …

**3** Wie spät ist es? *What's the time?* Some of these are unusual.
You don't have to be able to say them all, but you should be
able to work out what they mean.

a Zwanzig nach vier
b Zehn nach zwei
c Halb zehn
d Fünf nach halb elf
e Fünf vor halb vier

f Fünf nach halb sieben
g Viertel vor neun
h Halb drei
i Drei viertel vier
j Zehn vor neun

**4** What times do the various timepieces show – and which is which in German?

a die Kuckucksuhr
b der Radiowecker
c die Armbanduhr

d die (Wand) Uhr
e der Wecker

**5** **Anagrams. Welcher Tag?** Which day is represented by each of these anagrams?

a STAGDINE
b GATEFIR
c MANGOT
d MAGASST

e TITCHMOW
f SONGANT
g SNNOGDATER

**6** Why can't these people answer when you ask **Wie spät ist es?**

a Ich brauche eine Batterie für meine Uhr.

b Ich habe meine Armbanduhr verloren.

c Meine Uhr ist kaputt.

ich brauche — *I need*
verloren — *lost*

82

# Der Stadtplan
## The street map

In this unit you will learn how to
- *Recognize names of important buildings in a German town*
- *Ask where places are*
- *Say what street they are in*
- *Help yourself understand new words*

## Wo ist ...? *Where is ...?*

◀) **CD2, TR 10**

| | |
|---|---|
| **dort drüben** | *over there* |
| **der Bahnhof** | *station* |
| **die Bibliothek** | *library* |
| **die Brücke** | *bridge* |
| **der Dom** | *cathedral* |
| **der Flughafen** | *airport* |
| **das Freibad** | *open-air swimming pool* |
| **das Informationsbüro** | *information office* |
| **die Jugendherberge** | *youth hostel* |
| **das Kino** | *cinema* |
| **die Kirche** | *church* |
| **die Kneipe** | *pub* |
| **das Krankenhaus** | *hospital* |
| **der Marktplatz** | *marketplace* |

QUICK VOCAB

| das Rathaus | *town hall* |
| das Schloss | *castle* |
| der Schnellimbiss | *snack bar* |
| die Straße | *street* |
| die Hauptstraße | *main street* |

And these shouldn't present much difficulty.

| die Bank | die Post |
| der Park | das Hotel |
| das Restaurant | das Theater |

## Insight

Most people nowadays prefer to get their money from a cash machine or ATM rather than carry traveller's cheques. In German a cash machine is called **ein Geldautomat** and they usually have instructions in a choice of languages so if you are in any doubt just click on the Union Jack!

### LANGUAGE NOTES

There are three German words meaning *the*: **der**, **die** and **das**. **Der** indicates a masculine word, **die** a feminine word and **das** a neuter word. Learn the **der**, **die** or **das** with each word: eg. **der Bahnhof** *the station*.

### PRONUNCIATION TIPS

**der** sounds like **dare**
**die** sounds like **dee**
**das** sounds like **das**

### LEARNING TIPS

1 Practise saying the new words aloud.
2 Check the pronunciation with the recording.
3 Cover up the English and see how many you can recognize.
4 Choose ten to learn today.

## DIALOGUE 17

| | |
|---|---|
| **Sie** | Entschuldigen Sie bitte. Ist das die Bank? |
| **Passant** | Nein. Das ist das Rathaus. |
| **Sie** | Wo ist die Bank? |
| **Passant** | Die Bank ist dort drüben. |
| **Sie** | Danke. |
| | |
| **Sie** | Entschuldigung! Wo ist der Bahnhof? |
| **Passant** | Der Bahnhof? Dort drüben! |
| **Sie** | Danke. |
| **Sie** | Entschuldigen Sie bitte. Ist das das Hotel Zur Post? |
| **Passant** | Nein. Das ist das Hotel Modern. |
| **Sie** | Wo ist das Hotel Zur Post? |
| **Passant** | Es tut mir Leid. Ich weiß es nicht. |
| | |
| **Sie** | Wo ist das Informationsbüro? |
| **Passant** | Dort drüben. |
| **Sie** | Vielen Dank. Auf Wiedersehen. |
| **Passant** | Nichts zu danken. Auf Wiedersehen. |

### LEARNING TIP

**1** Read your part of the dialogue out loud.

### Exercise 1

A German visitor to your town asks you:

a **Ist das die Bank?** *Tell him, no it's the post office.*
b **Wo ist die Bank?** *Tell him, it's over there.*
c **Danke.** *Say, don't mention it.*
d **Wo ist das Hotel Star?** *Say you are sorry, you don't know.*
e **Wo ist das Informationsbüro?** *Tell him, it's over there.*
f **Vielen Dank. Auf Wiedersehen.** *Say goodbye.*

### WORD PATTERNS: 'THE' AND GENDER

This section is about the structure of the language. If all you want to do is speak and understand the language at a basic level you don't need to study it. It is better to concentrate on learning the **Key words** and useful phrases, but if you want to know more about the language and to be able to read and write it you should also try to learn something about its patterns.

A noun is a naming word, or a word that you can put *the* in front of in English, e.g. the table, the town centre, the hotel, the party, the pain, the shopping.

In German all nouns are masculine, feminine or neuter, i.e. **der**, **die** or **das** words. **Der, die** and **das** all mean *the*. In modern English there is only one word for *the*, but in German the word for *the* changes to match the word it is going with.

**Der** words are masculine words:  der Mann – *the man*
**Die** words are feminine words:  die Frau – *the woman*
**Das** words are neuter words:  das Haus – *the house*

Something else you may have noticed about nouns in German is that they all start with a capital letter.

Occasionally you can tell or guess whether the word is going to be masculine, feminine or neuter, but mostly you can't! So it's best to try to learn the **der, die** or **das** with new words or try to learn words in phrases or useful expressions, rather than as single words. You will probably find some shortcuts, however. For example, see what you notice in Exercise 2: What do you notice about (most) words which end with an 'e'? What about words which end with an 'o'? And foreign words (e.g. Café)?

If you want to say 'a' instead of 'the' you use **ein** or **eine**.

der words: **ein**
die words: **eine**
das words: **ein**

| **der Wagen** | *the car* | **ein Wagen** | *a car* |
| **die Katze** | *the cat* | **eine Katze** | *a cat* |
| **das Haus** | *the house* | **ein Haus** | *a house* |

## Exercise 2
**Masculine, feminine or neuter?**

Bahnhof Bank Bibliothek Brücke Café Flughafen Freibad
Hotel Informationsbüro Jugendherberge Kino Kirche Kneipe
Krankenhaus Marktplatz Park Post Rathaus Reisebüro Restaurant
Schloss Schnellimbiss Straße

| der | die | das |
|-----|-----|-----|
|     |     |     |

## Exercise 3
Fill in the rows, using these clues, to reveal another important
building in column A.

**a** a bridge
**b** a church
**c** a theatre
**d** a bank
**e** a marketplace
**f** a pub

**g** a cinema
**h** an airport
**i** a station
**j** a town hall
**k** a post office

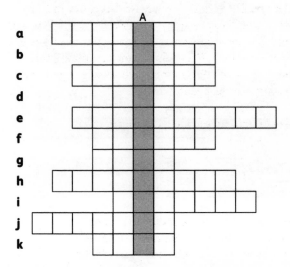

## Listening exercise 16
🔊 **CD2, TR 12**

Where do these people want to go?

## Wo ist ...? *Where is ...?*

**Legende** *Key*

| die Kirche | die Toiletten | der Park |
|---|---|---|
| das Kino | das Informationsbüro | das Hotel |

| das Theater | der Parkplatz | das Freibad |
|---|---|---|
| der Bahnhof | die Post | das Krankenhaus |
| das Restaurant | die Bank | der Biergarten |

## Exercise 4
Können Sie die Lücken ausfüllen? Can you fill in the gaps?

**a** Das Rathaus ist am …platz.
**b** Der Bahnhof ist in der …straße.
**c** Die Post ist in der …straße.
**d** Das Freibad ist in der …Allee.
**e** Die Bank ist in der …straße.
**f** Das Restaurant ist am …platz.
**g** Das Informationsbüro und die Toiletten sind (are) in der …straße.
**h** Das Kino ist in der …allee.

## Exercise 5
Ask where these places are …
**Wo ist hier ein/eine …?** *Where is there a … (here)?*

**a** die Kirche
**b** das Theater
**c** das Restaurant
**d** das Informationsbüro
**e** die Post
**f** der Park
**g** das Freibad
**h** der Biergarten
**i** das Kino
**j** der Bahnhof
**k** die Toilette
**l** der Parkplatz
**m** die Bank
**n** das Hotel
**o** das Krankenhaus
**p** der Campingplatz

Now give the full answer (without looking at **Exercise 2** if possible), e.g. Die Kirche ist in der ... Straße.

### WORD PATTERNS: TRIGGER WORD [PREPOSITION] 'IN'

A trigger word is a word which sometimes changes the word which comes after it.

You might have noticed that the word for street is **die Straße,** but when you say *in the street* it becomes **in der Straße**. This is because the word **in** is a trigger word which sometimes changes **die** to **der**.

**in + die = in der**   in der Hauptstraße

**In** also sometimes changes **der** and **das** to produce in **dem**, and this is almost always shortened to **im**:

**in + der = in dem** (im)   im Park
**in + das = in dem** (im)   im Hotel

It is the trigger words (or prepositions) that make people think German is a difficult language to learn.

## Insight

It is perfectly possible to speak understandable German without learning all the rules. The best thing is to learn some useful phrases by heart so that you are used to the pattern of the words and then use them as models to build phrases of your own, e.g.

**Ich bin im Hotel Stern in der Hauptstraße.**

*I am at the Star Hotel in the main street.*

Then change the name of the hotel and the street as necessary.

# TEST YOURSELF

**1** Pair up the English and the German words.

| | | | |
|---|---|---|---|
| **a** | der Bahnhof | **i** | the bridge |
| **b** | die Bar | **ii** | the café |
| **c** | die Bibliothek | **iii** | the church |
| **d** | die Brücke | **iv** | the youth hostel |
| **e** | das Café | **v** | the restaurant |
| **f** | der Dom | **vi** | the library |
| **g** | der Flughafen | **vii** | the pub |
| **h** | das Informationsbüro | **viii** | the hospital |
| **i** | die Jugendherberge | **ix** | the cathedral |
| **j** | das Kino | **x** | the town hall |
| **k** | die Kirche | **xi** | the castle |
| **l** | die Kneipe | **xii** | the cinema |
| **m** | das Krankenhaus | **xiii** | the airport |
| **n** | der Marktplatz | **xiv** | the snack bar |
| **o** | das Rathaus | **xv** | the street |
| **p** | das Restaurant | **xvi** | the bar |
| **q** | das Schloss | **xvii** | the station |
| **r** | der Schnellimbiss | **xviii** | the marketplace |
| **s** | die Straße | **xix** | the information office |

**2** Work out what these words mean by breaking them up (here are a few extra clues: **Haupt** *main*, **Auskunft** *information*, **Stelle** *place*).

der Campingplatz
die Hauptpost
das Auskunftsbüro
die Polizeiwache
die Bushaltestelle
die Autobahnbrücke

die Fußgängerzone
der Hauptbahnhof
der Sportplatz
der Busbahnhof
die Tankstelle
die Landungsbrücke

**Richtig oder falsch?** *True or false?*

|   |   | R | F |
|---|---|---|---|
| **a** | Die Kirche ist in der Griechstraße. | ☐ | ☐ |
| **b** | Die Bar ist in der Neustraße. | ☐ | ☐ |
| **c** | Die Post ist in der Rheinallee. | ☐ | ☐ |
| **d** | Das Café ist in der Burgstraße. | ☐ | ☐ |
| **e** | Die Bank ist am Marktplatz. | ☐ | ☐ |
| **f** | Die Kneipe ist in der Bahnhofstraße. | ☐ | ☐ |
| **g** | Die Toiletten sind am Parkplatz. | ☐ | ☐ |
| **h** | Das Informationsbüro ist am Rathausplatz. | ☐ | ☐ |
| **i** | Der Parkplatz ist in der Bonner Allee. | ☐ | ☐ |
| **j** | Die Jugendherberge ist am Rheinweg. | ☐ | ☐ |

**Sign language**

Which sign is it?

i **Bahnhof**   ii **Stadtmitte**   iii

iv **Schwimmbad**   v *Fußballstadion*   vi *Rathaus*

**a** the football stadium
**b** the post office
**c** the town centre
**d** the station
**e** the town hall
**f** the swimming pool

# 9

---

# Wie komme ich zur Post?
## How do I get to the post office?

In this unit you will learn how to
- *Ask for directions*
- *Give directions*
- *Ask and say how far somewhere is*

◄) **CD2, TR 14**

---

Wie komme ich dorthin? *How do I get there?*

### WORD PATTERNS: TRIGGER WORD 'ZU'

**Zu** is a trigger word which changes    **die** to **der**
    **der** to **dem**
    **das** to **dem**
    **die** (plural) to **den**

**Zum** is an abbreviation of    **zu + dem.**
**Zur** is an abbreviation of    **zu + der.**
So with **der** and **das** words you use    **zum: zum** Bahnhof.
With **die** words you use    **zur: zur** Post.
With plural words you use    **zu den: zu den** Toiletten.

| Wie komme ich **zum** Bahnhof? | *How do I get to the station?* |
| | *(lit. how come I ...)* |
| **zur** Post | *to the post office* |
| **zum** Rathaus | *to the town hall* |

Memorize the phrases **zum Bahnhof, zur Post** and **zu den Toiletten** and use them to remind yourself of the correct forms.

Don't worry – even if you don't get them right, Germans will still be able to understand where you are asking for!

**Exercise 1**: *zum* **or** *zur*?
How would you ask the way to these places?

(First decide whether they are der, die, or das words.)

Wie komme ich zu ...
 **a** Rathaus?
 **b** Krankenhaus?
 **c** Hotel?
 **d** Café?
 **e** Restaurant?
 **f** Bank?
 **g** Freibad?
 **h** Supermarkt (m.)?
 **i** Tankstelle?
 **j** Campingplatz?
 **k** Parkplatz?
 **l** Busbahnhof?

**DIALOGUE 18**

| **Sie** | Wie komme ich am besten zur Post? |
| **Passant** | Sie gehen hier geradeaus. Die Post ist auf der rechten Seite. |
| **Sie** | Vielen Dank. Auf Wiedersehen. |
| **Passant** | Wie komme ich am besten zum Freibad? |

| Sie | Sie nehmen die erste Straße links. Das Freibad ist auf der linken Seite. |
| Passant | Vielen Dank. Auf Wiedersehen. |
| Sie | Wie komme ich am besten zum Bahnhof? |
| Passant | Sie nehmen die erste Straße rechts und die zweite Straße links. |

| | |
|---|---|
| **links/rechts** | *left/right* |
| **geradeaus** | *straight ahead* |
| **die erste Straße rechts** | *the first street right* |
| **die zweite Straße links** | *the second street left* |
| **auf der linken Seite** | *on the left (side)* |
| **auf der rechten Seite** | *on the right (side)* |
| **Sie nehmen ...** | *you take ...* |
| **zum/zur** | *to the* |

## PRONUNCIATION TIPS

**ch** as in loch
**ei** as in eye
**ge** as in grass

### LEARNING TIP

**1** Check you understand the German and then practise saying the dialogues.

Exercise 2
Tell your German friend the following directions:

**a** *straight ahead, on the right*
**b** *first right, on the left*
**c** *second left, on the left*
**d** *first left, on the right*
**e** *second right, on the right*
**f** *straight ahead, on the left*

## Im Informationsbüro *At the information office*

| | |
|---|---|
| **Gibt es … in der Nähe?** | *Is there a … near here?* |
| **Ich rufe mal an** | *I'll give them a ring. (lit. I call just up)* |
| **noch** | *still* |
| **frei** | *free, available* |
| **Einzel- oder Doppelzimmer** | *single or double room* |
| **mit Dusche** | *with shower* |
| **mit Bad** | *with bath* |
| **zu Fuß** | *on foot* |
| **mit dem Auto** | *(with the) by car* |
| **entlang** | *along* |
| **die Einbahnstraße** | *one-way street* |

**Entlang** means *along* but instead of saying *along the street* in German it is more correct to say 'the street along': **die Straße entlang.**

### PRONUNCIATION TIP

**Nähe** sounds like **nay-er.**

### LANGUAGE NOTES

| | m. | f. | n. |
|---|---|---|---|
| Gibt es | einen Parkplatz? | eine Bank? | ein Hotel? |

There are two ways of saying *I go* or *I am going* in German. If you are walking you say: **ich gehe** and if you are driving or being driven you use: **ich fahre**.

| **Ich fahre** | **mit dem Auto.** | *I am going* | *by car.* |
| | **mit dem Bus.** | | *by bus.* |
| | **mit dem Zug.** | | *by train.* |
| | **mit der Straßenbahn.** | | *by tram.* |
| | **mit der U-Bahn.** | | *by underground.* |

## Exercise 3
How do you ask if there is ... near here?

**a**  *a station*
**b**  *a campsite*
**c**  *a post office*
**d**  *a car park*
**e**  *a bank*
**f**  *a pub*
**g**  *a bus stop*
**h**  *an hotel*

## Exercise 4
What would you ask? You want a room with:

## Exercise 5

How do you say you are travelling:

a                         b

c                d             e

## DIALOGUE 19

**CD2, TR 16**

| | |
|---|---|
| **Sie** | Entschuldigen Sie bitte. Gibt es ein Hotel in der Nähe? |
| **Empfangsdame** | Ja. Das Hotel Zur Post. |
| **Sie** | Haben Sie noch Zimmer frei? |
| **Empfangsdame** | Ich rufe mal an. (Sie telefoniert) Ja. Einzel- oder Doppelzimmer? |
| **Sie** | Doppelzimmer. |
| **Empfangsdame** | Ja. Mit Bad oder Dusche? |
| **Sie** | Mit Bad. Wie komme ich zum Hotel? |
| **Empfangsdame** | Zu Fuß, oder mit dem Auto? |
| **Sie** | Zu Fuß. |
| **Empfangsdame** | Sie gehen die Hauptstraße entlang, und es ist in der zweiten Straße links auf der rechten Seite. |
| **Sie** | Vielen Dank. Auf Wiedersehen. |
| **Empfangsdame** | Auf Wiedersehen. |
| | |
| **Sie** | Wie komme ich zum Bahnhof? |
| **Empfangsdame** | Zu Fuß, oder mit dem Auto? |
| **Sie** | Mit dem Auto. |
| **Empfangsdame** | Sie nehmen die zweite Straße links und die erste Straße rechts. Die erste Straße links ist eine Einbahnstraße. |

## LEARNING TIPS

**1** Practise both parts of the dialogue.
**2** Now adapt the dialogue. You want a single room, and the hotel is on the first street on the right, on the left-hand side.

Exercise 6
How do you ask:

  **a** *Is there a hotel near here?*
  **b** *Have they still got rooms available?*
  **c** *How do I get to the hotel on foot? and by car? and by bus?*

Exercise 7
Describe where the destination marked X is in each of these diagrams (you are standing at point A).

## Ist es weit? *Is it far?*

| | |
|---|---|
| **Ist es weit?** | *Is it far?* |
| **dort drüben** | *over there* |
| **da** | *there* |
| **hier vorne** | *in front (of you)* |
| **hier hinten** | *behind (you)* |
| **gleich hier** | *right there* |
| **um die Ecke** | *around the corner* |
| **gegenüber** | *opposite (trigger word)* |

**Wo kann ich Briefmarken kaufen?** *Where can I buy stamps?*
**Ich weiß es nicht.** *I don't know.*
**Ich bin hier fremd.** *I am a stranger here (myself).*

## PRONUNCIATION TIPS

w sounds v
d at the end of a word sounds t
ei sounds eye

When asked how far away somewhere is, Germans usually reply by telling you how long it takes to get there. **Z.B.** (Zum Beispiel – for example). **Wie weit ist es zum Bahnhof? Fünf Minuten zu Fuß.** *Five minutes on foot.*

## LEARNING TIPS

**1** Practise the new words and phrases. Say them out loud.
**2** Cover up the English and see how many you can understand.
**3** Decide which you should learn well enough to be able to use, and which you should be able to understand.
**4** Now cover up the German and see how many you can remember.

Exercise 8
Refer again to the map in Unit 8.

You are standing in front of the information office. To which building do the following directions refer?

**a** Gleich hier um die Ecke.
**b** Gegenüber dem Freibad.
**c** Nehmen Sie die erste Straße links und dann geradeaus.
**d** Auf der rechten Seite.
**e** Gleich hier vorne.
**f** Dort drüben, links.
**g** Gegenüber der Bank.

## DIALOGUE 20

You are looking for the Frauenkirche in München. Ask this lady:

CD2, TR 17

| | |
|---|---|
| **Sie** | Entschuldigen Sie, bitte. Wo ist die Frauenkirche? |
| **Dame** | Es tut mir Leid. Ich weiß es nicht. Ich bin hier fremd. |

*So you decide to go into the Informationsbüro instead.*

| | |
|---|---|
| **Sie** | Wo ist der Dom? |
| **Dame** | Hier gleich vorne. |
| **Sie** | Und wo sind die Toiletten? |
| **Dame** | Dort drüben. |
| **Sie** | Wo ist das Hotel Zum Garten? |
| **Dame** | Hier rechts, geradeaus und dann auf der rechten Seite. |
| **Sie** | Ist das weit? |
| **Dame** | Nein. Fünf Minuten zu Fuß. |
| **Sie** | Wo kann ich hier Briefmarken kaufen? |
| **Dame** | Die Post ist hier um die Ecke. |
| **Sie** | Und wo ist das Rathaus? |
| **Dame** | In der Fußgängerzone. Da, sehen Sie, dort hinten. |

## LEARNING TIPS

**1** Read the dialogues and make sure you understand everything in them. Which phrases do you know already?

**2** Look at the new phrases and choose three that you think it would be useful to learn. Write them down in English and see if you can put them back into German.

### Exercise 9

Ask where these places are and if they are far:

**a** *post office*
**b** *station*
**c** *church*
**d** *bank*
**e** *cinema*
**f** *hotel*
**g** *supermarket*

## Exercise 10

Now it's your turn to give directions. Use the plan to answer the following questions in German.

a Wie komme ich zum Hotel Alpblick?
b Gibt es eine Bank hier in der Nähe?
c Wo kann ich hier Briefmarken kaufen?
d Gibt es ein Kino in der Nähe?
e Wie komme ich zum Bahnhof?
f Wo ist hier ein Restaurant?
g Wie komme ich zum Schloss?
h Ist es weit?

| | |
|---|---|
| Schloss 3 km Restaurant ↑ | ↑ Hotel Alpblick 2 km Kino |
| Post | Bank |
| ← DB | |

Sie sind hier

## LANGUAGE NOTES

In this unit you have met some more trigger words:

| auf | [die Seite] **auf** der rechten Seite |
| mit | [das Auto] **mit** dem Auto |
| gegenüber | [der Bahnhof] **gegenüber** dem Bahnhof |

## TEST YOURSELF

**1** Can you ask the following:
- **a** the way to the station?
- **b** is it far?
- **c** where you can buy stamps?
- **d** where there is a bank?
- **e** if there is a hotel nearby?
- **f** if it still has rooms free?

**2** Check that you can say the following:
- **a** first on the right
- **b** second on the left
- **c** straight ahead
- **d** around the corner
- **e** on the left-hand side
- **f** on the right-hand side
- **g** a single room with bath
- **h** a double room with shower
- **i** in a car
- **j** on foot

And can you still say the following?
- **a** I'm sorry.
- **b** I don't understand.
- **c** I don't know.
- **d** Excuse me, please.
- **e** Pardon?
- **f** Thank you.

If not you will find them all in Unit 1.

### Sign language

What do these signs mean?

**a** + Post  **b** Bank  **c** Rathaus  **d** Kino  **e** Hallenbad

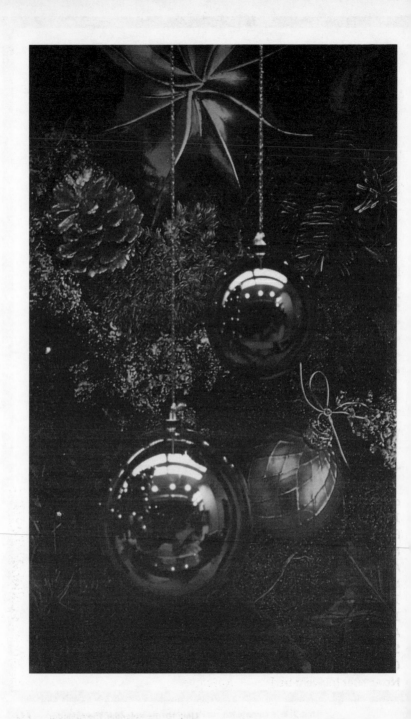

# 10

# Der Kalender
## The calendar

In this unit you will learn how to
* *Say the months of the year*
* *Say public holidays, days and dates*
* *Say when your holidays are*
* *Understand an invitation*
* *Invite someone to stay*
* *Make arrangements*

## Wann kommen Sie? *When are you coming?*

◀)) CD2, TR 18

| | |
|---|---|
| **die Monate** | *the months* |
| **Januar** [yan-oo-ar] | *January* |
| **Februar** [feb-roo-ar] | *February* |
| **März** [meh-rts] | *March* |
| **April** [a-pril] | *April* |
| **Mai** [my] | *May* |
| **Juni** [yoo-ny] | *June* |
| **Juli** [yoo-ly] | *July* |
| **August** [ow-gust] | *August* |
| **September** [zep-tem-ber] | *September* |
| **Oktober** [ok-to-ber] | *October* |
| **November** [no-vem-ber] | *November* |

QUICK VOCAB

| | |
|---|---|
| **Dezember** [day-tsember] | *December* |
| **die Feiertage** | *public holidays* |
| **Sommerferien** | *summer holidays* |
| **Winterferien** | *winter holidays* |
| **Osterferien** | *Easter holidays* |
| **Herbstferien** | *autumn holidays* |

## PRONUNCIATION TIPS

The italic parts of the sounds shown in brackets for the months are stressed. Remember also: j sounds y (**yuh**).

## LEARNING TIPS

**1** Read the names of the months out loud.
**2** Which month is it? Say out loud the full word for each of these abbreviations:

| | | | | | |
|---|---|---|---|---|---|
| **Mai** | **Dez** | **Jul** | **Feb** | **Jun** | **Sept** |
| **Jan** | **Aug** | **Mär** | **Okt** | **Apr** | **Nov** |

**3** Which holiday is it?

| Wo 1 **Januar**<br>**1**<br>**Donnerstag**<br>Neujahr | Wo 16 **April**<br>**17**<br>**Freitag**<br>Karfreitag | Wo 16 **April**<br>**19**<br>**Sonntag**<br>Ostersonntag |
|---|---|---|
| Wo 17 **April**<br>**20**<br>**Montag**<br>Ostermontag | Wo 22 **Mai**<br>**29**<br>**Sonntag**<br>Pfingsten | Wo 52 **Dezember**<br>**24**<br>**Donnerstag**<br>Heiligabend |
| Wo 52 **Dezember**<br>**25**<br>**Freitag**<br>1. Weihnachtstag | Wo 53 **Dezember**<br>**31**<br>**Donnerstag**<br>Silvester | |

## DIALOGUE 21

Practise the dialogue.

CD2, TR 18, 00:35

| | |
|---|---|
| **Fräulein Schneider** | Wann kommen Sie nach Deutschland? |
| **Sie** | Ich komme am 14. März. |
| **Fräulein Schneider** | Wie lange bleiben Sie? |
| **Sie** | Eine Woche. |
| **Fräulein Schneider** | Wann fahren Sie ab? |
| **Sie** | Am 22. März. Wann kommen Sie nach England? |
| **Fräulein Schneider** | Am 15. Oktober. |
| **Sie** | Wie lange bleiben Sie? |
| **Fräulein Schneider** | Zwei Wochen. |
| **Sie** | Wann fahren Sie ab? |
| **Fräulein Schneider** | Am 1. November. Wann kommen Sie zu uns? |
| **Sie** | Ich komme vom 4. bis zum 7. Juni, wenn das geht. |
| **Fräulein Schneider** | Ja. Das geht. Ich freue mich schon darauf. |

**Wann fahren Sie ab?** *When are you leaving?*
**Wie lange bleiben Sie?** *How long are you staying?*
**wenn das geht** *if that is all right*

QV

### WORD PATTERNS

**Am ...** *On the ...*
**am ersten** *on the first*
**am zweiten** *on the second*
**am dritten** *on the third*
**am fünften** *on the fifth*
**usw. (und so weiter)** *etc.*
  *(and so on)*

**am zehnten** *on the tenth*
**am zwanzigsten** *on the twentieth*
**am einundzwanzigsten** *on the 21st*
**am dreißigsten** *on the 30th*

**Vom ... bis zum ...** *From ... to ...*
**vom 8. Juli bis zum 1. August** *from 8 July to 1 August*
(**vom achten Juli bis zum ersten August**)

**an** (*on*) is a trigger word and **am** is an abbreviation of **an dem**.
**von** (*from/of*) is a trigger word and **vom** is an abbreviation of
**von dem**.

**zu** (*to*) is a trigger word and **zum** is an abbreviation of **zu dem**.
A trigger word is a word which may change      **der** to **dem**.
                                          **die** to **der**.
                                          **das** to **dem**.

---

## Eine Einladung *An invitation*

| | |
|---|---|
| **Möchten Sie uns besuchen?** | *Would you like to visit us?* *(lit. would you like us visit)* |
| **Ja, gerne.** | *Yes, I would. (lit. yes, willingly)* |
| **Wann können Sie kommen?** | *When can you come?* |
| **Ich weiß es nicht.** | *I don't know. (lit. I know it not)* |
| **Wann passt es Ihnen?** | *When does it suit you?* |
| **genau** | *exactly* |
| **nur** | *only* |
| **frei** | *free* |
| **zu Weihnachten** | *at/for Christmas (lit. to Christmas)* |
| **zu Ostern** | *at Easter* |
| **Geht das?** | *Is that OK? (lit. goes that?)* |
| **Ja, das geht.** | *Yes, that's OK. (lit. yes, that goes)* |
| **Ich freue mich schon darauf.** | *I'm already looking forward to it.* |
| **Vielen Dank für die Einladung** | *Many thanks for the invitation* |
| **Nichts zu danken.** | *Don't mention it.* |
| **Auf Wiederhören.** | *(on the phone) Goodbye.* |

### PRONUNCIATION TIPS

| | |
|---|---|
| v sounds f | ei as eye |
| ö as ur | au as ow in owl |
| ge as gue in guest | freue – froy-uh |

## LEARNING TIPS

**1** Practise reading all the words and phrases out loud (repeating after the recording if you have it).
**2** Cover up the English and see if you can remember what all the German words and phrases mean.
**3** Cover up the German and see if you can remember it.
**4** Count how many words and phrases you know already and choose three new ones to try to learn.

Exercise 1
Saying *thank you*. How do you say the following using the phrases in the box?

**a** *Thank you very much.*
**b** *Thanks.*
**c** *Many thanks.*
**d** *Don't mention it.*

| i Danke schön | iii Danke. |
| ii Nichts zu danken. | iv Vielen Dank. |

## DIALOGUE 22

CD2, TR 19

| Fräulein Hoffman | Hallo! Wie geht's? |
| Sie (am Telefon) | Gut danke. Und Ihnen? |
| Fräulein Hoffman | Gut. Möchten Sie uns in Deutschland besuchen? |
| Sie (am Telefon) | Ja, gerne. |
| Fräulein Hoffman | Wann können Sie kommen? Ich weiß nicht. Wann passt es Ihnen? |
| Fräulein Hoffman | Wann sind die Sommerferien? |
| Sie (am Telefon) | Vom 15. Juli bis zum 8. August. |
| Fräulein Hoffman | Und wann sind die Weihnachtsferien? |
| Sie (am Telefon) | Vom 20. Dezember bis zum 3. Januar. |
| | *(Contd)* |

| | |
|---|---|
| **Fräulein Hoffman** | Wann sind die Osterferien? |
| **Sie (am Telefon)** | Das weiß ich nicht genau. |
| **Fräulein Hoffman** | Ostersonntag ist am 4. April. |
| **Sie (am Telefon)** | Ich habe nur zwei Tage frei. |
| **Fräulein Hoffman** | Möchten Sie zu Weihnachten kommen? |
| **Sie (am Telefon)** | Gerne. Ich habe vom 20. bis 28. Dezember frei. Geht das? |
| **Fräulein Hoffman** | Ja. Das geht. Ich freue mich schon darauf. |
| **Sie (am Telefon)** | Vielen Dank für die Einladung. |
| **Fräulein Hoffman** | Nichts zu danken. Auf Wiederhören. |
| **Sie (am Telefon)** | Auf Wiederhören. |

### LEARNING TIPS

**1** Read the text carefully and make sure you understand everything.
**2** Practise reading it out loud. See if you can get someone to read the other part with you.
**3** Try to substitute the dates of your own holidays. If you don't know them use these:

Easter: 2–7 April. Christmas: 23 December–3 January. Summer: 14–30 July.

## Wann treffen wir uns? *When shall we meet?*

QUICK VOCAB

| | |
|---|---|
| **ins** | *in + das = ins (in) to the* |
| **nächste Woche** | *next week* |
| **nächsten Montag** | *next Monday* |
| **morgens** | *in the morning* |
| **nachmittags** | *in the afternoon* |
| **abends** | *in the evening* |
| **heute** | *today* |
| **morgen Abend** | *tomorrow evening* |

| | |
|---|---|
| **Wie wäre es mit Dienstag?** | *What about Tuesday? (lit. how would it be with Tuesday?)* |
| **Das geht leider nicht.** | *That won't do/I can't make it. (lit. that goes unfortunately not)* |
| **Prima!** | *Great!* |
| **keine Zeit** | *no time* |

### LANGUAGE NOTES

Das Datum: *the date*

Dates are written like this: **den 14. Juni** or **14. 6.**
and read like this: **den vierzehnten Juni** or
                    **den vierzehnten sechsten**

The full stop after the figure represents **-ten** which is like the
English *-th* in *4th, 5th, 10th*, etc, or *-rd* in *23rd*.

Now read these dates out loud remembering to add the **-ten**
(or **-sten** if the number is more than 20) wherever there is a
full stop.

| | | | |
|---|---|---|---|
| **a** 5. März | **d** 10. Feb | **g** 13. 5. | **j** 27. 4. |
| **b** 19. Nov | **e** 8. Okt | **h** 7. 9. | **k** 1. 8. |
| **c** 21. Jul | **f** 30. Jan | **i** 12. 5. | **l** 28. 10 |

**Wann haben Sie Geburtstag?** *When is your birthday?*

**Mein Geburtstag ist am …** or **Ich habe am … Geburtstag.**
And can you say when the birthdays ringed below are?

| | JAN | | | | |
|---|---|---|---|---|---|
| Mo | | 7 | 14 | 21 | 28 |
| Di | 1 | 8 | 15 | 22 | 29 |
| Mi | 2 | 9 | 16 | 23 | 30 |
| Do | 3 | 10 | 17 | 24 | (31) |
| Fr | 4 | 11 | 18 | 25 | |
| Sa | 5 | 12 | 19 | 26 | |
| So | 6 | 13 | 20 | 27 | |

| | MAI | | | | |
|---|---|---|---|---|---|
| Mo | | 6 | 13 | 20 | 27 |
| Di | | 7 | 14 | 21 | 28 |
| Mi | 1 | 8 | 15 | 22 | 29 |
| Do | 2 | 9 | 16 | 23 | 30 |
| Fr | 3 | 10 | 17 | 24 | 31 |
| Sa | 4 | 11 | 18 | 25 | |
| So | 5 | 12 | 19 | 26 | |

| | SEPT | | | | |
|---|---|---|---|---|---|
| Mo | | 2 | 9 | 16 | 23 30 |
| Di | | 3 | 10 | 17 | 24 |
| Mi | | 4 | 11 | 18 | 25 |
| Do | | 5 | 12 | 19 | 26 |
| Fr | | 6 | 13 | 20 | 27 |
| Sa | | 7 | 14 | 21 | (28) |
| So | 1 | 8 | 15 | 22 | 29 |

| | FEB | | | | |
|---|---|---|---|---|---|
| Mo | | 4 | 11 | 18 | 25 |
| Di | | 5 | 12 | 19 | 26 |
| Mi | | 6 | 13 | 20 | 27 |
| Do | | 7 | 14 | 21 | 28 |
| Fr | 1 | 8 | 15 | 22 | |
| Sa | 2 | 9 | 16 | 23 | |
| So | 3 | 10 | 17 | 24 | |

| | JUN | | | | |
|---|---|---|---|---|---|
| Mo | | 3 | 10 | 17 | 24 |
| Di | | 4 | 11 | 18 | 25 |
| Mi | | 5 | 12 | 19 | 26 |
| Do | | 6 | 13 | 20 | 27 |
| Fr | | 7 | 14 | 21 | 28 |
| Sa | 1 | 8 | 15 | 22 | 29 |
| So | 2 | 9 | (16) | 23 | 30 |

| | OKT | | | | |
|---|---|---|---|---|---|
| Mo | | 7 | 14 | 21 | 28 |
| Di | 1 | 8 | 15 | 22 | 29 |
| Mi | 2 | 9 | 16 | 23 | 30 |
| Do | 3 | 10 | 17 | 24 | 31 |
| Fr | 4 | 11 | 18 | 25 | |
| Sa | 5 | 12 | 19 | 26 | |
| So | 6 | 13 | 20 | 27 | |

| | MÄR | | | | |
|---|---|---|---|---|---|
| Mo | | 4 | 11 | 18 | 25 |
| Di | | 5 | 12 | 19 | 26 |
| Mi | | 6 | 13 | 20 | 27 |
| Do | | 7 | 14 | 21 | 28 |
| Fr | 1 | 8 | 15 | 22 | 29 |
| Sa | 2 | 9 | 16 | 23 | 30 |
| So | 3 | 10 | 17 | 24 | 31 |

| | JUL | | | | |
|---|---|---|---|---|---|
| Mo | 1 | 8 | 15 | 22 | 29 |
| Di | 2 | 9 | 16 | 23 | 30 |
| Mi | 3 | 10 | 17 | 24 | 31 |
| Do | 4 | 11 | 18 | 25 | |
| Fr | 5 | 12 | 19 | 26 | |
| Sa | 6 | 13 | 20 | 27 | |
| So | 7 | 14 | 21 | 28 | |

| | NOV | | | | |
|---|---|---|---|---|---|
| Mo | | 4 | 11 | 18 | 25 |
| Di | | 5 | 12 | (19) | 26 |
| Mi | | 6 | 13 | (20) | 27 |
| Do | | 7 | 14 | 21 | 28 |
| Fr | 1 | 8 | 15 | 22 | 29 |
| Sa | 2 | 9 | 16 | 23 | 30 |
| So | 3 | 10 | 17 | 24 | |

| | APR | | | | |
|---|---|---|---|---|---|
| Mo | 1 | 8 | 15 | 22 | 29 |
| Di | 2 | 9 | 16 | 23 | 30 |
| Mi | 3 | 10 | 17 | 24 | |
| Do | 4 | 11 | 18 | 25 | |
| Fr | 5 | 12 | 19 | 26 | |
| Sa | 6 | 13 | 20 | 27 | |
| So | 7 | 14 | 21 | 28 | |

| | AUG | | | | |
|---|---|---|---|---|---|
| Mo | | 5 | 12 | 19 | 26 |
| Di | | 6 | 13 | 20 | 27 |
| Mi | | 7 | 14 | 21 | 28 |
| Do | 1 | 8 | 15 | 22 | 29 |
| Fr | 2 | 9 | 16 | 23 | 30 |
| Sa | 3 | 10 | 17 | 24 | 31 |
| So | 4 | 11 | 18 | 25 | |

| | DEZ | | | | |
|---|---|---|---|---|---|
| Mo | | 2 | 9 | 16 | 23 30 |
| Di | | 3 | 10 | 17 | 24 31 |
| Mi | | 4 | 11 | 18 | 25 |
| Do | | 5 | 12 | 19 | 26 |
| Fr | | 6 | (13) | 20 | 27 |
| Sa | | 7 | 14 | 21 | 28 |
| So | 1 | 8 | 15 | 22 | 29 |

What date are you arriving and leaving?

**Ich komme ...** *I'm arriving ...*

**Ich fahre ...** *I'm going/leaving ...*

e.g. 20. 7.–1. 8.: **Ich komme am zwanzigsten siebten.**
**Ich fahre am ersten achten.**

**a** 13. 07.–25. 07.

**b** 16. 08.

**c** 21. 12.–27. 12.

**d** 4. 03.–18. 03.

## DIALOGUE 23

| | |
|---|---|
| **Herr Braun** | Gehen wir ins Kino? |
| **Sie** | Ja, gerne. Wann? |
| **Herr Braun** | Nächste Woche, am Montag? Geht das? |
| **Sie** | Ja. Um wie viel Uhr? |
| **Herr Braun** | Um sieben Uhr abends. |
| **Sie** | Gehen wir in die Pizzeria? |
| **Herr Braun** | Ja, gerne. Wann? |
| **Sie** | Morgen Abend? |
| **Herr Braun** | Nein. Das geht leider nicht. Wie wäre es mit Mittwochabend? |
| **Sie** | Ja, prima. Um wie viel Uhr? |
| **Herr Braun** | Um halb sieben? |
| **Sie** | Ja, bis dann. Tschüss. |
| **Sie** | Spielen wir heute Nachmittag Tennis? |
| **Herr Braun** | Heute habe ich keine Zeit. Wie wäre es mit Samstag? |
| **Sie** | Ja, gut. Um wie viel Uhr? |
| **Herr Braun** | Um zwei Uhr nachmittags. |

### LEARNING TIP

**1** Read both parts of the dialogues.

### Exercise 2
How would you invite someone to do the following? Note that the day of the week and/or times come earlier in the German sentence:

*Example:* Go to the theatre with you on Friday evening?

*Answer:* Gehen wir Freitagabend ins Theater?

**a** *Play tennis with you on Monday evening.*
**b** *Go to the cinema with you tomorrow evening.*
**c** *Go to the pizzeria with you today at 8 pm.*

Now use what you have learned to invite someone to:

**d** *Go swimming (**schwimmen**) Wednesday afternoon.*
**e** *Play squash Saturday at 11.00.*
**f** *Go to a restaurant (**das Restaurant**) Friday evening.*

## Exercise 3

Frau Fischer invites you to their house that evening. Complete this short conversation.

| | |
|---|---|
| **Fr. Fischer** | Kommen Sie heute Abend zu uns? |
| **You** | Say you can't make it tonight. |
| **Fr. Fischer** | Oh, das tut mir Leid. Wann können Sie kommen? |
| **You** | Ask if Thursday evening would be all right. |

## Exercise 4
**Rollenspiel** *Role play*

**Am Telefon** *On the phone*: You are going to visit Herr Braun in Köln. Say your part of the dialogue.

| | |
|---|---|
| **Herr Braun** | Hallo. … Wie geht's? |
| **a You** | Well, thank you and you? |
| **Herr Braun** | Gut, danke. Wann kommen Sie? |
| **b You** | On Monday, 15 July. |
| **Herr Braun** | Wann kommen Sie in Köln an? (When do you get in to Cologne?) |
| **c You** | At 18.35. |
| **Herr Braun** | Wann fahren Sie von London ab? (When do you leave London?) |
| **d You** | At 9.30am. |
| **Herr Braun** | Wie lange bleiben Sie? (How long are you staying?) |
| **e You** | Until Friday evening. |
| **Herr Braun** | Um wie viel Uhr fahren Sie ab? |
| **f You** | At 19.30. |
| **Herr Braun** | Wann kommen Sie in London an? |

| g You | At 7.30am. |
| **Herr Braun** | Gut. Ich freue mich schon darauf. |
| h You | Goodbye. |
| **Herr Braun** | Auf Wiederhören. |

## Insight

Germans like to celebrate their birthdays and often take cakes or buns to work to share with their colleagues on their birthday.

If you are giving flowers as a present you should always buy an odd number and unwrap them as you hand them over.

*eine Geburtstagskarte*

*eine Weihnachtskarte*

Listening exercise 18

◀ **CD2, TR 21**

**Wann treffen wir uns?** *When shall we meet?*
Note down the times and dates of these eight meetings.

# TEST YOURSELF

1 Making arrangements. **Wann treffen wir uns?** *When shall we meet?* Tell your friend you will see her on:
   a Monday 2 May at 12.30
   b Friday 24 December at 14.30
   c next Saturday at 11.15
   d next week, on Thursday at 16.30
   e Wednesday 16 April 9.15
   f Saturday 1 September at 17.00
   g next Tuesday at 13.30
   h Friday at 8pm

## UNIT 6

1 A double room with a shower is
   a ein Doppelzimmer ohne Bad
   b ein Doppelzimmer mit Dusche
   c ein Einzelzimmer mit Bad.

2 **Im dritten Stock** means
   a it is out of stock
   b it is nearly out of stock
   c it is on the third floor

## UNIT 7

3 Re-arrange the words to ask what the time is: **Uhr es viel ist wie?**

4 **Um halb acht** means
   a at half past eight
   b at half past nine
   c at half past seven

## UNIT 8

**5** How would you ask where the station is
    **a** Wie ist der Bahnhof?
    **b** Wer ist der Bahnhof?
    **c** Wo ist der Bahnhof?

**6** Complete the sentences:
der words are ...
die words are ...
das words are ...

## UNIT 9

**7** True or false? A trigger word [or preposition] is a word which may trigger a change in the following word.

**8** I am going by train. Fill in the missing words: **Ich fahre __ __ Zug.**

## UNIT 10

**9** Fill in the missing verb to go:
    You use __ when you go on foot and __ when you go on transport.

**10** Put the days of the week in the right order starting with Monday:
    Do Di So Mi Mo Sa Fr

Any problems with questions

1 and 2 go back to Unit 6
3 and 4 Unit 7
5 and 6 Unit 8
7 and 8 Unit 9
9 and 10 Unit 10

# 11

## German verbs

In this unit you will learn how to
- *Identify a verb*
- *Know which form of the verb to use*
- *Make the correct form of the verb*
- *Talk about what is happening (present tense) and what has happened (past tense)*
- *Look up verbs in the dictionary*

This unit does not work in the same way as the preceding and following ones. Do not try to learn everything in it at once. Use it for reference and come back to it as and when you need it.

If you know what a verb is go on to **B**.

**A** Verbs are 'doing words': go, sleep, run, eat, talk, think, understand, speak – all things which one can 'do'.

To check if a word is a verb try saying it after:

I ... *or* I can ...

You can learn to speak a language at a simple and effective level by using phrases which you have learned which already include the verb in its correct form, e.g.

Wie **heißen** Sie?          Ich **wohne** in ...          Wann **treffen** wir uns?

But there will come a time when you want to say something which you haven't learned and you will want to make up a sentence of your own. To do this you need to learn something more about the patterns of the language.

If you know about the pattern of English verbs go on to **C**.

**B** Look at the pattern of a verb in English:

*to make (infinitive)*

| *(singular)* | | *(plural)* | |
|---|---|---|---|
| *I* | *make* | *we* | *make* |
| *you* | *make* | *you* | *make* |
| *he/she/it* | *make**s*** | *they* | *make* |

**C** Now look at the same verb in German:

*machen (infinitive)*

| *(singular)* | | *(plural)* | |
|---|---|---|---|
| *ich* | *mach**e*** | *wir* | *mach**en*** |
| *du* | *mach**st*** | *ihr* | *mach**t*** |
| *er/sie/es* | *mach**t*** | *sie* | *mach**en*** |
| | | *Sie* | *mach**en*** |
| | | *(you – polite form)* | |

It is obviously easier to learn an English verb than a German one, because it is the same as the infinitive except that you add an s in the *he/she/it* form. (The infinitive is the form of the verb that you will find if you look it up in a dictionary.)

If you are not ready to learn all about the German verbs yet leave this and come back to it later.

**D** The German verb has seven forms (or persons):

The **ich** form, **du** form, **er** form, **wir** form, **ihr** form, **sie** form and **Sie** form.

You already know some of them:

**ich** form – Ich wohne, ich heiße
**du** form – Wann kommst du?
**wir** form – Wann treffen wir uns?
**Sie** form – Wie heißen Sie?

We are leaving the **ihr** form out for now. So that leaves us with:

**er** form (*he/she/it*)
**sie** form (*they*)

Now look at the German verb again and you will find that these two forms are: **er/sie/es macht** and **sie machen**.

You make the correct form by taking the **-en** off the infinitive – this gives you the 'stem' of the verb – you then add the ending that you need: **-e, -st, -t** or **-en**. Here is a short summary of all the endings:

The **ich** form ends in **-e**   The **wir** form ends in **en** [The **ihr** form ends in **-t**]
The **du** form ends in **-st**   The **sie** form ends in **-en**
The **er** form ends in **-t**    The **Sie** form ends in **-en**

## Exercise 1
**a** I eat (I am eating) … I am called … I live …
You are talking about yourself so what will the verb end with?
**a** – e **b** – st **c** – en

**b** What is your name? Where do you live (you – polite form)?
You are talking to a stranger so what will the verb end with?
**a** – e **b** – st **c** – en

**c** What is your name? Would you like an ice-cream?
You are talking to a younger person so what will the verb end with?
**a** – e **b** – st **c** – en

**d** You are talking about yourself and someone else (John and I …).
Which form will you use? What will the verb end with?
**a** – e **b** – st **c** – en

## WORD PATTERNS: ICH FORM – I

When you are talking about yourself in German the verb almost always ends with an -e although it is not always pronounced clearly in spoken German. Remember: ich form: ich __e

What is the **ich** form of these verbs?

| infinitive | | ich form | |
|---|---|---|---|
| **haben** | *to have* | **ich ....** | *I have* |
| **spielen** | *to play* | **ich ......** | *I play* |
| **machen** | *to make* | **ich .....** | *I make* |
| **gehen** | *to go* | **ich ....** | *I go* |
| **schwimmen** | *to swim* | **ich ......** | *I swim* |
| **essen** | *to eat* | **ich ....** | *I eat* |
| **trinken** | *to drink* | **ich ......** | *I drink* |
| **fahren** | *to drive* | **ich .....** | *I drive* |
| **sehen** | *to see* | **ich ....** | *I see* |
| **kommen** | *to come* | **ich .....** | *I come* |

If you know the infinitive it is easy, but what happens when you don't know the word you need? You look it up in the dictionary.

You want to say you will *fetch* the book, so you look up the word *fetch* in the dictionary and this is what it says:

**fetch** [fetʃ] vt. **holen;** (in sale) **einbringen, erzielen.**

The word in brackets [fetʃ] is the phonetic pronunciation of the English word *fetch*. You know how to pronounce it already so you can ignore this.

You don't want to say how much something fetches in a sale so you can ignore all the second part; the word you want is **holen.**

**holen** is the infinitive, so what is the **ich** form going to be?

**holen** *to fetch*   **ich hole** *I fetch*

Try it again. You want to say I'll *bring* the book.

Look up *to bring*:

**bring** [briŋ] vt. irreg. **bringen;** – about **zustande bringen ...**

From 'vt.' you know that it is a verb; 'irreg.' tells you that it is an irregular verb; **bringen** tells you the infinitive of the verb that you want, so you can ignore the rest of the text.

**bringen** is the infinitive, so the **ich** form will be **ich bringe.**

---

## The present tense

You use the present tense to say what you are doing now (or do regularly).

### Talking about yourself (I)
Use the **ich** form, ending in **-e.**

| | | |
|---|---|---|
| I go | *or* I am going | **ich gehe** |
| I eat | *or* I am eating | **ich esse** |
| I drink | *or* I am drinking | **ich trinke** |
| I go/drive | *or* I am going/driving | **ich fahre** |

**gehen** means to go when you go on foot; **fahren** is used if you go by transport.

Talking about yourself and someone else (we)
Use the **wir** form, ending in **-en**.

| | | |
|---|---|---|
| we go | *or* we are going | **wir gehen** |
| we eat | *or* we are eating | **wir essen** |
| we drink | *or* we are drinking | **wir trinken** |
| we/go drive | *or* we are going/driving | **wir fahren** |

Talking about one other person (he or she)
Use the **er/sie** form, ending it **-t**.

| | | |
|---|---|---|
| he/she goes | *or* he/she is going | **er/sie geht** |
| he/she eats | *or* he/she is eating | **er/sie issen** |
| he/she drinks | *or* he/she is drinking | **er/sie trinken** |
| he/she goes/drives | *or* he/she is going/driving | **er/sie fähren** |

**essen** and **fahren** are irregular verbs which don't always follow the normal pattern but they still take **-t**.

Talking about more than one other person (they)
Use the **sie** form, ending in **-en**.

| | | |
|---|---|---|
| they go | *or* they are going | **sie gehen** |
| they eat | *or* they are eating | **sie essen** |
| they drink | *or* they are drinking | **sie trinken** |
| they go/drive | *or* they are going/driving | **sie fahren** |

Using the **du** and **Sie** forms

Remember the normal form is the **Sie** form.

You use the **du** form only with people you know well and younger people.

Exercise 2

Which forms are you going to use?

**a** You are talking about your friend Harry.
   **i** ich **ii** er **iii** Sie

**b** You are talking about yourself and Monika.
   **i** ich **ii** sie **iii** wir

**c** You are talking about your friends Herr and Frau Schulz.
   **i** ich **ii** sie **iii** wir

**d** You are asking Herr Braun a question.
   **i** er **ii** sie **iii** Sie

**e** You are asking his young son a question.
   **i** ich **ii** Sie **iii** du

**f** You are talking about yourself.
   **i** ich **ii** du **iii** er

## LANGUAGE NOTES

There are some special verbs which don't end in -e in the **ich** form.
They are.

| | | | |
|---|---|---|---|
| ich **weiß** | *I know* | ich **will** | *I want to* |
| ich **bin** | *I am* | ich **darf** | *I may* |
| ich **kann** | *I can* | ich **soll** | *I should* |
| ich **mag** | *I like* | | |

## WORD PATTERNS: REGULAR VERBS AND IRREGULAR VERBS

Regular verbs are ones which follow a special pattern.
Unfortunately, there are also some irregular verbs which
don't always follow the pattern.

Present tense
(What you are doing now or usually do)

English has two forms of the present tense, for example:

I play/I am playing   I go/I am going

German only has one, so:

| | | |
|---|---|---|
| **Ich spiele** means | *I play* and | *I am playing* |
| **Ich gehe** means | *I go* and | *I am going* |

Past tense
(What you have done or what you did in the past)

| | | |
|---|---|---|
| Past: | I played | I went |
| Perfect: | I have played | I have gone |

If you were learning English verbs you would have to learn,
for example:

| Regular verbs | | | Irregular verbs | | |
|---|---|---|---|---|---|
| Infinitive | Past | Past participle | Infinitive | Past | Past participle |
| play | played | played | go | went | gone |
| dance | danced | danced | bring | brought | brought |
| clean | cleaned | cleaned | drink | drank | drunk |
| wash | washed | washed | eat | ate | eaten |
| | | | swim | swam | swum |
| | | | come | came | came |

The first column is the infinitive, the second is the past tense and the third is the past participle (the part used after *have* in forming the perfect tense: *I have played*). Another way of talking about what you did in the past in English is to say, *I was playing, I was going*; this is known as the imperfect tense.

Here are the same verbs in German. Can you work out which verbs they are?

## Insight

If a verb begins with **ge-** take off the **ge-** and you can often find which English verb it is related to. **ge-** is the equivalent of the English **-ed** as in *danced*. They put **ge** at the front of a verb, we put **-ed** at the back!

| Infinitive | Past (Imperfect) | Past participle |
|---|---|---|
| trinken | trank | getrunken |
| waschen | wusch | gewaschen |
| kommen | kam | gekommen |
| essen | aß | gegessen |
| gehen | ging | gegangen |
| bringen | brachte | gebracht |
| *spielen | spielte | gespielt |
| *putzen | putzte | geputzt |

*These verbs are regular.

Now what do you think these verbs might mean?

| | | |
|---|---|---|
| singen | sang | gesungen |
| fallen | fiel | gefallen |
| finden | fand | gefunden |
| tanzen | tanzte | getanzt |
| schwimmen | schwamm | geschwommen |

## Insight

Some English words which begin with a 'd' begin with a 't' in German: **die Tür** – *the door*; **tanzen** – *to dance*; **trinken** – *to drink*.

If you say the sound [duh] and [tuh] aloud you will find that they are made in the same way; [duh] is voiced (you make more effort to say it) and [tuh] is not voiced but they are basically the same sound.

Remember this is a reference chapter. If you do not need to know this yet leave it and come back at a later date.

### Forming the past tense in German
This is the pattern of a regular verb in German:

| 1 Infinitive | 2 Present er form | 3 Imperfect ich/er form | 4 Past participle |
|---|---|---|---|
| machen | macht | machte | gemacht |

### How to use the table
**1** The first column tells you the infinitive of the verb.
**2** The second column tells you the **er** form in the present tense because the **du** and **er** forms are sometimes irregular. In the case of this verb it is what you would expect: **-t**.
**3** The third column tells you how to form the imperfect tense – how to say: *I was doing/I was making*. **Ich machte**. (The imperfect tense is usually used to say what was happening when something

else happened e.g. I was doing it when I cut myself/I was driving when I hit the wall. It is an 'imperfect' or 'interrupted' action.)
**4** The fourth column tells you the past participle of the verb. You need the past participle to make the perfect tense. You add the past participle to *I have* … **Ich habe gemacht.**

| | |
|---|---|
| *I did it/have done it.* | **Ich habe es gemacht.** |
| *I played/have played tennis.* | **Ich habe Tennis gespielt.** |

Notice how the past participle goes to the end of the sentence.

The **perfect tense** is the one that you use most when talking about what you have done. This is the past tense that you should try to learn first.

### Word patterns for past participles
The past participle of a regular verb is made by adding **ge-** to the front of the word and using the **-t** ending:

| | | |
|---|---|---|
| machen | **ge** + mach + **t** | **gemacht** *made/did* |
| kaufen | **ge** + kauf + **t** | **gekauft** *bought* |

If you are looking up a word which begins with **ge-** in the dictionary and can't find it, it is probably a past participle. Try taking off the **ge-** and looking for the rest of the word.

Exercise 3
What are the infinitives of these verbs? i.e. what should you look up?

**a** geholt      **c** gearbeitet      **e** gesagt
**b** gelernt      **d** gefragt      **f** getanzt

Exercise 4
How would you make the past participle of these verbs?

**a** hören      **c** führen      **e** haben
**b** brauchen      **d** spielen      **f** kochen

Irregular verbs
Since most of the verbs in common use are irregular ones (just as in English – and they are usually the same ones as in English as our languages have some of the same origins) there is a list of them in most dictionaries and textbooks.

There is a list of the most useful ones in the grammar summary at the back of this book.

This is how irregular verbs are shown in most dictionaries:

| 1 Infinitive | 2 Present | 3 Imperfect | 4 Past participle |
|---|---|---|---|
| beginnen | beginnst/beginnt | begann | begonnen – to begin |
| *bleiben | bleibst/bleibt | blieb | geblieben – to stay |
| denken | denkst/denkt | dachte | gedacht – to think |
| essen | isst/isst | aß | gegessen – to eat |
| fahren | fährst/fährt | fuhr | gefahren – to go/drive |

[In this case column 2 includes the **du** and the **er** forms]

How to use the table
**1** The infinitive: **beginnen** to begin.
**2** The present tense: **beginnst/beginnt**. This is what you would expect for the **du** and **er** forms so you know that **beginnen** is regular in the present tense.
**3** The imperfect tense: **ich begann** I began/I was beginning.
**4** The past participle (use with **ich habe: ich habe begonnen** *I began/I have begun*).

### bleiben

**1** The infinitive: **bleiben** *to stay, to remain*.
**2** The present tense: (regular) **du bleibst, er bleibt**.
**3** The imperfect: **ich blieb** *I stayed/I was staying* The vowels have changed round: **ei** to **ie**.
**4** The past participle **ich bin geblieben** *I stayed/I have stayed*.

*The asterisk tells you to use **ich bin** instead of **ich habe**: *I have stayed* **ich bin geblieben**.

Exercise 5
What is the infinitive of these words? (i.e. what would you look up to find out what these words mean?):

  **a**  gelesen
  **b**  gegeben
  **c**  geschlafen
  **d**  gerufen
  **e**  gesehen
  **f**  gefahren
  **g**  gewaschen

Using **sein** and **haben** for the perfect tense
The verbs *to be* and *to have* are called auxiliary verbs as they are used as 'helper' verbs to make other tenses.

The present tense of sein and haben

**sein** *to be*

| | | | |
|---|---|---|---|
| **ich bin** | *I am* | **wir sind** | *we are* |
| **du bist** | *you are* | **ihr seid** | *you are* |
| **er/sie/es ist** | *he/she/it is* | **sie sind** | *they are* |
| | | **Sie sind** | *you are (polite form)* |

**haben** *to have*

| | |
|---|---|
| **ich habe** | **wir haben** |
| **du hast** | **ihr habt** |
| **er/sie/es hat** | **sie haben** |
| | **Sie haben** |

Sein and haben are both used to make the perfect tense:

| | |
|---|---|
| **Ich** *habe* **Squash** *gespielt.* | **Ich** *bin* **in Hamburg** *geblieben.* |
| **Ich** *habe* **den Film** *gesehen.* | **Ich** *bin* **nach Köln** *gefahren.* |
| **Er** *hat* **Tennis** *gespielt.* | **Sie** *ist* **in München** *geblieben.* |
| **Wir** *haben* **007** *gesehen.* | **Wir** *sind* **nach Italien** *gefahren.* |

**Remember:** You are not supposed to learn everything in this unit at once. Only refer to it as and when you need it.

The main points to remember:

If you are talking about yourself use the **ich** form: after **ich** the verb ends in **-e**:

e.g. *Ich* **trink***e* **ein Glas Bier.**          *I'm drinking a glass of beer.*

If you are saying what you have done use: **Ich habe/ich bin** + the past participle.

Learn this sentence as a model.

**Ich bin in die Bar gegangen und ich habe ein Bier getrunken.**

*I am in the bar (ge)gone and I have a beer (ge)drunk.*

# 12

# Meine Familie
## My family

In this unit you will learn how to
- *Talk about your family*
- *Make plural forms*
- *Say what people are like*
- *Say what your job is*
- *Say what jobs other people do*

## Meine Familie *My family*

| | |
|---|---|
| **meine Verwandten** | *my relations* |
| **mein ...** | *my ...* |
| **mein Vater** | *my father* |
| **mein Vati** | *my dad* |
| **mein Stiefvater** | *my stepfather* |
| **mein Schwiegervater** | *my father-in-law* |
| **mein Großvater** | *my grandfather* |
| **mein Opa** | *my grandad* |
| **mein Urgroßvater** | *my great-grandfather* |
| **mein Bruder** | *my brother* |
| **mein Sohn** | *my son* |
| **mein Onkel** | *my uncle* |
| **mein Patenonkel** | *my godfather* |
| **mein Cousin** | *my cousin (male)* |

| mein Mann | my husband |
| mein Freund | my friend (male) |

| 1 meine ... | my ... |
| 2 meine Mutter | my mother |
| 3 meine Mutti | my mum |
| 4 meine Stiefmutter | my step-mother |
| 5 meine Schwiegermutter | my mother-in-law |
| 6 meine Großmutter | my grandmother |
| 7 meine Oma | my grandma |
| 8 meine Urgroßmutter | my great-grandmother |
| 9 meine Schwester | my sister |
| 10 meine Tochter | my daughter |
| 11 meine Tante | my aunt |

| meine Patentante | my godmother |
| meine Cousine | my cousin (female) |
| meine Frau | my wife |
| meine Freundin | my friend (female) |

## PRONUNCIATION TIPS

Cousin [cooseng], Cousine [cooseenuh]
ie = ee, ei = eye, ur- sounds oor
w sounds v, Sohn sounds zone

## WORD PATTERNS: HOW TO SAY 'MY'

To say *my father* you use **mein** Vater;
to say *my mother* you use **meine** Mutter;
to say *my parents* you say **meine** Eltern.
Use **mein** with masculine (and neuter) words and **meine** with
feminine words and with plural words.

## LEARNING TIP

**1** Choose the words you will need to talk about your family
and try to learn them.

## Exercise 1
How do you say the following?

a my father
b my sister
c my grandfather
d my parents
e my girlfriend
f my mother
g my brother
h my grandmother

i my wife
j my husband
k my son
l my daughter
m my grandma
n my grandad
o my mother-in-law

### DIALOGUE 24

Herr Fischer introduces you to his family:

| | |
|---|---|
| **Herr Fischer** | Darf ich Ihnen meine Frau vorstellen? |
| **Sie** | Sehr angenehm. |
| **Herr Fischer** | Und das ist meine Tochter Angelika. |
| **Sie** | Hallo, Angelika. |
| **Herr Fischer** | Mein Sohn Peter. |
| **Sie** | Hallo, Peter. |
| **Herr Fischer** | Und das ist meine Mutter. |
| **Sie** | Guten Tag, Frau Fischer. |
| *And you introduce Herr Fischer to your boss:* | |
| **Sie** | Darf ich Ihnen meinen Chef vorstellen? |
| | Herr Smith – Herr Fischer. |
| **Herr Fischer** | Sehr angenehm. |
| **Sie** | Haben Sie eine gute Reise gehabt? |
| **Herr Fischer** | Ja, danke. |

CD2, TR 22

**Haben Sie eine gute Reise gehabt?** *Did you have a good journey?*

QV

Listening exercise 19
◀ **CD2, TR 23**

Hannelore, Joachim and Katrin describe their family holiday photos. Which relatives are in the photos? Cross out the ones they mention.

**a** Vater Mutter Großmutter Großvater Bruder Schwester Sohn Tochter Hund
**b** Vater Mutter Großmutter Großvater Bruder Schwester Sohn Tochter Hund
**c** Vater Mutter Großmutter Großvater Bruder Schwester Sohn Tochter Hund

Exercise 2
**Darf ich meine Familie vorstellen?** May I introduce my family?

Tell your friend Uschi who these people are!

Hier ist ...

## WORD PATTERNS: SINGULAR AND PLURAL

If you have more than one ...

| *singular* | *plural* |
|---|---|
| **mein Bruder** | **meine Brüder** |
| **meine Schwester** | **meine Schwestern** |
| **mein Sohn** | **meine Söhne** |
| **meine Tochter** | **meine Töchter** |

The changes needed to make the plural form are usually shown in brackets after the noun in the vocabulary or in a dictionary, for example:

**1** **der Bruder** (¨) means that you add an Umlaut to the **u** to form the plural: **zwei Brüder**.
**2** **die Schwester** (n) means that you add an 'n' to form the plural: **eine Schwester, zwei Schwestern**.
**3** **das Fenster** (-) [window] means that the word doesn't change in the plural: **ein Fenster, zwei Fenster**.

In most dictionaries, if you want to find the plural form you will have to look up the word in the singular in the German–English section; it will not be listed in the English–German section.

Exercise 3
How do you make the plurals of these words?

  **a** **die Tochter** (¨) *daughter*
  **b** **der Tisch** (e) *table*
  **c** **der Stuhl** (¨e) *chair*
  **d** **das Haus** (¨er) *house*

## Leute beschreiben *Describing people*

| | |
|---|---|
| **ziemlich** | *rather* |
| **ganz** | *quite* |
| **sehr** | *very* |
| **nett** | *nice* |
| **groß/klein** | *big/small* |
| **lang/kurz** | *long/short* |
| **hell/dunkel** | *light/dark* |
| **schlank/dick** | *thin/fat* |
| **schulterlang** | *shoulder length* |
| **lockig** | *curly* |
| **blau** | *blue* |
| **grün** | *green* |
| **grau** | *grey* |
| **weiß** | *white* |
| **rot** | *red* |
| **schwarz** | *black* |
| **braun** | *brown* |
| **Mein Mann ist ziemlich groß.** | *My husband is rather tall.* |
| **Meine Frau ist ganz klein.** | *My wife is quite small.* |
| **45 Jahre alt** | *45 years old* |
| **sehr nett** | *very nice* |
| **Er/sie trägt eine Brille.** | *He/she wears glasses.* |
| **Kontaktlinsen** | *contact lenses* |
| **Er/sie hat blaue/grüne/ braune Augen.** | *He/she has blue/green/ brown eyes.* |
| **Er hat eine Glatze.** | *He is bald.* |
| **gefärbte Haare** | *coloured/dyed hair* |

### PRONUNCIATION TIPS

ziemlich – [tseemlich] **klein** – [kline]
e at the end of a word is always pronounced and sounds -uh

## WORD PATTERNS: DESCRIBING WORDS (ADJECTIVES)

Describing words (adjectives) all add an **-e** when used in front of a plural word. **Haare** is frequently plural in German (unless you literally mean a single hair), so the adjectives describing someone's hair are plural too, with an **-e**.

| Er  | hat   | lange        | blonde  | Haare |
|-----|-------|--------------|---------|-------|
| Sie | kurze | dunkle       |         |       |
|     |       | schulterlange | lockige |       |

German people usually know exactly how tall they are and will usually tell you they are 1,74 m etc. rather than say **ganz groß**. Find out how tall you are (in metric measurements!) and learn to say it in German.

### Exercise 4
Wie sehen sie aus? Tick the correct statements:

**a**
 **i** Er ist groß.
 **ii** Er ist klein.
 **iii** Er hat lange Haare.
 **iv** Er hat kurze Haare.
 **v** Er trägt eine Brille.
 **vi** Er hat dunkle Haare.
 **vii** Er hat blonde Haare.

**b**

   **i**    Sie ist groß.
  **ii**    Sie ist klein.
 **iii**    Sie hat lange Haare.
 **iv**    Sie hat kurze Haare.
  **v**    Sie trägt eine Brille.
 **vi**    Sie hat dunkle Haare
**vii**    Sie hat blonde Haare.

---

## Was sind Sie von Beruf? *What job do you do?*

| | |
|---|---|
| Was sind Sie von Beruf? | *What job do you do?* |
| | *(lit. what are you by job?)* |
| der Beruf | *job* |
| arbeiten | *to work* |
| Ich arbeite (als) ... | *I work as ...* |
| Ich bin/er ist/sie ist | *I am/he is/she is* |
| Ich bin selbständig. | *I am self-employed.* |
| der Lehrer | *teacher* |
| der Student | *student* |
| der Ingenieur | *engineer* |
| der Kfz-Mechaniker | *car mechanic* |
| der Verkäufer | *salesman* |
| der Polizist | *policeman* |
| der Zahnarzt | *dentist* |
| der Arzt | *doctor* |
| der Politiker | *politician* |

| | |
|---|---|
| der Programmierer | *computer programmer* |
| der Schauspieler | *actor* |
| der Moderator | *radio/TV presenter* |
| der Kellner | *waiter* |
| der Vertreter | *sales rep* |
| der Angestellte | *the employee* |
| der Beamte | *the official* |
| der Arbeiter | *the worker* |

## WORD PATTERNS: MASCULINE AND FEMININE

All the 'job' words make the feminine form by adding -in, e.g.:
der Sekretär, die Sekretärin; **Arzt** also adds an Umlaut: der Arzt,
die **Ärztin**.

Note that some jobs end in -**mann**. These usually change their
ending to -**frau** if the person is a woman, and to -**leute** if there is
more than one:

| | | |
|---|---|---|
| **der Mann –** *man* | **die Frau –** *woman* | |
| **der Geschäftsmann** | **die Geschäftsfrau** | *businessman/woman* |
| **der Kaufmann** | **die Kauffrau** | *buyer/salesperson* |
| **die Leute –** *people* | | |
| **die Geschäftsleute –** | | |
| *business people* | | |
| *also:* | | |
| **der Frisör/Friseur** | **die Frisörin** *hairdresser* | |

An -**in** ending usually means that a word is feminine.

**Der Freund** is a friend (male); **die Freundin** is a (female) friend.

**Der Journalist** is a male journalist, so a female one is **die Journalistin**.

### LEARNING TIPS

**1** Read the words out loud.
**2** Select the ones which you think you would find most useful and
learn them.

### DIALOGUE 25 ICH BIN ... *I AM ...*

| | |
|---|---|
| **Fräulein Fischer** | Was sind Sie von Beruf? |
| **Sie** | Ich bin Autoelektriker. |
| **Fräulein Fischer** | Was ist Fräulein Smith von Beruf? |
| **Sie** | Sie ist Krankenschwester. |
| | *(Contd)* |

CD2, TR 24

| | |
|---|---|
| **Fräulein Fischer** | Und was macht Herr Black? |
| **Sie** | Er ist Kfz-Mechaniker. |
| **Fräulein Fischer** | Was machen Herr und Frau Shaw? |
| **Sie** | Er ist Elektriker und sie hilft ihm im Geschäft. |
| **Fräulein Fischer** | Was macht ihre Tochter? |
| **Sie** | Sie ist Buchhändlerin. Sie arbeitet bei einer kleinen Firma. |
| **Fräulein Fischer** | Was macht ihr Sohn? |
| **Sie** | Er ist Grafiker, aber er ist im Moment arbeitslos. |

## LEARNING TIPS

**1** Read the dialogue out loud.
**2** There are some new words:
   **a** Krankenschwester
   **b** Elektriker
   **c** Buchhändlerin
   **d** Grafiker

Cross out the ones you already know or can guess. See how many of the clues you need to get the other ones!

**a** **Kranken** *the sick*, **Schwester** *sister*, so **Krankenschwester** *a nurse* (female)
**b** **der Elektriker** *electrician*
**c** **das Buch** *the book*, **handeln** *to trade*, so **der Buchhändler/ die Buchhändlerin** *bookseller*
**d** **der Grafiker** *graphic designer*

**3** Now re-read the dialogue substituting your family or friends and saying what jobs they do.

## Insight

German words are often made up of two or more parts.
If you know one part you have a clue to the meaning of the whole word. e.g. If you see the word **Arbeit** you know it is to do with 'work'.

| | |
|---|---|
| **arbeiten** | *to work* |
| **Ich arbeite als ...** | *I work as a ...* |
| **der Arbeiter/-in** | *worker* |
| **arbeitslos** | *without work (unemployed)* |
| **der Arbeitgeber** | *employer (lit. work giver)* |
| **der Arbeitnehmer** | *employee (lit. work taker)* |
| **das Arbeitsamt** | *employment exchange* |
| **das Amt** | *office* |

## WORD PATTERNS: VERBS

Talking about yourself – the verb ends with -e:

*I work*      **ich arbeite**

Talking about other people – the verb ends with -t:

*he works*      **er arbeitet**
*she works*      **sie arbeitet**

Talking about yourself and someone else -en:

*we work*      **wir arbeiten**

Talking about two or more people -en:

*they work*      **sie arbeiten**

### WORD BUILDING

**Arbeit(s-)** means *work*      **die Kleidung** means *clothes*
                                    **der Platz** means *?*

So, using the word-building principle it's easy to work out how you would say work clothes and workplace: die **Arbeitskleidung, der Arbeitsplatz.**

Remember that the gender of the new noun is the same as that of the last word.

Exercise 5
What new words can you make with **Arbeits-** and these words?

**a  der Beginn** *beginning*
**b  die Pause** *break*
**c  das Zimmer** *room*
**d  das Ende** *end*
**e  der Tisch** *table*
**f  die Zeit** *time*
**g  die Woche** *week*
**h  der Schluss** *end*
**i  der Vertrag** *contract*

Exercise 6
Using the following vocabulary clues, make the German equivalents of the English **a–d**.

**die Post** *post*          **das Amt** *office*
**Verkauf**-*sales*         **das Büro** *office*
**Reise**-*travel*          **Auskunfts**-*information*

**a**  *sales office*
**b**  *information office*
**c**  *post office*
**d**  *travel agency*

Exercise 7
Look at the pictures of Herr Braun and Silke Müller. Which questions would be suitable to ask each of them, and which replies belong to which person?

a  Was sind Sie von Beruf?
b  Was machst du?
c  Wo arbeitest du?
d  Wo arbeiten Sie?
e  Was machen Sie?

f  Was bist du ...?
g  Ich bin Studentin.
h  Bei BMW.
i  Ich bin Kfz-Mechaniker.
j  Auf einer Hotelfachschule.

Listening exercise 20
◄ CD2, TR 25

What do these eight people do for a living?

# Einkaufen
## Shopping

In this unit you will learn how to
- *Find your way around the shops*
- *Buy presents and souvenirs*
- *Buy clothes*
- *Ask about sizes, materials and colours*
- *Ask to try something on*

---

## Das Citycenter *The town centre*

QUICK VOCAB

| | |
|---|---|
| **das Geschäft\*** | *shop (or business)* |
| **der Laden\*** | *shop* |
| **die Apotheke** | *(dispensing) chemist* |
| **die Buchhandlung** | *bookshop* |
| **die Drogerie** | *chemist (not dispensing)* |
| **das Elektrogeschäft** | *electrical goods* |
| **das Fotogeschäft** | *photographer's* |
| **der Geschenkladen** | *gift shop* |
| **der Gemüseladen** | *greengrocer's* |
| **das Kaufhaus** | *department store* |
| **die Reinigung** | *cleaner's* |
| **der Schreibwarenladen** | *stationer's* |
| **das Schuhgeschäft** | *shoe shop* |
| **der Souvenirladen** | *souvenir shop* |

| der Tante-Emma-Laden | corner shop (lit. Aunt Emma's shop) |
| der Zeitungskiosk | newspaper shop |
| das Einkaufscenter | the shopping centre |
| Wo ist hier ein Supermarkt? | Is there a supermarket near here? (lit. Where is here a supermarket?) |
| Ausverkauf | sale |
| Zu Verkaufen | for sale (lit. to sell) |
| der Winterschlussverkauf | winter sales |
| der Sommerschlussverkauf | summer sales |
| die Bäckerei | bakery |
| die Konditorei | cake shop |
| der Supermarkt | supermarket |
| das Blumengeschäft | florist |
| die Metzgerei | butcher's (southern Germany) |
| der Schlachter | butcher/butcher's (northern Germany) |
| der Tabakhändler | tobacconist |

*These two words for shop are often interchangeable.

Exercise 1
Which shop would you go to?

148

## Wo kann ich hier ... kaufen? *Where can I buy ...?*

| | |
|---|---|
| **eine Ansichtskarte** | *a picture post card* |
| **Briefpapier/Schreibpapier** | *writing paper* |
| **ein Buch** | *a book* |
| **eine CD/Compact Disc** | *a compact disc* |
| **Medikamente** | *medicine* |
| **ein Paar Schuhe** | *a pair of shoes* |
| **eine Zahnbürste** | *a toothbrush* |
| **eine Flasche Parfüm** | *a bottle of perfume* |
| **eine Flasche Wein** | *a bottle of wine* |
| | |
| **Andenken** | *souvenirs* |
| **Blumen** | *flowers* |
| **Briefmarken** | *stamps* |
| **Brot** | *bread* |
| **eine DVD** | *a dvd* |
| **ein Geschenk** | *a present* |
| **einen Kuchen** | *a cake* |
| **einen Mantel** | *a coat* |
| **Zahnpasta** | *toothpaste* |
| **Batterien** | *batteries* |
| **Weingläser** | *wine glasses* |
| **einen Bierkrug** | *a beer mug* |
| **einen Schal** | *a scarf* |
| **Ohrringe** | *earrings* |

Exercise 2

What do you think they might be buying? Fill in a suitable word and then practise the dialogues.

(**Passantin** *passerby*)

> **Touristin**    Wo kann ich hier einen (a) ... kaufen?
> **Passantin**    Das Fotogeschäft ist hier gleich um die Ecke.
> **Touristin**    Ich möchte eine (b) ... Gibt es ein Musikgeschäft hier in der Nähe?
>
>                                               *(Contd)*

As well as at the post office you can usually buy stamps anywhere that sells picture postcards and at most newsagents and tobacconists (who usually sell tickets for local transport).

In an **Apotheke** you can get a prescription made up, but you can also buy medication without a prescription and the **Apotheker** is qualified to suggest remedies for most minor ailments.

---

## Im Geschäft *In the shop*

| | |
|---|---|
| **Ich suche ...** | *I am looking for ...* |
| **Wie viel kostet ...?** | *How much does ... cost?* |
| **etwa** | *about* |
| **Haben Sie etwas Billigeres?** | *Have you anything cheaper?* |
| **Kann ich Ihnen helfen?** | *Can I help you?* |
| **Sonst noch etwas?** | *Anything else?* |
| **ein Geschenk für** | *a present for* |
| **ein Geschenk für meinen Mann/meine Frau** | *a present for my husband/wife* |
| **ein Geschenk für meinen Bruder/meine Schwester** | *a present for my brother/sister* |
| **ein Geschenk für meinen Vater/meine Mutter** | *a present for my father/mother* |
| **ein Geschenk für meinen Freund/meine Freundin** | *a present for my friend, boyfriend/girlfriend* |
| **ein Geschenk für meinen Sohn/meine Tochter** | *a present for my son/daughter* |
| **Könnten Sie es/sie als Geschenk einpacken?** | *Could you wrap it/them as a present?* |
| **Sie bezahlen an der Kasse.** | *You pay at the cash desk.* |

| Haben Sie eine Tüte, bitte? | *Have you a carrier bag, please?* |
| Das reicht, danke. | *That's enough, thank you.* |
| Haben Sie ...? | *Have you ...?* |
| Ich möchte... | *I would like ...* |
| Ich nehme ... | *I'll take ...* |
| Ich brauche ... | *I need ...* |

## Exercise 3

You want to buy presents for your family and friends. How would you say *I am looking for a present for ...*?

Ich suche ein Geschenk für ...

**a** *my girlfriend*        **e** *my husband*
**b** *my brother*          **f** *my mother*
**c** *my grandmother*      **g** *my boyfriend*
**d** *my wife*             **h** *my son*

## Exercise 4

**a** Ask if they have:
   **i** *a book*
   **ii** *writing paper*
   **iii** *a bottle of perfume*

**b** Say you're looking for:
   **i** *a bottle of wine*
   **ii** *wineglasses*
   **iii** *a beer mug*

**c** Say you'd like:
   **i** *a scarf*
   **ii** *earrings*
   **iii** *a cake*

A gift-wrapping service is offered free in most German shops. You will usually be asked:

**Soll ich das als Geschenk einpacken?**  *Shall I gift-wrap it for you?*
**Soll ich den Preis abmachen?**  *Shall I take the price off?*

### DIALOGUE 26

| | |
|---|---|
| **Verkäuferin** | Kann ich Ihnen helfen? |
| **Sie** | Ich möchte ein Geschenk für meine Tochter. |
| **Verkäuferin** | Wie alt ist sie? |
| **Sie** | Zwei Jahre. |
| **Verkäuferin** | Wie wäre es mit einem Stofftier? |
| **Sie** | Wie viel kosten sie? |
| **Verkäuferin** | Von etwa €25 bis €100. |
| **Sie** | Wie viel kostet der Teddybär? |
| **Verkäuferin** | Der kleine Bär kostet €22, und der große kostet €45,50. Der Hund kostet €48 und die Katze €36. |
| **Sie** | Ich nehme die Stoffkatze. Könnten Sie es als Geschenk einpacken? |
| **Verkäuferin** | Ja, natürlich. Sonst noch etwas? |
| **Sie** | Haben Sie Computerspiele? |
| **Verkäuferin** | Ja. Skifahrer – das ist neu. |
| **Sie** | Wie viel kostet es? |
| **Verkäuferin** | €43. |
| **Sie** | Haben Sie etwas Billigeres? |
| **Verkäuferin** | Ja, Autocops. €18. |
| **Sie** | Ich nehme es. |
| **Verkäuferin** | Sonst noch etwas? |
| **Sie** | Nein, danke, das ist alles. Was macht das? |
| **Verkäuferin** | €54. |
| **Sie** | Bitte schön. |
| **Verkäuferin** | Danke. Auf Wiedersehen. |
| **Sie** | Auf Wiedersehen. |

### LEARNING TIPS

**1** Read the dialogue and make sure you understand everything.

**2** Read it out loud, playing each part in turn.

Listening exercise 21
�»)) **CD2, TR 27**

What are these six customers buying, and for whom?

**Plastikgeld:** Although paying by credit card is becoming more acceptable in Germany, in some restaurants this is still not the case. The most widely used cards are Visa and Eurocard and Maestro.

---

## Im Kaufhaus *In the department store*

**ICH MÖCHTE .../HABEN SIE ...** *I WOULD LIKE .../HAVE YOU ...*

| | |
|---|---|
| **einen Pullover** | *a jumper* |
| **eine Hose** | *trousers (lit. a trouser)* |
| **einen Schal** | *a scarf* |
| **ein Paar Handschuhe** | *a pair of gloves* |
| **einen Anzug** | *a suit* |
| **einen Schlafanzug** | *pyjamas (lit. a sleeping suit)* |
| **ein Kleid** | *a dress* |
| **einen Jogginganzug** | *a track suit* |
| **einen Badeanzug** | *a swim suit* |
| **einen Mantel** | *a coat* |
| **einfarbig** | *plain (lit. one-coloured)* |
| **aus ...** | *made of ...* |
| **aus Wolle** | *made of wool* |
| **aus Baumwolle** | *made of cotton* |
| **aus Leder** | *made of leather* |
| **aus Seide** | *made of silk* |
| **die Größe** | *size* |
| **eine Bluse Größe 36** | *a blouse size 36* |
| **das ist zu teuer** | *that's too expensive* |
| **Ich nehme es/sie** | *I'll take it/them* |

QUICK VOCAB

| | |
|---|---|
| **Was für ...?** | *What kind of ...?* |
| **einen Schlips** | *a tie* |
| **ein Hemd** | *a shirt* |
| **eine Bluse** | *a blouse* |
| **einen Rock** | *a skirt* |
| **die Farben** | *colours* |
| **rot** | *red* |
| **rosa(rot)** | *pink* |
| **blau** | *blue* |
| **grün** | *green* |
| **grau** | *grey* |
| **schwarz** | *black* |
| **weiss** | *white* |
| **dunkelblau** | *dark blue* |
| **hellblau** | *light blue* |
| **türkis** | *turquoise* |
| **violet** | *purple* |
| **gelb** | *yellow* |
| **braun** | *brown* |
| **bunt** | *colourful* |
| **gemustert** | *patterned* |
| **kariert** | *check* |
| **gestreift** | *striped* |

## LEARNING TIP

**1** Read all the new words out loud. Select the ones you think would be the most useful to you and learn them.

Exercise 5
How would you ask for:

  **a**  *a blue jumper size 38?*
  **b**  *a red blouse size 34?*
  **c**  *a pair of brown trousers size 36?*
  **d**  *a green wool scarf?*
  **e**  *a pair of black gloves?*
  **f**  *a white cotton shirt?*

## Exercise 6

You are buying various items in a department store. Complete your part of the dialogue.

| | | |
|---|---|---|
| **a You** | You would like to buy a scarf for your mother. | |
| **Verkäuferin** | Welche Farbe? | |
| **b You** | Blue. | |
| **Verkäuferin** | Dunkelblau oder hellblau? | |
| **c You** | Dark blue. | |
| **Verkäuferin** | Dieser Schal hier ist sehr schön. | |
| **d You** | Is it wool? | |
| **Verkäuferin** | Ja, natürlich. 100-prozentig. | |
| **e You** | How much does it cost? | |
| **Verkäuferin** | €62,50. | |
| **f You** | That's a bit expensive. Ask if they have anything cheaper. | |
| **Verkäuferin** | Der karierte Schal kostet €28. | |
| **g You** | You'll take it. | |

*CD2, TR 28*

Now you want a pair of gloves for your friend.

| | |
|---|---|
| **h You** | Say you'd like a pair of gloves. |
| **Verkäuferin** | Was für Handschuhe? |
| **i You** | Black, leather. |
| **Verkäuferin** | Welche Größe? |
| **j You** | You don't know. |
| **Verkäuferin** | Groß oder mittelgroß? |
| **k You** | Big. |
| **Verkäuferin** | Die kosten €43,50. |
| **l You** | Say you'll take them. And ask her to gift-wrap them. |

Now you want a road map (**eine Straßenkarte**).

| | |
|---|---|
| **m You** | Have you got a road map? |
| **Verkäuferin** | In der Buchabteilung. |
| **n You** | Where is the book section? |
| **Verkäuferin** | Im vierten Stock. |
| **o You** | Ask where the lift is. |
| **Verkäuferin** | Dort drüben. |
| **p You** | Say thank you. |

Listening exercise 22
◀) **CD2, TR 29**

What are these six customers buying?

**LANGUAGE NOTES**

Here are some more useful phrases to do with shopping:

| | |
|---|---|
| **Ich kaufe ...** | *I am buying* |
| **Ich kaufe ein ...** | *I am shopping* |
| **Ich gehe einkaufen.** | *I do the shopping.* |
| **Ich habe gekauft** | *I have bought* |
| **Ich habe einen Mantel gekauft.** | *I have bought a coat.* |

Notice the word order in the last example. *I have a coat bought.*

**Insight**

Opening hours have changed across Germany and you can now expect most shops to stay open till 8 pm or even later, especially in the larger cities, big shopping centres and tourist venues where many shops are now even open on Sundays.

Exercise 7
Look at the floor plan below. On which floor would you find...?

| | | | |
|---|---|---|---|
| **a** | *leather goods* | **g** | *car parts* |
| **b** | *books* | **h** | *tennis rackets* |
| **c** | *trainers* | **i** | *model aircraft* |
| **d** | *records* | **j** | *toilets* |
| **e** | *men's clothing* | **k** | *confectionery* |
| **f** | *children's clothing* | **l** | *ladies' clothing* |

| Untergeschoss | 2. Obergeschoss |
|---|---|
| Autozubehör | Restaurant/Café |
| Werken und Basteln | Reisebüro |
| Lebensmittel | WC |

| Erdgeschoss | 3. Obergeschoss |
|---|---|
| Lederwaren | Sportartikel |
| Schreibwaren | Sportkleidung |
| Tabakwaren | Schwimmsport |
| Bonbons | Sportschuhe |
| Kosmetik | |
| Schmuck | |
| Herrenbekleidung | |

| 1. Obergeschoss | 4. Obergeschoss |
|---|---|
| Kinder-und Damenbekleidung | Buchhandlung |
| | Musikgeschäft |
| | Elektrogeschäft |
| | Hauswaren |

| | |
|---|---|
| **Schmuck** | *jewellery* |
| **Autozubehör** | *car accessories* |
| **Werken und Basteln** | *hobby and crafts* |
| **die Rolltreppe** | *escalator* |
| **der Fahrstuhl/der Aufzug** | *lift* |

QUICK VOCAB

# 14

---

# Wann fährt der Zug?
## When does the train leave?

In this unit you will learn how to
- *Use public transport in Germany*
- *Ask for travel information*
- *Buy tickets*
- *Read the signs at the station*
- *Work out what names mean*

---

## Am Bahnhof *At the station*

| | |
|---|---|
| **der Zug** | *train* |
| **mit dem Zug** | *by train* |
| **der Bus** | *bus* |
| **mit dem Bus** | *by bus* |
| **wann?** | *when?* |
| **das Gleis** | *platform, track* |
| **fahren** | *to go* |
| **ab/fahren** | *to depart* |
| **kommen** | *to come* |
| **an/kommen** | *to arrive* |
| **um** | *at* |
| **ab** | *from* |
| **Wann fährt der Zug ab?** | *When does the train leave?* |
| **Um wie viel Uhr fährt der Zug?** | *At what time does the train leave?* |

| Wann kommt er in München an? | When does it arrive in Munich? (lit. when comes he in Munich in?) |
| Wo fährt der Zug nach München ab? | Where does the Munich train leave from? |
| Wann kommt der Bus aus London an? | When does the bus from London arrive? |

Word patterns in questions
Look at the word order in the questions:

| **Wann** *fährt* **der Zug?** | lit. *When* **goes** *the train?* |
| **Wie** *schreibt* **man das?** | *How* **write** *you that?* |
| **Wie** *geht* **es Ihnen?** | *How* **goes** *it to you?* |
| **Wo** *wohnen* **Sie?** | *Where* **live** *you?* |

### LANGUAGE NOTE

**Nach** usually means *after* as in **Nachmittag** *afternoon*, but it means *to* in expressions like **nach München, nach Italien.**

Exercise 1
Put the words in each of these sentences in the right order.

a der Zug in München wann kommt an?
b ab der Zug wann fährt?
c man schreibt wie das?
d wie es Ihnen geht?
e Sie wohnen wo?

Exercise 2
*How would you say ...?*

a *to Munich*
b *to Italy*
c *from England*
d *from London*

## DIALOGUE 27

🎧 CD2, TR 30

| | |
|---|---|
| **Sie** | Wann fährt der Zug nach Hamburg? |
| **Bahnbeamter** | Der nächste Zug nach Hamburg fährt um 11 Uhr 10. |
| **Sie** | Wann kommt er in Hamburg an? |
| **Bahnbeamter** | Um 14 Uhr 46. |
| **Sie** | Wo fährt er ab? |
| **Bahnbeamter** | Ab Gleis 7. |
| **Sie** | Und der nächste Zug nach Köln? |
| **Bahnbeamter** | Der fährt um 11 Uhr 39. |
| **Sie** | Wann kommt er in Köln an? |
| **Bahnbeamter** | Um 16 Uhr 27. |
| **Sie** | Wo fährt er ab? |
| **Bahnbeamter** | Ab Gleis 14. |

## Abfahrt

## Ankunft

### PRONUNCIATION TIPS

**ab** *sounds* **ap**
**nächste** *[next-uh]*

**fährt** *[fair-t]*
**Köln** *[curl-n]*

### LEARNING TIPS

**1** Read Dialogue 27 and check that you can understand everything.
**2** Practise reading it out loud.
**3** Ask for information about the trains to Hamburg and Köln. What questions are you going to ask?
**4** Now make up a different dialogue. Say that the train to Hamburg leaves at 12.15 from platform 8 and gets in at 15.13. The train to Köln leaves at 14.05 from platform 2 and gets in at 17.44.

Before using public transport, buy a ticket from a machine (**Fahrausweise**). On boarding, you must get your ticket stamped in a ticket-cancelling machine (**Entwerter**) – often found at the top or bottom of the steps as you enter the vehicle.

---

## Einmal nach Köln, bitte *A ticket to Cologne, please*

| | |
|---|---|
| **Sondertarife** | *special fares* |
| **die Fahrkarte** | *ticket* |
| **der Fahrplan** | *timetable* |
| **die Auskunft** | *information* |
| **die Abfahrt** | *departure(s)* |
| **die Ankunft** | *arrival(s)* |
| **der Bahnsteig** | *platform* |
| **der Fahrkartenschalter** | *ticket office* |
| **der Fahrscheinautomat** | *automatic ticket machine* |
| **Schliessfächer** | *(left luggage) lockers* |
| **das Gepäck** | *luggage* |
| **der Koffer** | *suitcase* |
| **der Kofferkuli** | *luggage trolley* |
| **der Speisewagen** | *dining car* |
| **der Schlafwagen** | *sleeping car* |
| **erste/zweite Klasse** | *first/second class* |
| **Raucher/Nichtraucher** | *smoker/non-smoker* |
| **Ich möchte ...** | *I would like ...* |
| **Ich möchte einen Platz reservieren.** | *I would like to reserve a seat.* |
| **Ich möchte eine Rückfahrkarte.** | *I would like a return ticket.* |
| **Ich möchte einmal einfach nach Hamburg.** | *I would like a single to Hamburg.* |
| **Ich möchte zweimal nach Bonn, hin und zurück.** | *I would like 2 returns to Bonn.* |
| **Ich möchte zweieinhalb.** | *I would like two-and-a-half, i.e. 2 adults, 1 child.* |

QUICK VOCAB

| | |
|---|---|
| **Ich möchte anderthalb.** | *I would like one-and-a-half, i.e. 1 adult, 1 child.* |
| **einsteigen** | *to get on* |
| **umsteigen** | *to change* |
| **aussteigen** | *to get off* |
| **Ich steige in Hamburg ein.** | *I get on in Hamburg.* |
| **Ich steige in Köln um.** | *I change in Cologne.* |
| **Ich steige in Stuttgart aus.** | *I get off at Stuttgart.* |
| **Was kostet es?** | *How much is it?* |
| **Ist dies der Zug nach Trier?** | *Is this the train for Trier?* |
| **Hat der Zug nach Dortmund Verspätung?** | *Is the Dortmund train late?* |
| **Muss ich umsteigen?** | *Do I have to change?* |
| **Wo muss ich umsteigen?** | *Where do I have to change?* |

## Exercise 3
How would you ask for:

**a** *1 single to Berlin?*

**b** *1 return to Salzburg?*

**c** *3 returns to Mannheim?*

**d** *2 returns to Koblenz?*

**e** *2 singles to Osnabrück?*

**f** *1 return to Innsbruck?*

**Abkürzungen** *Abbreviations*

| DB | Deutsche Bahn | German railways |
|---|---|---|
| EC | Eurocity | |
| ICE | InterCity Express | |
| D-Zug | [Durch Zug] | express train [through train] |
| RE | Regional-Express | |
| U-Bahn | Untergrundbahn | underground (railway) |
| S-Bahn | Schnell- oder Stadtbahn | suburban railway |

## Exercise 4

Complete the dialogues following the guidelines given, and then practise them.

| | |
|---|---|
| **a** | You want a return ticket to Köln. |
| **Bahnbeamtin** | Erste oder zweite Klasse? |
| **b You** | Second. Ask how much it is. |
| **Bahnbeamtin** | €32. |
| **c You** | Ask when the train goes. |
| **Bahnbeamtin** | Um halb elf. |
| **d You** | Ask where it goes from. |
| **Bahnbeamtin** | Gleis 8. |
| **e You** | Say thank you. |
| *On your return journey …* | |
| **f You** | Ask when the next train leaves for München. |
| **Bahnbeamtin** | Es gibt einen InterCity um 10.53 Uhr und einen D-Zug um 11.18 Uhr. |
| **g You** | Ask how much it costs. |
| **Bahnbeamtin** | Mit dem InterCity €63 und mit dem D-Zug €42. |
| **h You** | D-Zug! Do you have to change? |
| **Bahnbeamtin** | Ja, in Koblenz. |
| **i You** | When do you get to München? |
| **Bahnbeamtin** | Um 16.44 Uhr. |
| **j You** | Where does the train leave from? |
| **Bahnbeamtin** | Ab Gleis 3. |

## Listening exercise 23
🔊 **CD2, TR 32**

Listen to the three customers, and for each, answer the following questions:

**a** Where are they going?
**b** What sort of ticket do they buy?
**c** When does the train leave?
**d** When does it get in?
**e** Do they have to change?
**f** How much does it cost?
**g** Which platform are they going from?

While staying in Germany you are going to ring the station to find out details about trains. Prepare a list of questions you are going to ask in each of these two situations:

**a** You are going on a business trip to Hamburg with a colleague.
**b** Going to Rüdesheim for the day with your friend.

## Insight

For information about trains on the internet go to: Deutsche Bahn or www.bahn.de

## Am Flughafen *At the airport*

| | |
|---|---|
| **das Flugzeug** | *aeroplane* |
| **der Flughafen** | *airport* |
| **der Flug** | *flight* |
| **die Flugnummer** | *flight number* |
| **der Flugsteig** | *gate* |
| **die Abflughalle** | *departure lounge* |
| **die Bordkarte** | *boarding card* |
| **fliegen** | *to fly* |
| **die Maschine** | *plane* |

QUICK VOCAB

| der Fensterplatz | *window seat* |
| der Gangplatz | *aisle seat* |
| Wie lautet die Flugnummer? | *What's the flight number?* |
| Wann ist Meldeschluss? | *What is the latest checking-in time?* |
| Wann startet die Maschine? | *When does the plane take off?* |
| Wann landet die Maschine? | *When does the plane land?* |
| Was für eine Maschine ist es? | *What type of plane is it?* |
| Wie war die Reise? | *How was the journey?* |
| Ich bin müde. | *I am tired.* |
| Ich bin hungrig. | *I am hungry.* |
| Ich bin durstig. | *I am thirsty.* |
| Ich bin schläfrig. | *I am sleepy.* |
| Es geht mir gut. | *I am fine.* |

## Exercise 5

You are going to Germany. Prepare what you would tell your
German friend on the phone. These are your flight details:

| dep: Manchester | 11.15 |
| arr: London Heathrow | 12.00 |
| dep: London Heathrow | 13.45 |
| arr: Hamburg Fuhlsbüttel | 14.15 (local time) |
| Flight number BA 5377 | |

## Exercise 6

You have rung up to find details of your return flight. How do
you ask:

a *When do you leave Hamburg?*

b *Is it a direct flight?*

c *What is your flight number?*

d *When are you due in Manchester?*

## Exercise 7

Complete your part in these telephone conversations with Fräulein Dellmann and Monika.

| | |
|---|---|
| **You** | Hallo. How are you? |
| **Frl. Dellmann** | Gut danke und dir? |
| **You** | You are fine too. |
| **Frl. Dellmann** | Wann kommst du nach Düsseldorf? |
| **You** | Sunday 26 October. |
| **Frl. Dellmann** | Wann kommst du in Düsseldorf an? |
| **You** | 16.00. |
| **Frl. Dellmann** | Wie lautet die Flugnummer? |
| **You** | LH 123. Ask where you will meet. |
| **Frl. Dellmann** | Ich hole dich vom Flughafen ab. (I'll fetch you from the airport.) |
| **You** | Say you are looking forward to it. |
| **Frl. Dellmann** | Bis dann. Tschüss! |
| **You** | Tschüss! Bye! |
| **You** | Hallo. How are you? |
| **Monika** | Gut danke, und dir? |
| **You** | You are fine too. Ask when she is coming. |
| **Monika** | Dienstag den 4. |
| **You** | Ask at what time she is due in. |
| **Monika** | Um 18.45 Uhr. |
| **You** | Ask what the flight number is. |
| **Monika** | BA 345. |
| **You** | Say you will meet her at the airport. |
| **Monika** | Gut. Ich freue mich schon darauf. |
| **You** | Say till then, goodbye. |
| **Monika** | Auf Wiederhören. |

## Exercise 8

How would you say you are arriving at:

a  *14.30 in Düsseldorf*
b  *9.05 in Munich/München*
c  *11.30 in Cologne/Köln*
d  *18.35 in Hamburg*
e  *21.20 in Vienna/Wien*
f  *17.45 in Frankfurt*

Listening exercise 24
🔊 **CD2, TR 33**

When are these six travellers arriving and what are their flight numbers?

### LANGUAGE NOTES: WHAT'S IN A NAME?

Many German placenames give you a clue about the whereabouts or origin of the place by including a word you already know. Here are a few examples:

| | |
|---|---|
| **die Brücke** *the bridge* | **Innsbruck** *bridge over the river Inn*<br>**Saarbrücken** *bridges over the river Saar* |
| **die Burg** *the castle* | **Freiburg, Hamburg, Augsburg ... etc.** |
| **-chen** *little* | **München** *little monks* **München** *was originally a small settlement of monks* |
| **der Berg** *mountain* | **Nürnberg** *Nürn mountain,* **Königsberg** *King's mountain* |
| **das Dorf** *village* | **Düsseldorf** *village on the river Düssel* |
| **die Stadt** *the town* | **Friedrichstadt** *Frederick's town* |
| **der Mund** *mouth* | **Dortmund** *mouth of the river Dort* |
| **new** *new* | **Neustadt** *new town* |
| **der Bach** *stream* | **Marbach** *the Marbrook* |
| **der Wald** *wood* | **Mittenwald** *in the middle of the wood* |
| **das Tal** *valley* | **Wuppertal** *valley of the river Wupper* |
| **Baden** *baths (spa)* | **Wiesbaden** *spa on the Wiese (meadow)* |
| **der Hafen** *harbour* | **Bremerhaven** *port of Bremen* |
| **die Kirche** *church* | **Oberkirch** *upperchurch* |
| **das Heim** *home* | **Rüdesheim** *Rudi's home* |
| **der See** *lake* | **Bodensee** *(Lake Constance)* |
| **das Feld** *field* | **Bielefeld** |

Exercise 9
What do you think these names mean?

| | | |
|---|---|---|
| **a** Wolfsburg | **c** Neuburg | **e** Gelsenkirchen |
| **b** Fischbach | **d** Bad Ischl | **f** Ingolstadt |

| g | Ammersee | m | Chiemsee | s | Osnabrück |
|---|----------|---|----------|---|-----------|
| h | Heidelberg | n | Baden Baden | t | der Schwarzwald |
| i | Neunkirchen | o | berstdorf | u | Neustadt |
| j | Friedrichshafen | p | Mühlsdorf | v | Rheinburg |
| k | Zweibrücken | q | Steinbach | w | Guntersdorf |
| l | Salzburg | r | Magdeburg | x | Mannheim |

Names which we spell (or say) differently:

**München** *Munich*, **Wien** *Vienna*, **Köln** *Cologne*, **der Rhein** *Rhine (river)*, **die Mosel** *Moselle (river)*, **Braunschweig** *Brunswick*, **Hannover** *Hanover*, **Hameln** *Hamelin*.

# 15

## Essen und trinken
Eating and drinking

In this unit you will learn how to
- *Recognize meal times*
- *Ask for breakfast in a hotel*
- *Ask for room service*
- *Buy a snack*
- *Call the waiter/waitress*
- *Say you need something*
- *Buy ice-creams and drinks*

Zimmerservice *Room service*

| | |
|---|---|
| das Frühstück | *breakfast* |
| das Mittagessen | *lunch* |
| das Abendessen | *evening meal* |
| ein Imbiss | *a snack* |
| Kaffee und Kuchen | *coffee and cakes* |
| die Sahne | *cream/evaporated milk* |
| die Milch | *milk* |
| Ei(er) (gekocht) | *egg(s) (boiled)* |
| Rührei | *scrambled egg* |
| Spiegelei(er) | *fried egg(s)* |
| das Brot/Brötchen | *bread/roll(s)* |

QUICK VOCAB

| Joghurt, Cornflakes und Müsli | yoghurt, cornflakes and muesli |
|---|---|
| **Was essen Sie zum Frühstück?** | *What do you eat for breakfast?* |
| **der Schinken** | *ham* |
| **der Speck** | *bacon* |
| **die Wurst** | *sausage* |
| **der Käse** | *cheese* |
| **die Butter** | *butter* |
| **der Zucker** | *sugar* |
| **die Konfitüre** | *jam* |
| **der Honig** | *honey* |
| **der Toast** | *toast* |
| **der Saft** | *juice* |

Exercise 1
At what time ...

**a** *can you have breakfast?*  **c** *can you get an evening meal?*
**b** *is lunch served?*  **d** *can you get a cup of coffee?*

| MAHLZEITEN | |
|---|---|
| **FRÜHSTÜCKSBÜFFET** | 6.00–9.30 |
| **MITTAGESSEN** | 12.00–14.00 |
| **ABENDESSEN** | 18.00–22.00 |
| **KAFFEE IN DER KAFFEESTUBE** | 10.00–18.00 |

### DIALOGUE 28

| **Kellner** | Guten Morgen. Tee oder Kaffee? |
|---|---|
| **Sie** | Kaffee, bitte. |
| **Kellner** | Fruchtsaft oder Cornflakes? |
| **Sie** | Orangensaft. |
| **Kellner** | Essen Sie ein Ei? |
| **Sie** | Nein, danke. |
| **Kellner** | Toast oder Brötchen? |
| **Sie** | Brötchen. Haben Sie noch Milch? |
| **Kellner** | Bitte schön. |

You would like to take breakfast in your room. Fill out the breakfast order.

---

**TRUSTEE** • Park Hotel • München

Guten Morgen!

Zimmer-Frühstücksbestellung

---

| Zimmer Nr. | Gast | Personenzahl |
|---|---|---|

---

Frühstück
Wann möchten Sie Ihr Frühstück – bitte kreuzen Sie die gewünschte Uhrzeit an:

☐ 7.00 Uhr ☐ 7.30 Uhr ☐ 8.00 Uhr
☐ 8.30 Uhr ☐ 9.00 Uhr ☐ 9.30 Uhr
☐ 10.00 Uhr ☐ 10.30 Uhr

Bitte hängen Sie die ausgefüllte Frühstückskarte bereits am Abend an den Türknopf.

---

"Trustee Frühstück" €20

☐ Kaffee ☐ Tee mit Zitrone ☐ Schokolade
☐ Orangensaft ☐ Tee mit Sahne ☐ Milch kalt
☐ Grapefruitsaft ☐ Ei gekocht ☐ Milch heiß
☐ Schinken ☐ Wurst ☐ Käse
☐ Brot (Schwarzbrot/Weißbrot), Brötchen, Croissant,
  Butter, Konfitüre, Honig

---

Auf Ihren Wunsch
☐ 2 Spiegeleier ☐ 2 Rühreier €3,20
☐ Mit Schinken ☐ Mit Speck €4,90

---

Unterschrift Total

---

Die Preise enthalten Service und gesetzliche Mehrwertsteuer.
Etagenaufschlag €5,-

| der Türknopf | door knob |
| auf Ihren Wunsch | at your request (extras) |

**LEARNING TIP**

**1** Practise the dialogue, ordering different things.

---

## Ich habe Hunger! *I'm hungry!*

| eine Portion | a portion |
| Bratwurst | grilled sausage |
| Bockwurst | boiled sausage (Frankfurter type) |
| die Pommes (frites) | chips |
| der Senf | mustard |
| mit Ketchup | ketchup |
| die Mayonnaise | mayonnaise (now also written as **Majonäse**) |
| Reibekuchen mit Apfelmus | thin potato fritters with apple purée |
| Waffeln mit Kirschsoße | waffles with cherry sauce |
| eine Dose Cola | a can of cola |
| ein Glas Limo | a glass of lemonade |
| eine Flasche Sprudel | a bottle of carbonated water |
| Wasser | water |
| einen Apfelsaft | apple juice |
| Apfelschorle (Apfelsaft mit Limo) | apple juice with lemonade |
| ein Bier | beer |
| ein Glas Wein | a glass of wine |
| Kleingeld | (small) change |
| und | and |
| Bitte schön. | Here you are. |
| zurück | change (lit. back) |
| Einmal Bratwurst mit Kartoffelsalat. | Sausage and potato salad for one. |
| Zweimal Currywurst mit Püree. | Curried sausage with potato purée for two. |

## Exercise 2
How would you order these?

**a** chips; **b** 2 grilled sausages; **c** sausage (frankfurter) and chips x 2; **d** can of coke; **e** a beer; **f** 2 waffles

## Listening exercise 25
🔊 **CD2, TR 35**

What have these eight customers ordered?

## Exercise 3
**Ich möchte ...**

Complete your part of the dialogue.

| | | |
|---|---|---|
| **a You** | *You would like a sausage and chips.* | CD2, TR 36 |
| **Kellner** | Ketchup oder Mayo? | |
| **b You** | *Ketchup.* | |
| **Kellner** | Bitte schön. Sonst noch etwas? | |
| **c You** | *Your friend wants a curry sausage and potato salad.* | |
| **Kellner** | Bitte schön. Und zu trinken? | |
| **d You** | *You want a coke and your friend wants a beer. That's all. Ask how much it is.* | |
| **Kellner** | Das macht €22. | |
| **e You** | *Here you are: €50.* | |
| **Kellner** | Haben Sie Kleingeld? | |
| **f You** | *I have €2.* | |
| **Kellner** | So, €30 zurück. | |

## Exercise 4
Where would you expect to get the following meals or snacks? Match each one with a place.

**a** a quick snack; **b** coffee and cakes; **c** a pizza; **d** a self-service meal; **e** a meal and a drink (more than one place); **f** an ice-cream

i **Café-Konditorei**
ii **Schnellimbiss**
iii *Eiscafé*
iv **Pizzeria**
v **Gaststätte**
vi *Wirtschaft*
vii **Selbstbedienung**

**LEARNING TIP**

**1** Choose a snack for yourself and two friends and work out what you would have to say to order it.

## An dem Tisch *At the table*

| | |
|---|---|
| der Suppenteller | *soup bowl* |
| der Becher (–) | *beaker/mug* |
| noch | *more* (lit. *still*)/*another* |
| die Soße | *sauce* |
| der Teller (–) | *plate* |
| die Tasse (n) | *cup* |
| die Untertasse (n) | *saucer* |
| die Schüssel (n) | *bowl* |
| das Messer (–) | *knife* |
| das Glas (¨er) | *glass* |
| das Salz | *salt* |
| der Pfeffer | *pepper* |
| die Gabel (n) | *fork* |
| der Löffel (–) | *spoon* |
| der Ketchup | *ketchup* |
| der Senf | *mustard* |

QUICK VOCAB

## WORD PATTERNS: EIN (A) AND KEIN (NO/NOT A)

| Ich habe | **keinen Teller** | *masculine* | (**der** words) I haven't a plate |
|---|---|---|---|
| | **keine Tasse** | *feminine* | (**die** words) I haven't a cup |
| | **kein Messer** | *neuter* | (**das** words) I haven't a knife |

| Ich brauche | **einen Teller** | (**der**) I need a plate |
|---|---|---|
| | **eine Tasse** | (**die**) I need a cup |
| | **ein Messer** | (**das**) I need a knife |

You won't be prevented from communicating effectively if you don't know whether a word is **der, die** or **das** because you can convey the meaning perfectly well without the ending. German speakers do not always pronounce them clearly themselves.

To get the waiter's/waitress's attention, you can use:

| **Fräulein!** | *Miss! (calling the waitress – whatever her age)* |
|---|---|
| **Herr Ober!** | *Waiter! (rather formal)* |

Or less formally

**Bitte!**   *Please!*

The standard reply is:

**(Ich) komme gleich.**   *(I'll) be right with you.*

## Insight

Warning! **Soße** as a word on its own usually means *custard*, *a sweet sauce* or *gravy*.

**Pudding** is blancmange; it doesn't mean pudding in the sense of dessert.

## Exercise 5
**a** How would you ask for:

**b** And how would you ask for more:

## Exercise 6
Complete your part of the dialogues.

| | | |
|---|---|---|
| **a You** | Attract the waiter's attention. | |
| **Kellner** | Ja? | |
| **b You** | You need another plate ... | |
| **Kellner** | Bitte schön. | |
| **c You** | And the salt pot is empty ... | |
| **Kellner** | Bitte schön. | |
| **d You** | And have they got any ketchup? | |
| **Kellner** | Sonst noch etwas? | |
| **e You** | No, thanks that's all! | |
| **f You** | Try to attract her attention. | |
| **Kellner** | Ja, bitte schön. | |
| **g You** | You need another glass. | |
| **Kellner** | Bitte schön. | |
| **h You** | Have they got any mustard? | |
| **Kellner** | Es tut mir Leid. | |
| **i You** | You would like another beer and a glass of lemonade. | |

## WORD BUILDING

Here are a few more examples of how German words are often combinations of two words:

**der Löffel** *spoon*     **Ess-** *eating/dining*
**Ess** löffel    **Ess** zimmer
**Tee** löffel    **Ess** ecke
**Kaffee** löffel    **Ess** bar
**Koch** löffel    **Ess** tisch

Exercise 7
**Taschen-** *pocket* **Küchen-** *kitchen* **Brot-** *bread*

How would you say:

**a** *pocket knife?*    **b** *kitchen knife?*    **c** *bread knife?*

---

## In der Eisdiele *At the ice-cream parlour*

### DIALOGUE 29

| | |
|---|---|
| **Kellnerin** | Was darf es sein? |
| **Sie** | Ich möchte ein Eis. |
| **Kellnerin** | Hier ist die Eiskarte. |
| **Sie** | Ich möchte einmal Pfirsich Melba und einmal Bananen-Split. |
| **Kellnerin** | Mit Sahne? |
| **Sie** | Ja, mit Sahne. |
| **Kellnerin** | Hat es geschmeckt? |
| **Sie** | Ja. Lecker! |

## DIE EISKARTE

| | |
|---|---|
| **Venediger** | Walnuss- und Pistazieneiscreme mit Nüssen und Schlagsahne |
| **Kopenhagener** | Vanilleeis mit warmer Schokosoße und Schlagsahne |
| **Schwarzwälder** | Schoko- und Vanilleeis mit Kirschwasser und Sauerkirschen und Schlagsahne |
| **Florentiner** | Schoko-, Nuss- und Vanilleeis mit Schlagsahne |
| **Kalifornien** | Pfirsich-Eiscreme mit Pfirsichstücken, Himbeersoße und Schlagsahne |
| **Wiener** | Mokka- und Vanilleneiscreme mit Baiserstückchen, Schlagsahne und Schokosoße |
| **Italiener** | Spaghettieis mit Erdbeersoße und Kokosflocken |

**QUICK VOCAB**

| | |
|---|---|
| **die Schlagsahne** | *whipped cream* |
| **das Schlagobers** | *whipped cream (southern Germany and Austria)* |
| **Mokka** | *coffee* |
| **das Baiser/die Meringe** | *meringue* |
| **die Kokosflocken** | *coconut flakes* |
| **der Streusel** | *hundreds and thousands* |
| **Welchen Geschmack?** | *Which flavour?* |
| **Hat es geschmeckt?** | *Did you like it? (lit. Has it tasted (good)?)* |
| **das Walnusseis** | *walnut ice-cream* |
| **das Vanilleeis** | *vanilla ice-cream* |
| **das Zitroneneis** | *lemon ice-cream* |
| **das Milcheis** | *milk ice-cream* |
| **das Fruchteis** | *fruit sorbet* |

## LEARNING TIPS

1 Choose an ice-cream for yourself and your friend.
2 Make up an ice-cream!

# Was kostet das? *What does it cost?*

Exercise 8
Was kostet das?

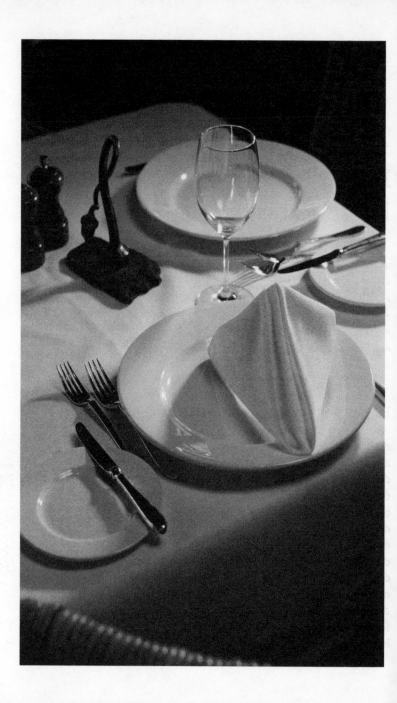

# 16

# Im Restaurant
In the restaurant

In this unit you will learn how to
- **Understand a menu**
- **Recognize the names of various dishes**
- **Say what you like and don't like**
- **Ask for recommendations**
- **Say you are vegetarian**

Ist hier noch frei? *Is anyone sitting here?*

| | |
|---|---|
| **die Speisekarte** | *menu* |
| **die Weinliste** | *wine list* |
| **das Tagesgericht** | *dish of the day* |
| **die Tagessuppe** | *soup of the day* |
| **die Fleischgerichte** | *meat dishes* |
| **die Fischgerichte** | *fish dishes* |
| **die Vorspeisen** | *hors d'oeuvres* |
| **das Hauptgericht** | *main course* |
| **das Gemüse** | *vegetables* |
| **der Nachtisch** | *dessert* |
| **die Getränke** | *drinks* |
| **frisch gemacht** | *freshly made* |
| **hausgemacht** | *home-made* |

| German | English |
|---|---|
| **Was können Sie empfehlen?** | *What can you recommend?* |
| **Ich bin Vegetarier/in.** | *I am a vegetarian.* |
| **Ich esse kein Fleisch.** | *I don't eat meat.* |
| **Mir schmeckt es nicht.** | *I don't like (the taste of) it.* |
| **Es schmeckt mir gut.** | *I like (the taste of) it.* |
| **Schmeckt's?** | *Do you like it?* |
| **Hat es geschmeckt?** | *Did you like it?* |
| **Ja, es schmeckt sehr gut.** | *Yes, it is very nice.* |
| **lecker** | *delicious* |
| **Es ist zu sauer.** | *It is too sour.* |
| **Es ist zu scharf.** | *It is too hot (sharp).* |
| **Es ist zu süß.** | *It is too sweet.* |

### LEARNING TIP

**1** See if you can pair these up without looking at the **Key words**:

| | |
|---|---|
| **die Speisekarte** | *soup of the day* |
| **die Weinliste** | *dish of the day* |
| **das Tagesgericht** | *dessert* |
| **die Tagessuppe** | *main course* |
| **die Fleischgerichte** | *the menu* |
| **die Fischgerichte** | *the wine list* |
| **die Vorspeisen** | *meat dishes* |
| **das Hauptgericht** | *drinks* |
| **das Gemüse** | *fish dishes* |
| **der Nachtisch** | *hors d'oeuvres* |
| **die Getränke** | *vegetables* |

**2** Now cover up the German and see if you can remember it.

### DIALOGUE 30

| | |
|---|---|
| **Sie** | Ist hier noch frei bitte? |
| **Kellner** | Der Tisch in der Ecke ist frei. |
| **Sie** | Die Speisekarte bitte. |
| **Kellner** | Bitte schön. |
| **Sie** | Was können Sie empfehlen? |
| **Kellner** | Die Leberklöße sind Frisch gemacht. |

| | |
|---|---|
| **Sie** | Das schmeckt mir nicht. |
| **Kellner** | Wie wäre es mit dem Schweinefilet mit Champignonrahmsauce und hausgemachten Nudeln? |
| **Sie** | Gut. Ich nehme es. Mein Freund ist Vegetarier. |
| **Kellner** | Wie wäre es mit einer hausgemachten Gemüselasagne? |
| **Sie** | Gut. Wir nehmen einmal Tagessuppe und einmal Aufschnittplatte als Vorspeise. |
| **Kellner** | Und als Nachtisch? |
| **Sie** | Einmal Rote Grütze. |
| **Kellner** | Mit Sahne, Milch oder Vanillesosse? |
| **Sie** | Mit Vanillesosse und einmal Apfelstrudel. |
| **Kellner** | Was trinken Sie? |
| **Sie** | Ein Glas Hauswein. |
| **Kellner** | Rot oder weiß? |
| **Sie** | Rot, und ein Glas Sprudel. |
| **Kellner** | Mit Geschmack? |
| **Sie** | Nein, ohne. |

| | |
|---|---|
| **Leberklöße** | *liver dumplings* |
| **die Champignonrahmsauce** | *cream of mushroom sauce* |
| **Nudeln** | *pasta/noodles* |
| **Gemüselasagne** | *vegetable lasagne* |
| **Aufschnittplatte** | *cold sliced meats (ham and salami)* |
| **die Rote Grütze** | *a compote of red fruit (redcurrants, raspberries, etc.)* |
| **der Hauswein** | *house wine* |
| **mit Geschmack** | *flavoured (lemonade/orangeade etc.)* |

QUICK VOCAB

### LEARNING TIPS

**1** Read the dialogue and check that you understand everything.
**2** Read it out loud.

## Die Speisekarte *The menu*

| | |
|---|---|
| **Fleischgerichte** | *meat dishes* |
| **das Rindfleisch** | *beef* |
| **das Schweinefleisch** | *pork* |
| **das Hammelfleisch** | *mutton* |
| **das Hackfleisch** | *minced meat* |
| **der Schaschlik** | *kebab* |
| **das Lammfleisch** | *lamb* |
| **Fischgerichte** | *fish dishes* |
| **das Fischfilet** | *fish fillet* |
| **der Kabeljau** | *cod* |
| **die Forelle** | *trout* |
| **der Lachs** | *salmon* |
| **der Hering** | *herring* |
| **der Matjes** | *pickled herring* |
| **Krabben** | *shrimps/prawns* |
| **das Geflügel** | *poultry* |
| **das Hähnchen** | *chicken* |
| **der Truthahn** | *turkey* |
| **die Gans** | *goose* |
| **die Ente** | *duck* |
| **das Omelett** | *omelette* |
| **das Gemüse** | *vegetables* |
| **Kartoffeln** | *potatoes* |
| | |
| **Folienkartoffeln** | *baked potatoes (cooked in foil)* |
| **Salzkartoffeln** | *boiled potatoes* (lit. *salt potatoes*) |
| | |
| **Bratkartoffeln** | *fried potatoes* |
| **Pommes (frites)** | *chips* |
| **Erbsen** | *peas* |
| **Bohnen** | *beans* |
| **Karotten** | *carrots* |
| **der Spinat** | *spinach* |
| **der Spargel** | *asparagus* |
| **Bambussprossen** | *bamboo shoots* |
| **der Blumenkohl** | *cauliflower* |

QUICK VOCAB

| der Kohl | cabbage |
|---|---|
| der Weisskohl | white cabbage |
| der Rotkohl | red cabbage |
| das Sauerkraut | sour pickled cabbage |
| der Salat | lettuce |

**Wienerschnitzel** (Viennese Schnitzel) is a thin slice of veal or pork, which is dipped in egg before being covered with breadcrumbs and lightly fried.

**Jägerschnitzel** (hunter's Schnitzel) is the same meat not covered in breadcrumbs, fried lightly and served with a tomato and mushroom sauce.

**Zigeunerschnitzel** (gypsy's Schnitzel) is the same meat again without breadcrumbs, fried lightly and served with a piquant sauce with spices and green pepper.

## DIALOGUE 31

| | | |
|---|---|---|
| **Sie** | Entschuldigung. Ist hier noch frei? | |
| **Kellner** | Ja, bitte schön. Hier ist die Speisekarte. | |
| **Sie** | Was für eine Tagessuppe gibt es heute? | |
| **Kellner** | Champignonrahmsuppe. | |
| **Sie** | Also, einmal Tagessuppe für mich und einmal Melone mit Parmaschinken. | |
| **Kellner** | Und als Hauptgericht? | |
| **Sie** | Ich möchte einmal Wienerschnitzel mit Pommes und grünem Salat und einmal Schweineroulade mit Butternudeln. | |
| **Kellner** | Was trinken Sie? | |
| **Sie** | Ein Glas Rotwein und ein Glas Sprudel. | |
| **Kellner** | Und als Nachtisch? | |
| **Sie** | Haben Sie Obstsalat? | |
| **Kellner** | Nein, leider nicht. Aber der Apfelstrudel ist gut. | |
| **Sie** | Was ist das? | |
| **Kellner** | Apfel, Rosinen und Zimt in Blätterteig mit Vanillesoße. | |

*CD2, TR 39*

*(Contd)*

| Sie | Das sieht gut aus. Einmal Apfelstrudel und einmal Erdbeertorte. |
| Kellner | Mit Sahne? |
| Sie | Nein danke, ohne Sahne. |

### LEARNING TIPS

**1** Read the dialogue carefully and make sure you understand everything. There are a few words that you have not met before. Can you work out what they mean?
**2** Read it out loud. Answer the questions for yourself and a friend.
**3** See if you can remember what the questions were.

Listening exercise 26
◀》 CD2, TR 40

What do these six customers order?

## Gern und lieber *Liking and preferring*

QUICK VOCAB

| | |
|---|---|
| **Essen Sie gern ...?/Isst du gern ...?** | *Do you like (to eat ...)?* |
| **Trinken Sie gern ...?** | *Do you like (to drink ...)?* |
| **Ich esse gern ...** | *I like (to eat ...)* |
| **Ich esse lieber ...** | *I prefer (I would rather eat ...)* |
| **Ich trinke gern ...** | *I like (to drink ...)* |
| **Ich trinke lieber** | *I prefer (I would rather drink ...)* |
| **Ich mag ...** | *I like ...* |
| **Ich mag keine Pommes.** | *I don't like chips. (lit. I like no ...)* |
| **Trinken Sie gern ein Glas Wein?** | *Would you like a glass of wine?* |

### WORD PATTERNS: LIKING (AND DISLIKING)

Here are two different ways of saying you like something:

Using gern ('willingly')
When you use **gern** you have to say what it is that you like doing.

| **Ich** | **esse** | *gern* | **Gehen** *Sie gern ins Restaurant?* |
| | **trinke** | | **Essen** *Sie gern Chinesisch?* |
| | **spiele** | | **Trinken** *Sie gern Bier?* |
| | **Tanze** | | |

Using ich mag ('I like')
This seems easier to use because it is more like the English:

| **Ich mag Bier.** | *I like beer.* |

but ...

| **Ich mag Bier sehr gern.** | *I like beer very much.* |
| **Ich mag kein Bier.** | *I don't like beer.* |

And you prefer ...

| **Ich mag Tee, aber ich trinke lieber Kaffee.** | *I like tea but I prefer (to drink) coffee.* |
| **Ich trinke gern schwarzen Tee, aber ich trinke lieber Früchtetee.** | *I like (to drink) tea but I prefer to drink) fruit/herbal tea.* |

Exercise 1
You want to know if your friend likes these. How would you ask?

Ordinary tea is sometimes called 'black tea' to distinguish it from the many herbal teas that are drunk in Germany.

### Exercise 2 **Im Restaurant** In the resturant

Complete your part of the dialogue, using the **Quick Vocab** or, if you prefer, the menu that follows Dialogue 30.

| | | |
|---|---|---|
| **a You** | Ask if this place is free. | |
| **Kellner** | Ja, bitte schön. Hier ist die Speisekarte. | |
| **b You** | Find out what the soup of the day is today. | |
| **Kellner** | Gemüsesuppe. | |
| **c You** | Ask if they have tomato soup. | |
| **Kellner** | Nein, heute nicht. | |
| **d You** | Ask for something else. | |
| **Kellner** | Und als Hauptgericht? Das Schnitzel ist gut. | |
| **e You** | No, you don't like Schnitzel. | |
| **Kellner** | Essen Sie gern Fisch? | |
| **f You** | Choose what you would like from the menu. | |
| **Kellner** | Und als Gemüse? | |
| **g You** | Choose a suitable vegetable or salad. | |
| **Kellner** | Was trinken Sie? | |
| **h You** | Choose something to drink. | |
| **Kellner** | Und als Nachtisch? | |
| **i You** | Ask what they recommend. | |
| **Kellner** | Erdbeertorte. | |
| **j You** | Say you'll take it. | |
| **Kellner** | Mit Sahne? | |
| **k You** | Say yes, with cream. | |
| **Kellner** | Trinken Sie einen Kaffee? | |
| **l You** | Say yes, please. | |

### LEARNING TIP

**1** Read the dialogue out loud and check that you understand all the German.

## Zahlen, bitte *The bill, please*

| | |
|---|---|
| **Zahlen, bitte.** | *Bill, please. (lit. pay please)* |
| **Zusammen oder getrennt?** | *Together or separate?* |
| **mit Bedienung** | *with service* |
| **ohne Bedienung** | *without service* |
| **MWSt (Mehrwertsteuer)** | *VAT* |
| **Ich bin satt.** | *I am full.* |
| **Hat es geschmeckt?** | *Did you like it? (lit. has it tasted (good)?)* |
| **Das ist für Sie.** | *That's for you.* |
| **das Kleingeld** | *change (lit. small money)* |
| **das Trinkgeld** | *tip (lit. drink money)* |

### DIALOGUE 32

| | |
|---|---|
| **Sie** | Zahlen, bitte. |
| **Kellnerin** | Hat es geschmeckt? |
| **Sie** | Ja, lecker. |
| **Kellnerin** | Zusammen oder getrennt? |
| **Sie** | Zusammen. |
| **Kellnerin** | Das macht €64,25. |
| **Sie** | Nehmen Sie Kreditkarten? |
| **Kellnerin** | Nein. Leider nicht. |
| **Sie** | Ich habe nur eine 100 Euro Banknote. |
| **Kellnerin** | Ich habe Kleingeld. |
| **Sie** | Das ist für Sie. |
| **Kellnerin** | Vielen Dank. Auf Wiedersehen. |

### LEARNING TIPS

**1** Read the dialogue and check you understand everything.
**2** Practise your part of the dialogue out loud.

Exercise 3
These are questions you might be asked. What do they mean?

**a** Trinken Sie etwas dazu?
**b** Möchten Sie einen Nachtisch?

c Welchen Geschmack?
d Möchten Sie Ketchup?
e Hat es geschmeckt?
f Zusammen oder getrennt?

The service charge is almost always included in the bill, but if you have been satisfied with the service it is normal to give an additional tip or to leave the small change, though anything under €0,60 might be considered insulting.
If you want to take the food with you, you would order: 'Zum Mitnehmen, bitte'.

**Kaffeetrinken** Modern coffees for the 'Starbucks brigade' include **Espresso, doppelter Espresso, Milchkaffee, Kaffee HAG (ohne Koffein)** and **Kapuziner** or **Cappuccino**.

| Kaffeespezialitäten | |
|---|---|
| Cappuccino mit Milch oder Sahne | €3,50 |
| Milchkaffee | €3,80 |
| Latte Macchiato | €4,00 |
| Kännchen Schoko-Kaffee: ½ Schoko, ½ Kaffee | €4,50 |
| Espresso | €2,40 |
| Espresso, doppelt | €4,10 |
| Tasse Kaffee | €2,30 |
| Kännchen Kaffee | €5,60 |
| Tasse Mocca | €2,60 |
| Kännchen Mocca | €4,60 |
| Tasse Kaffee, entkoffeiniert | €2,50 |
| Tasse Schokolade mit Sahne geschlagen | €4,80 |
| Sirup: Caramel, Vanille, Amaretto, Haselnuss | €0,80 |

# TEST YOURSELF

**1** True or false? In German the plural is made, as in English, by adding **s** to the word.

**2** Many words are made by adding two words together. Put these words in the right order to make the sentences:
  **i** Where can I buy batteries? **hier ich kann kaufen Batterien wo?**
  **ii** I would like a pair of dark blue cotton trousers. **dunkelblaue eine möchte aus Hose ich Baumwolle.**

**3** Fill in the missing words:
  **i** When does the train go to Hamburg?
  **Wann __ der Zug __ Hamburg?**
  **ii** When does it get into Berlin?
  **Wann __ er __ Berlin __?**

**4** How would you answer?
  **i** **Und zu trinken? a** ein Glas Wein **b** Haben sie Ketchup? **c** Mit Milch und Zucker.
  **ii** **Sonst noch etwas? a** Die Post ist um die Ecke **b** Nein danke **c** Ich möchte eine Ansichtskarte.

**5** **Ich esse gern italienisch** – She **a** likes Italy **b** likes Italian food **c** likes Chinese food.

**6** **Ich mag keine Pommes. a** I like apples **b** I don't like apples **c** I don't like chips.

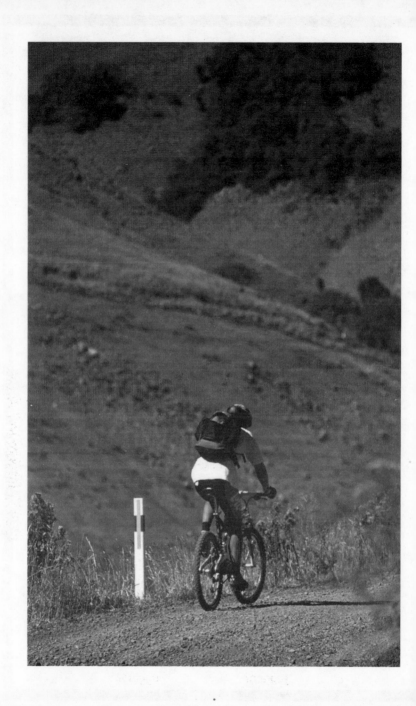

# 17

# Die Freizeit
Free time

In this unit you will learn how to
- *Say what you like doing in your free time*
- *Ask someone what they would like to do*
- *Take part in sports and hobbies*
- *Make arrangements*
- *Go about summer and winter activities*

| | |
|---|---|
| **Was machen Sie gern und was machen Sie nicht gern?** | *What do you like and not like doing?* |
| **in meiner Freizeit** | *in my free time* |
| **in Ihrer Freizeit** | *in your free time* |
| **Schwimmen Sie gern?** | *Do you like swimming?* |
| **Ich schwimme gern.** | *I like swimming.* |
| **Lesen Sie gern?** | *Do you like reading?* |
| **Ich lese gern.** | *I like reading.* |
| **Tanzen Sie gern?** | *Do you like dancing?* |
| **Ich tanze gern.** | *I like dancing.* |

## USING *GEHEN* WITH A SPORT OR PASTIME

| | | |
|---|---|---|
| **Gehen Sie gern** | **wandern** | *Do you like to go hiking?* |
| | **spazieren?** | *for walks?* |
| | **schwimmen?** | *swimming?* |
| | **ins Kino?** | *to the cinema?* |
| | **in ein Nachtlokal?** | *to a night club?* |
| | **joggen?** | *jogging?* |

## Using *spielen*

| **Spielen Sie gern** | **Tennis?** | *Do you like playing tennis?* |
|---|---|---|
| | **Karten?** | *cards?* |
| | **Snooker?** | *snooker?* |
| | **Schach?** | *chess?* |
| | **Squash?** | *squash?* |
| | **Fußball?** | *football?* |

## Separable verbs

**Ski laufen** *to ski*  **Laufen** sie gern **Ski?**  Ich **laufe** gern **Ski**.
**fernsehen** *to watch TV*  **Sehen** Sie gern **fern?**  Ich **sehe** gern **fern**.
**Rad fahren** *to ride a bike*  **Fahren** Sie gern **Rad?**  Ich **fahre** gern **Rad**.

These are all verbs which split up and the prefix (first part of the word) goes to the end of the sentence.

### Insight
**Ski** sounds *shee*. Just remember: *She goes skiing!*

## Exercise 1

What would you ask Fräulein Hoffmann to find out if she likes to:

**a** *go to the cinema?*  **d** *play cards?*
**b** *go dancing?*  **e** *go cycling?*
**c** *go swimming?*  **f** *watch TV?*

### DIALOGUE 33

◆ CD2, TR 42

| | |
|---|---|
| **Sie** | Was machen wir heute Abend? Spielen Sie gern Squash? |
| **Herr Schwarz** | Ja, sehr gern. |
| **Sie** | Gut. Wir spielen Squash. Schwimmen Sie auch gern? |
| **Herr Schwarz** | Ja. Ich schwimme gern. |
| **Sie** | Gut, wir spielen Squash und dann gehen wir schwimmen und danach gehen wir in ein Restaurant. |
| **Herr Schwarz** | Gut. Ich freue mich schon darauf! |
| **Sie** | Was machen wir heute Abend? Spielen Sie gern Tennis? |
| **Herr Schwarz** | Nein. Leider nicht. Mein Rücken tut weh. |
| **Sie** | Was machen Sie gern? |
| **Herr Schwarz** | Ich gehe gern tanzen oder ins Kino. |
| **Sie** | Gut. Wir gehen zuerst ins Kino und danach in ein Nachtlokal. |

| | |
|---|---|
| **dann/danach** | *then* |
| **zuerst** | *first* |

QV

## Exercise 2

How would you ask Herr Schwarz's 10-year-old son if he likes to:

**a** *play squash?*  **d** *play tennis?*
**b** *play football?*  **e** *ride a bike?*
**c** *ski?*  **f** *play chess?*

## Exercise 3
**Was machen Sie gern in Ihrer Freizeit?**

How would these people answer?

Listening exercise 27
🔊 **CD2, TR 43**

What do these six people like and not like doing?

---

## Haben Sie Lust mitzukommen?
*Would you like to come too?*

| | |
|---|---|
| **mitkommen** | *to come too (a splitting verb (lit. to come with (me/us/you))* |
| **ich komme mit.** | *I'll come too.* |
| **vorbeikommen** | *to come past* |
| **Ich komme ... vorbei.** | *I'm coming past ...* |
| **abholen** | *to fetch* |
| **Ich hole ... ab.** | *I'm fetching ...* |

| zurückkommen | to come back |
|---|---|
| **Ich komme um ... zurück.** | *I'm coming back at ...* |
| **das Spiel** | *game* |
| **gegen** | *against* |
| **danach** | *afterwards* |
| **vor** | *in front of* |

**Ich habe Lust Tennis zu spielen.**
*I would like to play tennis.*
**Haben Sie Lust Tennis zu spielen?/**
**Möchten sie Tennis spielen?**
*Would you like to play tennis?*
**Nein, ich habe keine Lust ...**
*No, I don't want to ...*
**Ich gehe lieber ...** *I would rather ...*

| **angeln** *to fish* | |
|---|---|
| **Ich bin noch nicht Ski gefahren.** | *I haven't skied before.* |
| **Wo/Wann treffen wir uns?** | *Where/When shall we meet?* |
| **Ich freue mich schon darauf.** | *I am looking forward to it.* |
| **heute** | *today* |
| **heute früh/morgen, heute Vormittag** | *morning* |
| **heute Nachmittag** | *afternoon* |
| **heute Abend** | *evening* |
| **morgen** | *tomorrow* |
| **morgen früh, morgen Vormittag** | *tomorrow morning* |
| **morgen Nachmittag** | *tomorrow afternoon* |
| **morgen Abend** | *tomorrow evening* |

Exercise 4

Hannelore is staying with you. Tell her:

**a** You are going to play tennis tomorrow morning. Would she like to come?

**b** You are going swimming tomorrow evening. Would she like to come?

**c** You are going to play cards this evening. Does she want to play?

**d** You are going fishing this afternoon. Does she want to come?

**e** You are going to a night club tonight. Is she going to come?

Jürgen is staying with you.

**f** Tell him you are going to the local football match on Saturday afternoon.

**g** Ask him if he would like to come with you.

**h** Tell him when the match begins.

**i** Ask him if he would like to play tennis afterwards.

## Exercise 5

Complete your part of the dialogues with Hans-Peter.

| | |
|---|---|
| **Hans-Peter** | Morgen Nachmittag gehen wir zum Fußball, Düsseldorf gegen Bayern-München. Haben Sie Lust mitzukommen? |
| **a You** | Yes, you would like to. What time? |
| **Hans-Peter** | Das Spiel beginnt um 14.30 Uhr. Wir treffen uns um 13.00 Uhr. |
| **b You** | Ask where you should meet. |
| **Hans-Peter** | Ich komme vorbei und hole Sie ab. |
| **Hans-Peter** | Morgen Nachmittag gehen wir zum Fußball, Düsseldorf gegen Bayern-München. Haben Sie Lust mitzukommen? |
| **c You** | No, you don't want to. You would rather play tennis. |
| **Hans-Peter** | Gut. Wir spielen danach Tennis. |
| **d You** | Ask what time. |
| **Hans-Peter** | Um sechs. |
| **e You** | Find out where to meet. |
| **Hans-Peter** | Vor der Tennishalle. |
| **Hans-Peter** | Wir fahren morgen Ski. Kommen Sie mit? |
| **f You** | Yes, I'll come too but I have not skied before! |
| **Hans-Peter** | Kein Problem! Jürgen ist Skilehrer. |
| **g You** | Find out when you are going. |
| **Hans-Peter** | Wir fahren um 7.30 Uhr ab. |
| **h You** | And when you are due back? |
| **Hans-Peter** | So, um halb zehn. |
| **i You** | Good. You are looking forward to it. |
| **Hans-Peter** | Bis dann. Tschüss. |

## Im Sommer *In summer*

QUICK VOCAB

| | |
|---|---|
| **am Strand** | *on the beach* |
| **in den Bergen** | *in the mountains* |
| **auf dem Land** | *in the country* |
| **in der Stadt** | *in the town* |
| **an der Küste** | *on the coast* |
| **am Mittelmeer** | *on the Mediterranean* |
| **die Ferien** | *holidays* |
| **das Angebot** | *offer* |

**Wo verbringen Sie Ihre Ferien?** *Where do you spend your holidays?*
**Ich verbringe meine Ferien in** *I spend my holidays in the*
**den Bergen/an der Küste/auf** *mountains/on the coast/on*
**dem Bauernhof.** *the farm.*

### WORD PATTERNS: MORE TRIGGER WORDS

**An, in** and **auf** are trigger words which sometimes (but not always) change **der, die** and **das** to **dem** and **der**.

| *masc.* | **der** *to* **dem** | *neut* | **das** *to* **dem** |
|---|---|---|---|
| *fem.* | **die** *to* **der** | *plural* | **die** *to* **den** |

an + dem = am    zu + dem = zum
in + dem = im    zu + der = zur

Exercise 6
Can you say which 13 activities are being offered at Sonnenstrand?

**Das Ferienangebot von Sonnenstrand**
Ein 12 km langer Sandstrand zum Sonnen, Baden und Spielen

| | | |
|---|---|---|
| Golf, Minigolf | Kegeln | Fahrradverleih |
| Strandsegeln | Angeln | Schwimmen |
| Tischtennis | Surfen | Tennis |
| Volleyball | Trimm-dich-Pfad | Segeln |
| Schach | | |

| Kegeln | bowling |
|---|---|
| Strandsegeln | sand yachting |
| Fahrradverleih | bicycle hire |
| Trimm-dich-Pfad | a fitness circuit laid out usually in a park or woodland |

## DIALOGUE 34: ICH SONNE MICH *I AM SUNBATHING*

| | |
|---|---|
| **Sie** | Wo verbringen Sie Ihre Ferien? |
| **Hannelore** | Im Winter verbringen wir unsere Ferien in den Alpen. Wir fahren gern Ski. |
| **Sie** | Und im Sommer? |
| **Hannelore** | An der Ostseeküste. |
| **Sie** | Was machen Sie dort? |
| **Hannelore** | Wenn das Wetter gut ist, gehen wir schwimmen und wir sonnen uns oder wir gehen surfen oder segeln. |
| **Sie** | Und wenn es schlecht ist? |
| **Hannelore** | Dann gehen wir ins Kino, oder wir machen einen Stadtbummel. Und Sie? |
| **Sie** | Wenn das Wetter schlecht ist, bleibe ich zu Hause, sehe fern oder lese ein Buch. |
| **Hannelore** | Wo verbringen Sie Ihre Ferien? |
| **Sie** | An der Küste oder in den Bergen. |
| **Hannelore** | Und was machen Sie? |
| **Sie** | Wir schwimmen und sonnen uns oder wir machen Wanderungen. |
| **Hannelore** | Was macht Herr Thomas? |
| **Sie** | Er spielt Golf oder geht angeln. |
| **Hannelore** | Und was machen die Kinder? |
| **Sie** | Peter spielt Tennis und fährt gern Rad und Mary verbringt den ganzen Tag am Strand. |

| den ganzen Tag | the whole day |
|---|---|
| Ich bleibe zu Hause. | I stay at home. |
| der Stadtbummel | stroll in town |

## Exercise 7

Was machen Sie gern, **a** wenn das Wetter gut ist? **b** wenn das Wetter schlecht ist? (Tick the appropriate activities.)

| | |
|---|---|
| **i** Ich sonne mich. | **vi** Ich spiele Karten. |
| **ii** Ich sehe fern. | **vii** Ich gehe surfen. |
| **iii** Ich lese ein Buch. | **viii** Ich gehe ins Kino. |
| **iv** Ich spiele Tennis. | **ix** Ich gehe joggen. |
| **v** Ich gehe schwimmen. | **x** Ich sehe fern. |

Listening exercise 28
◀ **CD2, TR 46**

**Was machen sie?** *What do they do?*

_____

## Im Winter *In winter*

| | |
|---|---|
| **die Möglichkeiten** | *possibilities* |
| **Pferdeschlittenfahrten** | *horse-drawn sleigh rides* |
| **der Schnee** | *snow* |
| **verschneit** | *snow-covered* |
| **der Weg (e)** | *path* |
| **durch den Wald** | *through the wood* |
| **die Piste** | *piste* |
| **schön** | *nice* |
| **geräumt** | *cleared* |
| **rodeln** | *to sledge, toboggan* |

QUICK VOCAB

| | |
|---|---|
| **die Rodelbahn** | *sledge track, toboggan run* |
| **Langlauf** | *cross-country skiing* |
| **die Loipe** | *cross-country ski route* |
| **Eislaufen** | *skating* (lit. *ice running*) |
| **am See** | *on the lake* |

| | |
|---|---|
| **oder** | *or* |
| **auf der Eislaufbahn** | *on the ice-rink* |
| **Eisstockschießen** | *a game rather like curling* |
| **die Gondelbahn** | *cable railway* |
| **der Sessellift** | *chair lift* |
| **der Schlepplift** | *drag lift* |
| **der Waldweg** | *woodland path* |
| **entspannen** | *to relax* |
| **Kegeln** | *bowling* |
| **die Kegelbahn** | *bowling alley* |

## WORD BUILDING

Use these vocabulary clues and words you already know to do Exercise 8:

| | | | |
|---|---|---|---|
| **der Schnee** | *snow* | **die Brille** | *glasses* |
| **die Schlacht** | *fight, battle* | **die Raupe** | *caterpillar* |
| **die Flocke** | *flake* | **der Sturm** | *storm* |
| **das Glöckchen** | *little bell* | **es schneit** | *it is snowing* |
| **die Kette(n)** | *chain(s)* | **verschneit** | *snow-covered* |

Exercise 8
How many of these new words can you make?

**a** *snowman*
**b** *snowball*
**c** *snowball fight*
**d** *snowflake*
**e** *snowdrop*

**f** *snowchains*
**g** *snow goggles*
**h** *snow-cat*
**i** *snow storm*

# 18

# Autofahren in Deutschland
## Motoring in Germany

In this unit you will learn how to
- *Buy petrol*
- *Drive on German motorways*
- *Use the emergency services*
- *Cope in the event of breakdown or accident*
- *Park*

## An der Tankstelle *At the petrol station*

| | |
|---|---|
| **die Tankstelle** | *petrol station* |
| **die Raststätte** | *service area* |
| **das Benzin** | *petrol* |
| **der Diesel** | *diesel* |
| **der/das Liter** | *litre* |
| **das Wasser** | *water* |
| **das Öl** | *oil* |
| **die Luft** | *air* |
| **volltanken** | *to fill up* |
| **prüfen** | *to check* |
| **der Reifen (-)** | *tyre* |
| **der Reifendruck** | *tyre pressue* |
| **Selbsttanken** | *self-service petrol* |
| **Münztank** | *coin-operated pump* |
| **Können Sie ...?** | *Can you ...?* |

QUICK VOCAB

| Können Sie den Reifendruck prüfen? | *Can you check the tyres?* |
|---|---|
| Können Sie den Ölstand prüfen? | *Can you check the oil?* |
| Können Sie die Windschutzscheibe putzen? | *Can you clean the windscreen?* |
| Hier ist meine Kreditkarte. | *Here is my credit card.* |

Most garages are now self-service, but if you buy petrol at the motorway services you will occasionally be served and the attendant will sometimes also wash the windscreen and expect a small tip.

### LEARNING TIPS

**1** Read all the words out loud.
**2** Cover up the English and see if you know what the German words mean.

Listening exercise 29
◄》 **CD2, TR 47**

What are these six customers asking?

### DIALOGUE 35

| Sie | Guten Tag. |
|---|---|
| Tankwart | Guten Tag. |
| Sie | Volltanken, bitte. |
| Tankwart | Benzin oder Diesel? |
| Sie | Diesel. |

◄》 CD2, TR 48

206

| Tankwart | So, bitte schön. |
| --- | --- |
| Sie | Wo muss ich zahlen? |
| Tankwart | An der Kasse, dort drüben. |
| Sie | Danke schön. |

## Auf der Autobahn *On the motorway*

| | |
| --- | --- |
| **die Autobahn** | *motorway* |
| **das Autobahndreieck** | *motorway junction* |
| **das Autobahnkreuz** | *motorway intersection* |
| **Stau auf der Autobahn** | *traffic jam on the motorway* |
| **Abstand halten** | *keep your distance* |
| **die Geschwindigkeitsbegrenzung** | *speed restriction* |
| **das Überholverbot** | *no overtaking* |
| **die Umleitung** | *diversion* |
| **zwischen** | *between* |
| **Wo stehen Sie?** | *Where are you?* |
| **Ich bin auf der A1 bei...** | *I'm on the A1 near...* |
| **Delmenhorst Richtung Hamburg.** | *Delmenhorst going towards Hamburg.* |
| **Achtung!** | *warning* |
| **Richtung** | *direction* |
| **die Baustelle** | *road works* |
| **das Glatteis** | *ice* |
| **die Raststätte** | *services* |
| **in der Nähe von/bei** | *near* |
| **der Nebel** | *fog* |
| **die Rutschgefahr** | *danger of skidding* |

QUICK VOCAB

Exercise 1
How would you ask someone to:

i *check the tyre pressures?*
ii *clean the windscreen?*
iii *check the oil?*

Exercise 2
What do these signs mean? Match each sign with its meaning.

**a** *car park*
**b** *one-way street*
**c** *motorway exit*
**d** *petrol station*
**e** *motorway services with restaurant*
**f** *way on to the motorway*

**LEARNING TIP**

**1** Practise saying all the new words and phrases.

Exercise 3
How would you tell someone you are ...?

**a** *on the A4 between Cologne (**Köln**) and Aachen travelling towards Aachen.*

**b** *near Solingen travelling towards Dortmund on the A1.*
**c** *on the A5 near Offenburg travelling towards Basel.*
**d** *on the A8 near Augsburg travelling to Munich (**München**).*
**e** *on the B10 near Geislingen between Stuttgart and Ulm, travelling towards Ulm.*

Listening exercise 30
🔊 **CD2, TR 49**

Where is the motorway blocked?

Motorway signs are blue and white and the motorways are numbered A1, A2, etc. The European equivalent numbers are prefixed with 'E'.

The motorways which link up with international routes also have European numbers which are in green. If the two numbers are different this can be confusing. It is usually easier to ignore the green signs and follow the blue ones.

Signs on the **Bundesstraßen** (*trunk roads*) are in yellow and black.

Distances are given in *kilometres* (**Kilometer**).

## Insight

To convert miles to kilometres: divide by 5 and multiply the answer by 8  20 miles ÷ 5 = 4 × 8 = 32 km

To convert kilometres to miles: divide by 8 and multiply the answer by 5  80 km ÷ 8 = 10 × 5 = 50 miles

### STAU AUF DER AUTOBAHN *CONGESTION ON THE MOTORWAY*

This is the sort of message you might hear on the car radio warning you about traffic problems ahead.

> Durch einen Unfall ist die Autobahn bei Friedberg blockiert. Der Stau ist 11 Kilometer lang. Reisende nach München werden gebeten, die Autobahn bei Augsburg zu verlassen und die Bundesstraße 2 zu benutzen.

Exercise 4
Read the passage and see if you can answer the questions:

**a** Where is the motorway blocked?
**b** Why is it blocked?
**c** Where should those travelling to Munich leave the motorway?
**d** What road should they use instead?

**STRASSENSCHILDER** *STREET SIGNS*

**Umleitung**

Umleitung
(diversion)

Vorfahrtstraße
(this road has the right of way)

Baustelle
(road works)

## Insight

When driving in Germany always have your **Führerschein** – (*driving licence*) and **Fahrzeugschein** (*vehicle documents*) with you.

In towns there is a speed limit of 50 km/h (sometimes 30 km/h). On other roads it is 100 km/h but there is no overall limit on the motorways although there are sometimes local restrictions.

Germans tend to drive very fast and very close on the motorways, but they are usually strict about obeying speed limits where they do exist. There are a lot of radar checks and if you are caught speeding you will be expected to pay the fine on the spot.

You must used dipped headlights if visibility is poor. Fog lights may only be used when visibility is less than 50 metres. If you break down you must display a red warning triangle about 100 metres behind your car.

## Ich habe eine Panne *My car has broken down*

| | |
|---|---|
| **Ich habe eine Panne.** | *My car has broken down.* |
| **Ich habe einen Unfall gehabt.** | *I have had an accident.* |
| **Was für ein Auto haben Sie?** | *What kind of a car have you got?* |
| **Welche Automarke haben Sie?** | *What make of car is it?* |
| **das Kennzeichen** | *car registration* |
| **Können Sie das Auto reparieren?** | *Can you repair the car?* |
| **Was ist los?** | *What is wrong?* |
| **Das Benzin ist alle.** | *I have run out of petrol.* |
| **Mein/e ... ist kaputt.** | *My ... is broken.* |
| **Sind Sie Mitglied eines Autovereins?** | *Are you a member of an automobile club?* |

QUICK VOCAB

On the motorways there is an emergency phone (**Notrufsäule**) every two kilometres. This will connect you with the nearest motorway control unit.

If you have to make a call on one you will probably be asked:

1 *your registration number*
2 *what number phone you are calling from*
3 *what road you are on*
4 *what direction you are travelling in*

Exercise 5
What are you being asked?

a **Was ist los?**
b **Was für ein Auto haben Sie?**
c **Wo stehen Sie?**
d **Welche Automarke haben Sie?**
e **Sind Sie Mitglied eines Automobilclubs?**

Listening exercise 31
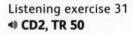 **CD2, TR 50**

What has happened to these seven motorists?

## DIALOGUE 36

CD2, TR 51

| | |
|---|---|
| **Sie** | Ich habe eine Panne. |
| **Autobahnhilfe** | Wo stehen Sie? |
| **Sie** | Ich bin auf der A8 in der Nähe von Rosenheim Richtung Salzburg. |
| **Autobahnhilfe** | Bei welchem Autobahn-kilometer stehen Sie? |
| **Sie** | 115. |
| **Autobahnhilfe** | Was für ein Auto haben Sie? |
| **Sie** | Einen Volkswagen Golf. |
| **Autobahnhilfe** | Kennzeichen? |
| **Sie** | GWY 622. |
| **Autobahnhilfe** | Was ist los? |
| **Sie** | Der Motor wird zu heiß. |
| **Autobahnhilfe** | Sind Sie Mitglied eines Autovereins? |
| **Sie** | Ja. AA. |
| **Autobahnhilfe** | Wie ist Ihre Mitgliedsnummer? |
| **Sie** | Das weiß ich im Moment nicht. Mein Ausweis ist im Auto. |
| **Autobahnhilfe** | OK. Jemand kommt gleich. |
| **Sie** | Wann wird er hier sein? |
| **Autobahnhilfe** | In zwanzig Minuten. |

## LEARNING TIPS

**1** Make sure you understand both parts of the dialogue.
**2** Practise reading your part of the conversation.
**3** Now vary it to say:

- you are on the A7 between Hannover and Hamburg travelling towards Hamburg, phone number 87.
- you have a Ford Focus, SP 09 ABC
- you are a member of the AA (your membership number is 16 5653 3789).
- your windscreen is broken.

## Wo kann ich hier parken? *Where can I park?*

| | |
|---|---|
| **die Parkuhr** | *parking meter* |
| **der Parkplatz** | *car park* |
| **die Tiefgarage** | *underground garage* |
| | *(lit. deep garage)* |
| **das Parkhaus** | *multi-storey car park* |
| **der Parkschein** | *parking ticket* |
| **die Parkgebühr** | *parking fee* |
| **Parkverbot** | *parking forbidden* |
| **die Einbahnstrasse** | *one-way street* |
| **die Ampel** | *traffic lights* |
| **biegen** | *to turn* |

**Hier dürfen Sie nicht parken.**
*You can't park here.*
**Hier ist Parkverbot.** *Parking is forbidden here.*

| | |
|---|---|
| **Wie komme ich zumParkplatz?** | *How do I get to the car park?* |
| **Hier dürfen Sie nicht fahren.** | *You can't go/drive here.* |
| **Es ist eine Einbahnstraße.** | *It's a one-way street.* |
| **Anlieger frei** | *residents only* |
| **Fussgängerzone** | *pedestrian area* |
| **Spielstrasse** | *children may be playing* |
| **Kennzeichen** | *registration number(s)* |

### Insight

You usually have to pay fines for illegal parking, as for speeding, on the spot.

### Exercise 6

You're about to park your car in the street, when you're approached by a traffic policeman. Complete your part of the conversation.

| | |
|---|---|
| **Polizist** | Hier dürfen Sie nicht parken. |
| **a You** | *Ask where you can park.* |
| **Polizist** | Es gibt ein Parkhaus vor dem Bahnhof. |

| | |
|---|---|
| **b You** | *Ask how to get to the station.* |
| **Polizist** | Sie biegen hier gleich links ab, dann geradeaus bis zur Ampel, dann links und wieder links. |
| **c You** | *Ask where you can park.* |
| **Passant** | Der Parkplatz ist voll. Sie müssen in der Tiefgarage einen Platz finden. |
| **d You** | *Ask where it is.* |
| **Passant** | Gegenüber der Stadthalle. |
| **e You** | *Ask if it is expensive.* |
| **Passant** | Ein Euro pro Stunde bis 20.00 Uhr. |
| **f You** | *And after 8.00pm?* |
| **Passant** | Nichts. |
| **g You** | *Ask if he/she has any change.* |
| **Passant** | Was brauchen Sie? |
| **h You** | *Two 50 cent coins.* |
| **Passant** | Nein, leider nicht. Sie müssen zum Kiosk gehen. |

## Exercise 7

What do these signs tell you?

You can tell where a German car is registered by the first letter or letters on the number plate, for example:

| | | | | | | | |
|---|---|---|---|---|---|---|---|
| **B** | Berlin | **BN** | Bonn | **D** | Düsseldorf | **DO** | Dortmund |
| **H** | Hannover | **HH** | Hamburg | **M** | München | **MR** | Marburg |
| **L** | Leipzig | | | | | | |

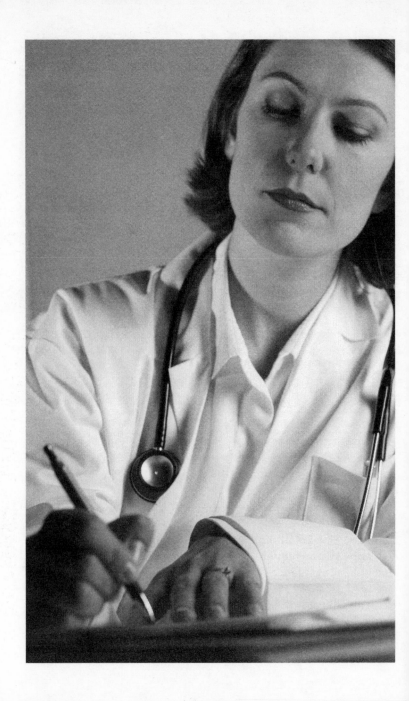

# 19

..........................................................................................

# Was ist mit Ihnen los?
## What's wrong with you?

In this unit you will learn how to

- *Say you don't feel well and ask for medicine*
- *Understand the instructions on the bottle*
- *Find out about opening times*

_____

Was ist mit Ihnen los? *What's the matter with you?*

| | |
|---|---|
| **Ich fühle mich nicht wohl.** | *I don't feel well* |
| **Ich habe...** | *I have ...* |
| **Ich habe Kopfschmerzen.** | *I have headache (lit. head pains).* |
| **Ich habe Ohrenschmerzen.** | *I have earache.* |
| **Ich habe Zahnschmerzen.** | *I have toothache.* |
| **Ich habe Halsschmerzen.** | *I have sore throat.* |
| **Ich habe einen Sonnenbrand.** | *I have sunburn.* |
| **Ich habe eine Grippe.** | *I have flu.* |
| **Ich habe eine Erkältung.** | *I have a cold.* |
| **Ich habe Heuschnupfen.** | *I have hay fever.* |
| **Ich habe eine Allergie.** | *I have an allergy.* |
| **Ich habe Husten.** | *I have a cough.* |
| **Ich habe Fieber.** | *I have a temperature.* |
| **Ich habe Durchfall.** | *I have diarrhoea.* |
| **Mein Bein tut weh.** | *My leg hurts.* |
| **Ich bin schlechter Laune.** | *I am in a bad mood.* |

QUICK VOCAB

| | |
|---|---|
| **Arm** | *arm* |
| **Fuss** | *foot* |
| **Magen** | *stomach* |
| **meine Hand** | *hand* |
| **Gesundheit!** | *Bless you!* |
| | *(lit. health)* |
| **Gesund** | *well, healthy* |
| **Krank** | *sick, ill* |

| | |
|---|---|
| **Haben Sie einMittel gegen ...?** | *Have you got something for ...?* |
| **Tabletten** | *tablets* |
| **schmerzstillende Tabletten** | *painkillers* |
| **Zäpfchen** | *suppositories* |
| **eine Salbe** | *cream, ointment* |
| **Hustentropfen** | *liquid cough medicine (lit. cough drops) (to put in water)* |
| **Hustenbonbons** | *cough sweets (to suck)* |

## Exercise 1

How would you say the following?

- **a** *You have a cold.*
- **b** *You don't feel well.*
- **c** *Have you got something for sunburn?*
- **d** *How often should I take them?*
- **e** *You have a cough.*
- **f** *You have toothache.*

**Listening exercise 32**
🔊 **CD2, TR 52**

Was ist mit ihnen los? *What is wrong with these four people?*

## In der Apotheke *At the chemist's*

Exercise 2

| **a You** | *Tell the chemist that you don't feel well.* |
|---|---|
| **Apothekerin** | Was ist mit Ihnen los? |
| **b You** | *Say you've got a temperature. You've got a headache and a sore throat.* |
| **Apothekerin** | Ach, Sie haben eine Grippe. Ich gebe Ihnen Tabletten gegen Halsschmerzen. |
| **c You** | *Ask her if she has anything for the headache.* |
| **Apothekerin** | Gegen Fieber nimmt man am besten Aspirin. |

Exercise 3

Wie oft soll ich sie einnehmen? *How often should I take them?*

See if you can match each instruction with one of the labelled medicines below.

  **a** *Every four hours with water.*
  **b** *Three times a day as required.*
  **c** *One tablet twice a day.*
  **d** *After meals, twice a day.*
  **e** *Every three hours.*
  **f** *Apply/rub in as required.*

You will receive free medical treatment at doctors' surgeries and hospitals if you have the European Health Insurance Card which is available from your local post office. Nearly all Germans have some form of private health insurance.

---

## Geschäftszeiten *Opening times*

| | |
|---|---|
| **Wann?** | *When?* |
| **Um wie viel Uhr?** | *At what time?* |
| **der Ruhetag** | *closing day (lit. rest day)* |
| **Betriebsferien** | *works/shop holiday* |
| **der Feierabend** | *end of the working day* |
| **Öffnungszeiten** | *opening times* |
| **offen/geöffnet** | *open* |
| **geschlossen** | *closed* |
| **um** | *at (time)* |

> **Öffnungszeiten**
> Montag–Mittwoch u. Freitag
> 8.30–13.00 Uhr u. 14.15–16.00 Uhr
> Donnerstag
> 8.30–13.00 Uhr u. 14.15–18.00 Uhr

Exercise 4
  **a** When is the chemist's open on a Thursday?
  **b** When is the chemist's open on a Monday?
  **c** Is the chemist's open on a Saturday?

Exercise 5
How would you tell your German friend:
  **a** when the chemist's is open where you live?
      **i** Am ... ist die Apotheke von ... Uhr bis ... geöffnet.
      **ii** Am ... ist die Apotheke nicht geöffnet.

**b** when you finish work?

**Wann haben Sie Feierabend?**

**Um ... Uhr ist für mich Feierabend.**

**c** which day the shops are closed where you live?
**Welcher Tag ist Ruhetag?**
_____ **ist hier Ruhetag.**

**d** what time the shops usually shut?
**die Geschäfte machen meistens um ... Uhr zu.**

## DIALOGUE 37

| | | |
|---|---|---|
| **Sie** | Bitte, gibt es eine Apotheke in der Nähe? | ⏺ CD2, TR 53 |
| **Freund** | Ja, in der Hauptstraße, aber sie ist im Moment geschlossen. | |
| **Sie** | Wann wird sie geöffnet? | |
| **Freund** | Um 14.00 Uhr. | |
| **Sie** | Bis wann? | |
| **Freund** | Bis 16.30 Uhr. | |
| **Sie** | Danke. | |
| **Freund** | Bitte. | |

Exercise 6
Put your part of this dialogue into German, then read through the whole dialogue out loud and check you understand it all.

| **a You** | _You want to go to buy some medicine. Ask if there is a chemist's nearby._ |
|---|---|
| **Freund** | Sie ist im Moment geschlossen. |
| **b You** | _Ask when it will open._ |
| **Freund** | Um 14.00 Uhr. |
| **c You** | _Ask when it shuts again._ |
| **Freund** | Um 16.30 Uhr. |

## LEARNING TIP

**1** Revise telling the time. How do you say these times?

| | | | |
|---|---|---|---|
| 10.15 | 2.30 | 14.45 | 3.05 |
| 6.20 | 17.40 | 11.30 | 12.00 |

## Exercise 7

**a** *When is this shop open?*

**b** *And when is this one not open?*

```
Öffnungszeiten
Montag bis Freitag
8.45–18.30 Uhr
Samstag 8.45–13.00 Uhr
la. Samstag 8.45–18.00 Uhr
```

```
Betriebsferien
14.–28. Juli
```

# 20

# Kontakt!
## Contact!

In this unit you will learn how to
- *Keep in contact using a computer and a mobile phone*
- *Ask for help with using your computer*
- *Make arrangements*

| | |
|---|---|
| **der PC oder der Computer** | *PC or computer* |
| **der Laptop** | *laptop* |
| **die Festplatte** | *hard drive* |
| **der Server** | *server* |
| **die Tastatur** | *keyboard* |
| **die Maus** | *mouse* |
| **der Speicher Stick** | *memory stick* |
| **die Akte** | *file* |
| **das E-Mail** | *email* |
| **die CD** | *CD* |
| **die Überspielbare CD** | *re-writeable CD* |
| **Wireless LAN/Drahtlos** | *WIFI* |
| **Alle Computer sind ausser Dienst.** | *All the computers are down.* |
| **Keine Verbindung zum Internet.** | *The internet is down.* |
| **Ich möchte ...** | *I would like to ...* |
| **meine E-Mails herunterladen** | *download my emails* |
| **ein E-Mail versenden** | *send an email* |
| **eine Anlage dazu versenden** | *send an attachment* |
| **eine Anlage sichern** | *save an attachment* |

| | |
|---|---|
| eine Akte entfernen/löschen | delete a file |
| eine Akte kopieren | copy a file |
| meinen Laptop anschliessen | connect my laptop |
| im Internet surfen | surf the internet |
| in meine Mailbox | get into my mailbox |
| einen Stadtplan ausdrucken | print a plan of the town |
| in Google surfen | (to) google (something) |
| den Zugfahrplan ansehen | look up train times |
| einen Flug buchen | book a flight |
| ein Hotel suchen | look for a hotel |
| ein Foto versenden | send a photo |
| die Wettervorhersage heraussuchen | look up the weather forecast |
| ein Podcast herunterladen | download a podcast |
| das Abendprogramm ansehen | find out what is on tonight |

What other things might you want to do on the computer? Here are some suggestions.

QUICK VOCAB

| | |
|---|---|
| das Internetcafé | internet café |
| der Internetanschluss | internet connection |
| Wo kann ich den (Internetanschluss) benutzen? | Where can I use it (internet connection)? |
| das USB-Kabel | USB cable |
| den Versand vornehmen | to send |
| selbstverständlich | of course |

### DIALOGUE 38

CD2, TR 54

| | |
|---|---|
| **Sie** | Ist hier in der Nähe ein Internetcafé? |
| **Empfangsdame** | Nein, aber das Hotel hat einen Internetanschluss. |
| **Sie** | Wo kann ich den benutzen? |
| **Empfangsdame** | Ein Anschluss ist in Ihrem Zimmer. Dort können Sie Ihr Laptop anschliessen oder Sie gehen in das Business Center und benutzen einen PC von uns. |

| | |
|---|---|
| **Sie** | Was kostet das? |
| **Empfangsdame** | €5,00 die Stunde. |
| **Sie** | Wie kann ich eine Akte über meinen PC versenden? Ich habe mein USB-Kabel nicht mit. |
| **Empfangsdame** | Haben Sie einen Speicher Stick? |
| **Sie** | Ja! |
| **Empfangsdame** | Dann können Sie den Versand über den Hotel-Computer vornehmen. |
| **Sie** | Kann ich es auch ausdrucken? |
| **Empfangsdame** | Ja, selbstverständlich. |

## Exercise 1
Match the German phrases to their English equivalents.

a **Ich komme nicht ins Internet, was muss ich tun?**
b **Haben Sie 'senden' angeklickt?**
c **Ich kann diese Akte nicht herunterladen.**
d **Es liegt eine Störung vor.**
e **Gehen Sie bitte an einen anderen PC.**

i *I can't download this file.*
ii *There is a problem.*
iii *I can't get onto the web, what should I do?*
iv *Please use another PC.*
v *Have you clicked on 'send'?*

## Listening exercise 33
🔊 **CD2, TR 55**

Was wollen sie machen? *What do they want to do?*

_____

## Wann treffen wir uns? *When shall we meet?*

In German a mobile phone is usually referred to as **ein Handy**.

## Dialogue 39

| | |
|---|---|
| **Sie** | Können Sie mich heute Abend anrufen? |
| **Kollege** | Wie ist Ihre Telefonnummer? |
| **Sie** | Sie brauchen die Ländervorwahl für Deutschland, +49, und meine Telefonnummer ohne die Null. |
| **Kollege** | Welche Telefonnummer haben Sie? |
| **Sie** | Also +49 für Deutschland; Hamburg hat die Vorwahl 040, ohne Null heisst es +49 40, und meine Telefonnummer… 1 23 45 67 89. |
| **Kollege** | Wie ist Ihre Handynummer? |
| **Sie** | +49 für Deutschland, dann 171 98 76 54 32, aber wo ich wohne gibt es nicht immer Funkkontakt. Falls es keinen Funkkontakt gibt, rufen Sie mich auf dem Festnetz an. |
| **Kollege** | OK. In Ordnung. Bis dann. |
| **Sie** | Tschüss. |

**Verstehen Sie SMS?** *Do you understand SMS?* [short message service]

Most SMS derive from the English so you may already know them.

| | |
|---|---|
| **cu – bis bald** | *See you soon* |
| **j4f – nur zum Spaß** | *Just for fun* |
| **np – null Problem** | *No problem* |
| **lg – liebe Grüsse** | *Loving greetings* |
| **gn8 – gute Nacht** | *Good night* |
| **mb – schreib zurück**k | *Mail bac* |

But some are German!

| | |
|---|---|
| **akla? – alles klar?** | *Understood?* |
| **as – antworte schnell!** | *Reply quickly* |
| **biba – bis bald** | *Till soon* |
| **bu – bin unterwegs** | *On the way/travelling* |

| | |
|---|---|
| **dad – denk an dich** | *Thinking about you* |
| **dwb – dumm wie Brot** | *Daft as bread/stupid* |
| **hdl – hab' dich lieb** | *Love you!* |
| **kgw – komme gleich wieder** | *I'll be straight back* |
| **kk – kein Kommentar** | *No comment* |
| **k – Kuss** | *Kiss* |
| **kes – komme etwas später** | *I am coming a bit later* |
| **vd – vermisse dich** | *Miss you* |

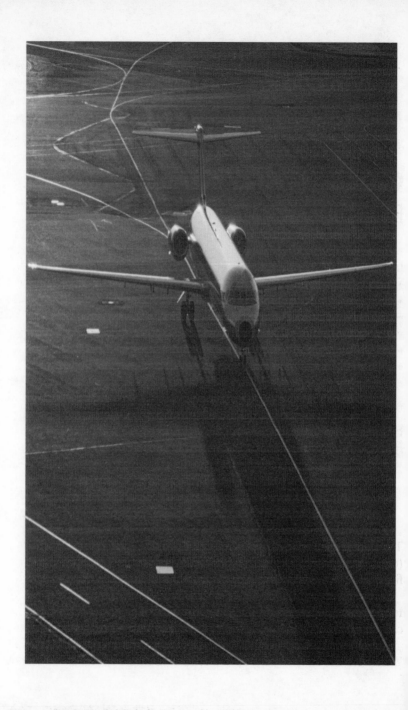

# 21

# Geschäftsreise oder Besuch?
## Business trip or visit?

In this unit you will learn how to
- *Make more detailed arrangements for accommodation*
- *Read signs about the town*
- *Ask the way to somewhere complicated*
- *Ask for things and say if something is wrong in more detail*
- *Read the signs at a trade fair*
- *Recognize the Länder*

---

## Haben Sie ein Zimmer frei?
*Have you a room available?*

| Zimmer |
|---|

### ÜBERNACHTUNG *ACCOMMODATION*

The town information bureau **Auskunftsbüro/Verkehrsamt** (or the organizers of the trade fair or conference) can help you find accommodation.

It is possible to stay in private houses and this is usually much cheaper than in hotels.

**Zimmernachweis** is where you can ask about rooms available.

| | |
|---|---|
| **die Messe** | *trade fair* |
| **das Hotel** | *a hotel (usually international standard)* |
| **das Gasthaus** ⎫<br>**der Gasthof** ⎭ | *a hotel, often typical of*<br> *the region, inn* |
| **die Pension** | *a cheaper hotel* |
| **Zimmer frei** | *rooms vacant* |
| **Zimmer belegt** ⎫<br>**Zimmer besetzt** ⎭ | *rooms taken*<br>*no vacancies* |
| **Wie komme ich zum/zur ...?** | *How do I get to the ...?* |
| **Vollpension** | *full board* |
| **zu teuer** | *too dear* |
| **Halbpension** | *half board* |
| **das Zimmer** | *room* |

Exercise 1
What do these signs mean?

Zimmer frei

Zimmer belegt

Zimmernachweis

Exercise 2
Match the sign to the facilities:

| | | |
|---|---|---|
| 1 Restaurant | 7 Schwimmbad | 12 Konferenzraum |
| 2 Parkplatz | 8 Doppelzimmer | 13 Kreditkarten |
| 3 Fax | 9 Einzelzimmer | 14 Sauna |
| 4 Airport-transfer | 10 Garage | 15 Für Behinderte geeignet |
| 5 Telefon | 11 Bar | 16 Fernseher |
| 6 Frühstücksbüffet | | |

## DIALOGUE 40

| | |
|---|---|
| **Sie** | Haben Sie noch ein Zimmer frei? |
| **Empfangsdame** | Einzel-oder Doppelzimmer? |
| **Sie** | Ein Einzelzimmer. |
| **Empfangsdame** | Mit Bad oder Dusche? |
| **Sie** | Mit Dusche. Haben Sie ein Zimmer mit Telefon? |
| **Empfangsdame** | Ja. Im Hotel Superdeluxe. €180 pro Nacht. |
| **Sie** | Das ist zu teuer. |
| **Empfangsdame** | Pension Sailer. Ein Einzelzimmer mit Bad kostet €50 inklusive Frühstück. |
| **Sie** | Gibt es einen Parkplatz? |
| **Empfangsdame** | Nein. Aber Sie können bis 8.00 Uhr auf der Straße parken. |
| **Sie** | Gut. Ich nehme es. Wie komme ich am besten zur Pension? |
| **Empfangsdame** | Sie fahren hier geradeaus und dann links. Die Pension Sailer ist auf der rechten Seite. |
| **Sie** | Vielen Dank. Auf Wiedersehen. |

**◀ CD2, TR 57**

**1** Practise the dialogue, reading both parts out loud.

---

## Ich bin zur Messe hier
*I have come to the trade fair*

### ANKOMMEN *GETTING THERE*

Here are some phrases that might be useful.

| | |
|---|---|
| Wie komme ich zur Messe? | *How do I get to the fair?* |
| mit der Straßenbahn Linie ... | *(with) tram number ...* |
| mit der U-Bahn | *(on the) underground* |
| mit dem Bus | *(on the) bus* |
| Wo ist die Haltestelle? | *Where is the stop?* |
| Wo ist die U-Bahnstation? | *Where is the underground station?* |
| die Fahrkarte | *ticket* |
| zu Fuss | *on foot* |
| Ist es weit? | *Is it far?* |
| Es ist gerade um die Ecke. | *It's just round the corner.* |
| Wie oft fährt der Bus?/die U-Bahn? | *How often does the bus/ underground run?* |
| alle 20 Minuten | *every 20 minutes* |
| Wo treffen wir uns? | *Where shall we meet?* |
| Wann treffen wir uns? | *When shall we meet?* |
| der Treffpunkt | *the meeting place* |
| eine Eintrittskarte | *an entry ticket* |
| Ich bin Aussteller. | *I am an exhibitor.* |
| Ich bin Einkäufer/in. | *I am a buyer.* |
| Meine Firma heißt ... | *My firm is called ...* |

## Exercise 3
Pair up the question words.

| | | | |
|---|---|---|---|
| i | Wo? | a | When? |
| ii | Wann? | b | Which? |
| iii | Was? | c | How much …? |
| iv | Was für …? | d | How? |
| v | Wie viel …? | e | Where? |
| vi | Welcher? | f | Who? |
| vii | Wie? | g | What kind of …? |
| viii | Wer? | h | What? |

If you are travelling by car and want to take it to the fair every day you will find it very helpful to book parking in advance.

Remember to drive on the right and to adapt your headlights accordingly.

## Exercise 4
Complete your part of the dialogue, and then read the whole dialogue out loud, checking that you understand it all.

⏺ CD2, TR 58

| a You | *How do I get to the fair?* |
|---|---|
| **Freund** | Mit dem Bus oder mit der U-Bahn? |
| b You | *Which bus?* |
| **Freund** | Linie 14. |
| c You | *How often does it run?* |
| **Freund** | Alle zwanzig Minuten. |
| d You | *Which U-Bahn?* |
| **Freund** | Linie 3 und Linie 5. |
| e You | *Do I have to change?* |
| **Freund** | Ja. Sie steigen am Bahnhof um. |
| f You | *How often does it run?* |
| **Freund** | Alle zehn Minuten. Die U-Bahn ist schneller. |
| g You | *Thank you.* |
| | *(Contd)* |

You arrive, but you haven't booked your ticket in advance …

**h You** *Say you would like an entrance ticket.*
**Beamter** Einkäufer oder Aussteller?
**i You** *You are a buyer.*
**Beamter** Name und Firma?
**j You** *Give your details.*
**Beamter** Unterschreiben Sie hier. Das kostet €10.

---

## In der Messehalle *At the trade fair*

| | |
|---|---|
| Wo bekommt man …? | *Where can you get …?* |
| Wo bekommt man einen Aschenbecher? | *Where can you get an ashtray?* |
| Wo bekommt man Wasser? | *Where can you get water?* |
| Wo bekommt man Blumen? | *Where can you get flowers?* |
| Wo bekommt man Getränke? | *Where can you get drinks?* |
| Wo bekommt man einen Imbiss? | *Where can you get a snack?* |
| Wo bekommt man ein Programm? | *Where can you get a programme?* |
| Wo bekommt man einen Schlüssel für Stand Nr …? | *Where can you get a key for stand no. …?* |
| Wo kann ich Fotokopien machen? | *Where can I get photocopies?* |
| Wo kann ich ein Fax abschicken? | *Where can I send a fax?* |
| Wo sind die Toiletten? | *Where are the toilets?* |
| Mein Telefon/Kühlschrank ist kaputt. | *My telephone/fridge doesn't work.* |
| Ich habe keinen Strom. | *I have no electricity.* |
| Ich habe kein Telefon. | *I have no telephone.* |
| Ich habe kein Wasser. | *I have no water.* |
| Ich habe ein Telefon bestellt. | *I ordered a telephone.* |

QUICK VOCAB

## Exercise 5

Complete your part of the dialogue.

| | |
|---|---|
| **a You** | *Say you want the key for your stand.* |
| **Hallenmeister** | Welche Nummer? |
| **b You** | *21.* |
| **Hallenmeister** | Bitte schön. |
| **c You** | *The electricity doesn't work.* |
| **Hallenmeister** | Ich schicke den Elektriker. |
| **d You** | *Where can you get ashtrays?* |
| **Hallenmeister** | Im Kiosk. |
| **e You** | *Where can you get water?* |
| **Hallenmeister** | Es gibt einen Wasserhahn in der Ecke. |

## Listening exercise 34
◀) **CD2, TR 59**

Wo? *Where?*

a *Where can you get photocopies?*
b *Where can you get a meal?*
c *Where can you get drinks?*
d *Where are the toilets?*
e *Where is the nearest phone?*

| | |
|---|---|
| **der Eingang** | entrance |
| **der Ausgang** | exit |
| **die Halle** | exhibition hall |
| **die Rolltreppe** | escalator |
| **der Aufzug/Fahrstuhl** | lift |
| **das Restaurant** | restaurant |
| **der Pendelbus** | shuttle bus service |
| **erste Hilfe** | first aid |
| **der Hallenmeister** | hall caretaker |

QUICK VOCAB

## Exercise 6
### Which sign is which?

a **KEIN AUSGANG**

b **NOTAUSGANG**

c **ROLLTREPPE**

d **NICHT RAUCHEN**

e **EINGANG**

f **IMBISS**

g **AUFZUG**

h **KEIN EINTRITT**

i **ERSTE HILFE**

| | | |
|---|---|---|
| **i** entrance | **iv** emergency exit | **vii** no smoking |
| **ii** snack bar | **v** escalator | **viii** no exit |
| **iii** lift | **vi** no entry | **ix** first aid |

---

## In der Stadt *In the town*

What do the signs tell you?

a RADFAHREN IM PARK NICHT GESTATTET

b BETRETEN DER BAUSTELLE VERBOTEN

c RASEN NICHT BETRETEN

d ACHTUNG FAHRZEUGVERKEHR VON RECHTS

e RAUCHEN VERBOTEN

f FUSSGÄNGERWEG GEGENÜBER BENUTZEN

g ACHTUNG SCHRANKE

h EINTRITT VERBOTEN

| German | English |
|---|---|
| **nicht gestattet** | *not permitted* |
| **nicht erlaubt** | *not allowed* |
| **verboten** | *forbidden* |
| **untersagt** | *not allowed* |
| **Achtung!** | *warning* |
| **Betreten** | *walking on* |
| **die Baustelle** | *building site* |
| **der Rasen** | *grass* (lit. *lawn*) |
| **Fahrzeugverkehr** | *traffic* |
| **die Schranke** | *level crossing barrier* |
| **Vorsicht!** | *Be careful! Watch out!* |
| **der Fußgängerweg** | *pavement* |
| **gegenüber** | *opposite* |
| **benutzen** | *to use* |

| *Land* *Region* | *Hauptstadt* *Capital city* |
|---|---|
| Baden-Württemburg | Stuttgart |
| Bayern | München |
| Berlin | Berlin |
| Brandenburg | Potsdam |
| Bremen | Bremen |
| Hamburg | Hamburg |
| Hessen | Wiesbaden |
| Mecklenburg-Vorpommern | Schwerin |
| Niedersachsen | Hannover |
| Nordrhein-Westfalen | Düsseldorf |
| Rheinland-Pfalz | Mainz |
| Saarland | Saarbrücken |
| Sachsen | Dresden |
| Sachsen-Anhalt | Magdeburg |
| Schleswig-Holstein | Kiel |
| Thüringen | Erfurt |

## Die Länder *The regions*

The Federal Republic of Germany consists of 16 regions (**Bundesländer**). Each **Land** (plural **Länder**) has its own regional parliament (**Landtag**) with much jurisdiction over regional affairs. Each **Land** or group of **Länder** has summer holidays at a different time on a rota so that not everyone is on the move at once.

## TEST YOURSELF

Can you answer the questions?

**1** How many genders are there in German? [cf Unit 8]

**2** How do you make the plural form? [cf Unit 12]

**3** What does a trigger word do? [cf Unit 8/9]

**4** What does the verb end with after **ich**? [cf Unit 11]

**5** Which form should you use when speaking to a stranger, **du** or **Sie**? [cf Unit 4]

**6** What does the verb end with in the **Sie** form? [cf Unit 4]

**7** If there are two verbs in a sentence where does the 'second' verb go? [cf Unit 6]

**8** What is a separable verb? [cf Unit 17]

**9** What does the prefix **ge-** usually indicate? [cf Unit 11]

**10** When should you use **gehen** and when do you use **fahren**? [cf Unit 11]

Congratulations on completing *Get started in German*!

I hope you have enjoyed working your way through the course.
I am always keen to receive feedback from people who have used
my course, so why not contact me and let me know your reactions?
I always welcome comments and suggestions and I do my best to
incorporate constructive suggestions into later editions.

You can contact me through the publishers at:

Teach Yourself Books, Hodder Headline Ltd, 338 Euston Road,
London NW1 3BH.

I hope you will want to build on your knowledge of German and
have made a few suggestions to help you do this in the section
entitled **Taking it further**.

**Alles Gute!**

*Rosi McNab*

# Taking it further

If you have enjoyed working your way through *Get started in German* and want to take your German further, why not try *Complete German*? You should find it ideal for building on your existing knowledge and improving your listening, reading and writing skills.

The following websites will help you take further your knowledge of German and the German-speaking world:

http://www.goethe.de The *Goethe Institut* is represented in most countries and staff may be able to inform you about German language courses in your area. They will also have information on short intensive courses based in Germany.

http://www.austria.org for information about Austrian life and culture.

http://www.swissinfo.org for information about Swiss life and culture.

The publisher has used its best endeavours to ensure that the URLs for external websites referred to in this book are correct and active at the time of going to press. However, the publisher has no responsibility for the websites and can make no guarantee that a site will remain live or that the content is or will remain appropriate.

## Try some real German!

Have a go at listening to German-speaking radio and TV stations and reading German newspapers and magazines.

Whatever you try, it's best to concentrate on small extracts at first – either a video or audio clip or a short article. See how much you can work out, going over the material several times. Then look up any words that you have not understood, and go on until you are satisfied that you have grasped the main ideas. If you do this on a regular basis, you'll find that your command of German increases steadily.

## Sources of real German

**1** Newspapers, magazines (e.g. *Bild-Zeitung*, *Stern*, *Focus*).

**2** Satellite and cable TV channels (e.g. ARD, RTL, SAT1, ZDF).

**3** Radio stations via satellite and, within Europe, on medium wave after dark.

**4** Internet – most German newspapers have websites where you can browse for short articles that interest you. TV and radio stations, too, have websites where you can often find audio and video clips of the latest newscasts. In some cases you will also find transcripts of the newscasts to help you if you run into difficulties with the spoken language. Use a German-language search engine or portal such as http://www.google.de, http://de.yahoo.com or http://www.tiscali.de to find any of the above and lots more besides.

**5** Last but not least, we would highly recommend that you try speaking German with native speakers, whether in your home country or in a German-speaking country. Explore Berlin, Vienna or Zürich (or any other German-speaking city) and make contact with the locals!

**Viel Spaß beim Weiterlernen!**

# Key to the exercises

## UNIT 1

1 a Guten Tag b auch c Herr d auf Wiedersehen e gut f Es geht mir gut g vielen Dank h Wie geht es Ihnen? i und 2 a geht b heiße c mir d Wiedersehen Listening exercise 1 1 iia 2 iiib 3 iva 4 ia 5 ic 6 ivb 7 iib 8 iiic 3 a Wie heißen Sie? b Ich verstehe nicht c Ich heiße d Entschuldigen Sie bitte e morgen f Herr Schulz ist nicht da g Auf Wiedersehen h Wie bitte? i ein bisschen Test yourself 1 a Guten Morgen b Guten Tag c Guten Tag d Guten Abend 2 c 3 c 4 i vee gate es ee-nen ii unt iii dankuh iv hair v fr-ow vi ow-uch vii owf-veeder-say-un. 5 a Sie b bitte c verstehe d heiße, heißen f nicht g Auf h bisschen 6 a ii b i c iv d iii Listening exercise 2 a iii b ii c ii d i

## UNIT 2

1 a Tee mit Milch b Kaffee c Kaffee mit Milch d Kaffee mit Sahne e Zitronentee mit Zucker f Apfelsaft g Orangensaft h Tomatensaft i eine Dose Fanta j eine Flasche Cola 2 a travel agents b traveller's cheques c travel costs d lemon tea 3 a ein Glas Zitronentee b ein Glas Rotwein c Kaffee mit Sahne d Tee mit Milch und Zucker e Bier f ein Glas Weißwein g Orangensaft Test yourself 1 a Wie war die Reise? b Trinken Sie … c Trinken Sie Kaffee mit Milch und Zucker? d Essen Sie ein Stück Kuchen? 2 a iv b i c iii d v e ii Listening exercise 3 a i b ii c i d iii Listening exercise 4 a i b ii c iii Sign language 1 cup or pot of coffee (also decaffeinated available), mocha drink, cup or pot of 1/2 hot chocolate and 1/2 coffee, cup or pot of hot chocolate, pot of hot chocolate with cream, pot of tea, cup of tea with rum, glass of camomile or peppermint tea 2 Bringen Sie mir einen Kaffee, einen Zitronentee mit Zucker, ein Bier, eine Cola, bitte

## UNIT 3

1 eins; zwei; drei; vier; fünf; sechs; sieben; acht; neun; zehn; elf; zwölf; dreizehn; vierzehn; fünfzehn; sechzehn; siebzehn; achtzehn; neunzehn; zwanzig 2 eins; dreizehn; sieben; zwei; fünf; elf; acht; neun; siebzehn; sechs; vier; achtzehn; zwanzig; drei 3 a vier b sechs c drei d zwei e fünf f zwei 4 a fünf Glas Rotwein b drei Glas Weißwein c sechs Tassen Tee d drei Tassen Kaffee e vier Flaschen Bier f zwei Dosen Cola Listening exercise 5 1–15 2–5 3–7 4–16 5–10 6–13 7–19 8–3 9–20 10–1 11–17 12–4 5 a einundzwanzig b fünfundzwanzig c zweiunddreißig d sechsunddreißig e dreiundvierzig f siebenundvierzig g vierundfünfzig h achtundfünfzig i einundsechzig j neunundsechzig k zweiundsiebzig l fünfundsiebzig m vierundachtzig n achtundachtzig o zweiundneunzig p neunundneunzig. Listening exercise 6 1–32 2–36 3–54 4–21 5–88 6–92 7–25 8–72 9–69 10–43 11–84 12–47 13–58 14–99 15–75 16–61 Listening exercise 7 a 24 b 23 c 52 d 46 e 83 f 67 g 93 h 92 i 84 j 62 Test yourself Listening exercise 8 a €5,20 b €12,80 c €16,50 d €43,60 e €50,00 f €4,75 g €40,10 h €54,00 i €25,00 j €27,90 1 a zwei Tassen Tee b drei Flaschen Bier c fünf Glas Rotwein d vier Stück Kuchen e acht Glas Weißwein

## UNIT 4

1 a Wie geht es Ihnen? b Wann kommen Sie nach London? c Was machen Sie morgen? d Spielen Sie gern Tennis? e Schwimmen Sie gern? f Trinken Sie gern eine Tasse Kaffee? 2 a l g e m h 3 a du b Wie geht es dir? c Trinkst du gern eine Tasse Kaffee oder ein Glas Orangensaft? Listening exercise 9 1 du 2 Sie 3 Sie 4 du 5 Sie 6 Sie 7 du 8 Ihnen/Sie 9 du 10 du Listening exercise 10 1 Friedrich Bittner 2 Ilse Egeberg 3 Reinhard Drexler 4 Wolf Kasselmann 5 Hans Kauffeld 6 Renate Walkemeier Listening exercise 11 i Braunschweig ii Heidelberg iii Wuppertal-Romsdorf iv Iserlohn v Offenbach vi Passau vii Magdeburg viii Erfurt ix Cuxhafen x Karlsruhe xi Mittenwald xii Ingolstadt Test yourself 1 a l b f c a d r e t f h g m h g 2 a Wie heißt du? b Woher kommst du? c Möchtest du ein Glas Limonade? d Spielst du gern Tennis? 3 a st b en c en d st e en f st g st h en i st j en k st l en Quiz 1 c 2 b 3 c 4 c 5 a 6 b 7 a

8 a Munich b Cologne c Stuttgart d Vienna 9 a Rhine b Moselle
c Danube d die Zugspitze is the highest mountain in Germany 10 a
11 see map end of Unit 21

## UNIT 5

1 a Deutschland b Frankreich c Italien d Polen e Irland
f Großbritannien g Belgien h Spanien i Österreich j England
k Schottland l Holland m Portugal n die Schweiz o Wales Listening
exercise 12 1 German from Stuttgart in Germany 2 Dutch from
The Hague in Holland 3 Belgian from Brussels 4 French from
Paris 5 Austrian from Vienna 6 Swiss from Zurich 7 Spanish
from Madrid 8 Italian from Milan 9 German from Munich
10 Scottish from Glasgow 2 a Helmut b Waldstraße 34, Stuttgart,
Germany c Austrian d single e 35 f 12 34 56 g Salzburg h 70597
Listening exercise 13 Name: Anna Hofmann Wohnort: Dortmund,
Neuburgring 38 Postleitzahl: 44267 Telefonnummer: 0230 22 34
56 Staatsangehörigkeit: German Familienstand: married with two
children Geburtsort: born 28/4/39 in Halle Ausweisnummer: 1984
2124 7D 3 a Haben Sie ein Zimmer frei? b (say your name) c (say
where you are from) d (say what nationality you are) e (give your
address) f (give your postcode) g (repeat it) h (give your telephone
number) i (give the dialling code) j (say thank you) 4 a Wie heißen
Sie? b und mit Vornamen? c Staatsangehörigkeit/Nationalität
d Wie ist Ihre Adresse? e und die Postleitzahl? f Wie ist Ihre
Telefonnummer? g Wie bitte? h Wie ist die Vorwahl? Test yourself
1 a 2 b 3 c 4 b 5 c 6 c 7 a 8 a 9 c 10 b

## UNIT 6

1 Haben Sie ein …? a Einzelzimmer mit Bad (mit Dusche also
correct) b Doppelzimmer mit Bad c Doppelzimmer mit Badewanne
und Dusche 2 a Wo ist das Zimmer? b Wo ist der Fahrstuhl?
c Wo ist das Telefon? Listening exercise 14 i double 3 nights ii 1
single and 1 double 1 night iii 2 doubles with bath for a week
iv single with shower for Monday night v room with 1 double and
an extra bed for 1 night (25 September) vi double for 2 nights
12 and 13 August 3 a Ich habe ein Zimmer reserviert b (give your

name) c nein. Einzelzimmer mit Dusche d Wie bitte? e Gibt es einen
Fahrstuhl? f Wann ist Frühstück? g Würden Sie mich um sieben
Uhr wecken? h Haben Sie ein Zimmer frei? i Für drei Nächte
j Doppelzimmer k Bad. Gibt es ein Telefon im Zimmer? l Was
kostet das? m Ist Frühstück inbegriffen? n Ich möchte zahlen / die
Rechnung bitte o Achthundertelf. Nehmen Sie Kreditkarten? p
Eine Quittung, bitte q Würden Sie mich wecken? r Um sieben Uhr
s Zweihundert sieben 4 a Entschuldigen Sie bitte b Mein Zimmer
ist zu laut c Gibt es eine Dusche? d Ich nehme es e Entschuldigen
Sie bitte. f Mein Zimmer ist zu heiß. Wie funktioniert die Heizung?
g Zimmerservice h Das Licht/ die Birne ist kaputt i Achtundvierzig
j Zimmerservice/ Zimmerdienst k Würden Sie mich um sechs Uhr
wecken? l Dreiundsechzig. Ich möchte im Zimmer frühstücken. m
Um sieben Uhr 5 a Ich möchte nach England anrufen b Ich möchte
Zimmer Nummer 25 anrufen c Wie mache ich ein Ortsgespräch?
Test yourself 1 Es gibt a kein Telefon b keine Bar c keinen
Fernseher in meinem Zimmer 2 Mein Zimmer ist a zu klein
b zu heiß c zu laut d zu kalt 3 a Ich möchte ein Doppelzimmer
b Ich möchte ein Einzelzimmer mit Bad c Ich möchte ein
Familienzimmer d Ich möchte ein Zweibettzimmer 4 a Der
Fernseher funktioniert nicht b Wie funktioniert die Klimaanlage?
c Gibt es einen Föhn?

## UNIT 7

1 a sechs Uhr b Mittag/zwölf Uhr c Viertel nach eins d zehn nach
zwei e zwanzig nach drei f Viertel vor fünf 2 a halb sechs b halb
acht c halb zehn d halb zwölf Listening exercise 1 5 a 9.30 b 5.30
c 7.30 d 11.30 3 a Wie viel Uhr ist es? b Wie viel Uhr ist es? c
Vielen Dank d Auf Wiedersehen e Es tut mir Leid. Ich weiß es nicht
4 halb neun; Viertel vor neun; Viertel nach zehn; Viertel vor drei;
halb sieben 5 a Montag Dienstag Mittwoch Donnerstag Freitag
Samstag Sonntag b 6.00 Uhr morgens; 9.00 Uhr früh; Mittag; 2.00
Uhr nachmittags; 4.ooh nachmittags; 6.ooh abends; 19.00 Uhr;
Mitternacht 6 a Montag um halb drei nachmittags b Donnerstag
um elf Uhr nachts c Samstag um sieben Uhr abends d Dienstag um
zehn Uhr zwanzig e Sonntag um Viertel vor sechs f Mittwoch um
halb sechs g Freitag um Viertel vor neun h Dienstag-mittag
i Donnerstagabend um Viertel nach sechs 7 a Auf Wiederhören

b Geht das? c Bis dann d Ich freue mich schon darauf Test
yourself 1 a Es ist sieben Uhr; b Viertel nach zwei; c halb fünf;
d Viertel vor zehn; e elf Uhr fünfundzwanzig; f zehn nach zwölf;
g acht Uhr fünfunddreißig; h zwanzig vor zwei; i halb zehn; j
fünf nach sechs 2 a Vierzehn Uhr vierundzwanzig; b um fünfzehn
Uhr siebenundzwanzig; c sechzehn Uhr zwölf; d neunzehn Uhr
neunundzwanzig; e zwanzig Uhr einundzwanzig; f zweiundzwanzig
Uhr zehn; g dreizehn Uhr sechsundfünfzig; h dreizehn Uhr
achtundvierzig 3 a 4.20 b 2.10 c 9.30 d 10.35 e 3.25 f 6.35 g 8.45
h 2.30 i 3.45 j 8.50 4 a vier Uhr; b Viertel vor sieben; c zwanzig
nach zwei; d halb elf; e fünf Uhr 5 a Dienstag b Freitag c Montag
d Samstag e Mittwoch f Sonntag g Donnerstag 6 a I need a battery
b I have lost my watch c My watch is broken

## UNIT 8

1 a Nein. Das ist die Post b Dort drüben c Bitte/Nichts zu
danken d Es tut mir Leid. Ich weiß es nicht e Dort drüben
f Auf Wiedersehen 2 der Bahnhof, die Bank, die Bibliothek, die
Brücke, das Café, der Flughafen, das Freibad, das Hotel, das
Informationsbüro, die Jugendherberge, das Kino, die Kirche,
die Kneipe, das Krankenhaus, der Marktplatz, der Park, die
Post, das Rathaus, das Reisebüro, das Restaurant, das Schloss,
der Schnellimbiss, die Straße 3 Krankenhaus a Brücke b Kirche
c Theater d Bank e Marktplatz f Kneipe g Kino h Flughafen
i Bahnhof j Rathaus k Post Listening exercise 16 1 Nikolai church
2 bank 3 hotel 4 restaurant 5 cinema 6 post office 7 pub 8 station
9 airport 10 information office 4 a Rathausplatz b Bahnhofstraße
c Einsteinstraße d Albrecht-Dürer-Allee e Einsteinstraße
f Rathausplatz g Rosenheimer Straße h Waldfriedhofallee 5 a in der
St-Martins-Straße b in der Rosen-heimerstraße c in der Albrecht-
Dürer Allee d in der Rosenheimerstraße e in der Einsteinstraße
f in der Albrecht-Dürer-Allee g in der Albrecht-Dürer-Allee h in der
Albrecht-Dürer-Allee i Waldfriedhofallee j in der Bahnhof-straße
k am Rathausplatz l in der Bahnhofstraße m in der Einsteinstraße
n in der Albrecht-Dürer-Allee o in der Rosenheimerstraße p in der
Bahnhofstraße Test yourself 1 a xvii b xvi c vii d i e ii f ix g xiii h
xix i iv j xii k iii l vi m viii n xviii o x p v q xi r xiv s xv. 2 campsite;
main post office; information office; police station; bus stop;

motorway bridge; pedestrian area; main station; sports ground;
bus station; petrol station; landing bridge Listening exercise
17 a R b F c F d R e R f F g F h F i R j F Sign language i d ii c iii b
iv f v a vi e

## UNIT 9

1 a zum b zum c zum d zum e zum f zur g zum h zum i zur j zum
k zum l zum 2 a geradeaus, auf der rechten Seite b die erste Straße
rechts, auf der linken Seite c die zweite Straße links, auf der linken
Seite d die erste Straße links, auf der rechten Seite e die zweite
Straße rechts, auf der rechten Seite f geradeaus auf der linken Seite
3 Gibt es ... in der Nähe? a einen Bahnhof b einen Campingplatz
c eine Post d einen Parkplatz e eine Bank f eine Kneipe g eine
Bushaltestelle h ein Hotel 4 a Einzelzimmer b Doppelzimmer
c (Doppelzimmer) mit Bad d (Einzelzimmer) mit Bad/mit Dusche
5 a mit dem Bus b mit dem Auto c mit der Bahn d mit der U-Bahn
e zu Fuß 6 a Gibt es ein Hotel in der Nähe? b Haben sie noch
Zimmer frei? c Wie komme ich zum Hotel ... zu Fuß; mit dem Auto;
mit dem Bus? 7 a Sie nehmen die erste Straße rechts und X ist auf
der linken Seite. b Sie gehen geradeaus bis zur zweiten Straße links
und X ist auf der rechten Seite. c Sie gehen geradeaus und X ist auf
der linken Seite nach der zweiten Straße links. d Sie nehmen die
erste Straße links und X ist auf der rechten Seite. 8 a toilets b hotel
c cinema d Rathausplatz e theatre f hospital g post office 9 Wo
ist... a die Post b der Bahnhof c die Kirche d die Bank e das Kino
f das Hotel g der Supermarkt? Ist es weit? 10 a Hier rechts, gleich
links und immer geradeaus b Ja, hier rechts, die erste Straße links,
erste Straße rechts, und die Bank ist auf der rechten Seite c Die Post
ist gegenüber vom Restaurant d Das Kino ist gegenüber der Bank
e Die erste Straße links und immer geradeaus f Links, erste Straße
rechts und erste Straße links. Das Restaurant ist gegenüber der
Post g Hier links, rechts und dann immer geradeaus h 3 Kilometer
Test yourself 1 a Wie komme ich zum Bahnhof? b Ist das weit?
c Wo kann ich hier Briefmarken kaufen? d Wo ist hier eine Bank?
e Gibt es ein Hotel in der Nähe? f Haben Sie noch Zimmer frei?
2 a die erste Straße rechts b die zweite Straße links c geradeaus
d um die Ecke e auf der linken Seite f auf der rechten Seite g ein

Einzelzimmer mit Bad h ein Doppelzimmer mit Bad/mit Dusche
i mit dem Auto j zu Fuß 3 a Es tut mir Leid b Ich verstehe nicht
c Ich weiß es nicht d Entschuldigen Sie, bitte e Wie bitte? f Vielen
Dank Sign language a Post office b Bank c Town hall d Cinema
e Swimming baths

## UNIT 10

1 a i b iii c iv d ii 2 a Spielen wir Montag-abend Tennis?
b Gehen wir morgen Abend ins Kino? c Gehen wir heute um
acht Uhr in die Pizzeria? d Gehen wir Mittwoch-nachmittag
schwimmen? e Spielen wir Samstag um elf Uhr Squash? f Gehen
wir Freitagabend ins Restaurant? 3 a Das geht leider nicht;
b Wie wäre es mit Donnerstag-abend? 4 a Gut, danke und Ihnen?
b Am Montag, den 15. Juli c Um achtzehn Uhr fünfunddreißig
d Um halb zehn e Bis Freitagabend f Um neunzehn Uhr dreißig
g Um halb acht h Auf Wiederhören Test yourself 1 a Montag den
zweiten Mai um halb eins b Freitag den 24. Dezember um vierzehn
Uhr dreißig c nächsten Samstag um Viertel nach elf d nächste
Woche am Donnerstag um sechzehn Uhr dreißig e am Mittwoch
den 16. April um Viertel nach neun f am Samstag den ersten
September um siebzehn Uhr g nächsten Dienstag um dreizehn Uhr
dreißig h am Freitag um acht Uhr Listening exercise 18 1 Café at
eleven tomorrow morning 2 Pub, tomorrow evening at 8.30
3 15 July at 2pm in Hamburg 4 6 April 8pm (other person's house)
5 24 October 7.30pm (speaker's house) 6 7 August 7.30pm
(speaker's house) 7 16.45 9 September at the station. 8 18.35
Friday 14 March at the airport Unit 6–10 Test yourself 1 b 2 c
3 Wie viel Uhr ist es? 4 c 5 c 6 masculine, feminine, neuter 7 true
8 mit dem 9 gehen, fahren 10 Mo Di Mi Do Fr Sa So

## UNIT 11

1 a -e b -en c -st d wir form -en 2 a er b wir c sie (plural) d Sie
(polite) e du f ich 3 a holen b lernen c arbeiten d fragen e sagen
f tanzen 4 a gehört b gebraucht c geführt d gespielt e gehabt
f gekocht 5 a lesen b geben c schlafen d rufen e sehen f fahren
g waschen

## UNIT 12

1 a mein Vater b meine Schwester c mein Großvater d meine
Eltern e meine Freundin f meine Mutter g mein Bruder h meine
Großmutter i meine Frau j mein Mann k mein Sohn l meine
Tochter m meine Oma n mein Opa o meine Schwiegermutter
Listening exercise 19 a Vater Oma Opa Schwester Hund b Vater
Mutter Sohn Tochter c Bruder Schwester Eltern Großeltern Hund
3 a die Töchter b die Tische c die Stühle d die Häuser 4 a i/ iv/
v/ vii b ii/ iii/ vi 5 a der Arbeitsbeginn b die Arbeitspause c das
Arbeitszimmer d das Arbeitsende e der Arbeitstisch f die Arbeitszeit
g die Arbeitswoche h der Arbeitsschluss i der Arbeitsvertrag
6 a das Verkaufsbüro b das Informationsbüro c das Postamt d das
Reisebüro 7 Herr Braun says b c f h i; Silke says a d e g j Listening
exercise 20 1 Car mechanic for BMW 2 Nurse 3 Business woman
4 Car electrician for a car firm 5 Hairdresser 6 Company rep
7 Business woman (in commerce) 8 Waiter

## UNIT 13

1 a Elektrogeschäft b Supermarkt c Kaufhaus d Konditorei e Bäckerei
f Metzgerei g Fotogeschäft h Gemüseladen i Drogerie j Apotheke
k Blumengeschäft l Zeitungskiosk m Tabakhändler 2 a Film
b CD/Kassette c Briefmarken d Zahnpasta 3 a meine Freundin
b meinen Bruder c meine Großmutter d meine Frau e meinen
Mann f meine Mutter g meinen Freund h meinen Sohn 4 a Haben
Sie …? i ein Buch ii Schreibpapier iii eine Flasche Parfüm b Ich
suche … i eine Flasche Wein ii Weingläser iii einen Bierkrug c Ich
möchte … i einen Schal ii Ohrringe iii einen Kuchen Listening exercise
21 1 book for father 2 winter coat for daughter 3 blue pullover
for husband 4 flowers for Frau Fischer 5 cake for Fräulein Sievers
6 toothpaste for self 5 a Ich möchte einen Pullover, blau Größe 38
b eine Bluse, rot, Größe 34 c eine Hose, braun, Größe 36 d einen
Wollschal, grün e ein Paar Handschuhe, schwarz f ein Hemd, weiß,
aus Baumwolle 6 a Ich möchte einen Schal für meine Mutter
b blau c dunkelblau d Aus Wolle? e Wie viel kostet er? f Das ist zu
teuer. Haben Sie etwas Billigeres? g Ich nehme ihn h Ich möchte ein
Paar Handschuhe i schwarz, aus Leder j Ich weiß es nicht

k groß l Ich nehme sie, könnten Sie sie als Geschenk einpacken?
m Haben Sie eine Straßenkarte? n Wo ist die Buchabteilung? o Wo
ist der Fahrstuhl? p Vielen Dank Listening exercise 22 1 road map
of North Germany 2 white shirt size 44 3 brown corduroy trousers
4 pair of jeans size 38 5 blue track suit 6 black lycra swimming
costume size 40 7 a ground floor b 4th c 3rd d 4th e ground floor
f 1st g basement h 3rd i basement j 2nd k ground floor l 1st

## UNIT 14

1 a Wann kommt der Zug in München an? b Wann fährt der Zug
ab? c Wie schreibt man das? d Wie geht es Ihnen? e Wo wohnen
Sie? 2 a nach München b nach Italien c aus England d aus London
3 a Nach Berlin, einmal einfach b Einmal nach Salzburg, hin
und zurück c Dreimal nach Mannheim, hin und zurück d Zwei
Rückfahrkarten nach Koblenz e Zweimal einfach nach Osnabrück
f Einmal nach Innsbruck, hin und zurück 4 a Einmal nach Köln
bitte, hin und zurück b Zweite. Wie viel kostet es? c Wann fährt
der Zug? d Wo fährt er ab? e Vielen Dank f Wann fährt der nächste
Zug nach München? g Wie viel kostet es? h D-Zug! Muss ich
umsteigen? i Wann kommt er in München an? j Wo fährt er ab?
Listening exercise 23 1 a Bremen b return c 14.49 d 16.12 e no
f €42,25 g 8 2 a Cologne b return c 9.39 d 13.48 e no f €108 g
10 3 a Vienna b single c 10.14 d 20.53 e no f €=143,50 g 9 5 Ich
fliege von Manchester um 11.15 Uhr ab. Ich komme in London
um 12.00 Uhr an. Ich fliege ab London um 13.45 Uhr. Ich komme
in Hamburg um 14.15 Uhr an. Die Flugnummer ist BA 5377 6 a
Wann ist der Flug nach Manchester? b Ist der Flug direkt? c Wie
lautet die Flugnummer? d Wann komme ich in Manchester an?
7 a Hallo. Wie geht es dir? b Auch gut. c Am Sonntag den 26.
Oktober. d Um 16 Uhr e LH 123 Wo treffen wir uns? f Ich freue mich
schon darauf g Tschüss h Hallo Wie geht's? i Auch gut danke. Wann
kommst du? j Um wie viel Uhr? Wann landet die Maschine? k Wie
ist die Flugnummer? l Wir treffen uns im Flughafen m Bis dann.
Tschüss 8 a um 14.30 in Düsseldorf an b um 9.05 in München an
c um 11.30 in Köln an d um 18.35 Uhr in Hamburg an e um 21.20
in Wien an f um 17.45 in Frankfurt an Listening exercise 24 1 Tues
21.35 flight LH12 2 Tues 13.45 BA52 3 Saturday 10.30 LH25 4

Thurs 8.15 BA 308 5 Fri 16th 11.05 LH 207 6 Weds 14th 15.30
BA 125 9 a wolf's castle b fish stream c new castle d Spa Ischl
e Gelsen churches f Ingol town g Ammer lake h Heather mountain
i new churches j Friedrich's harbour k two bridges l salt castle
m Chiem lake n Spa town o upper village p mill village q stony
stream r Magda's castle s Osna bridge t the Black Forest u new
town v Rhine castle w Gunter's village x Mann's home

## UNIT 15

1 a between 6 and 9.30 am b between 12 and 2 pm c yes (between
6 and 10 am) d yes (between 10 am and 6 pm) 2 a eine Portion
Pommes b zwei Bratwürste c Bockwurst und Pommes zweimal
d eine Dose Cola e ein Bier f zwei Waffeln Listening exercise 25
1 Sausage with potato salad and portion chips 2 Waffles with hot
cherry sauce 3 2 Curry sausage and potato purée 4 Frankfurter,
mustard and bread roll 5 Reibekuchen (potato fritter) with apple
sauce 6 Chips 7 1 ham sandwich and 1 cheese sandwich 8 2
beers and a coke 3 a Ich möchte einmal Bratwurst mit Pommes
b Ketchup c Ja, eine Currywurst mit Kartoffelsalat d Eine Cola und
ein Bier. Das ist alles. Was macht das? e So. 50 Euros f Ja, ich habe
zwei Euro 4 a ii b i c iv d vii e v and vi f iii 5 a Haben Sie …? ein
Messer; ein Glas; einen Löffel; einen Teller b Salz; Ketchup; Senf;
Zucker; Brot 6 a Bitte! b Ich brauche noch einen Teller c Haben Sie
Salz? d Haben Sie Ketchup? e Nein, danke das ist alles f Fräulein
g Noch ein Glas bitte h Haben Sie OK Sauce? i Noch ein Bier
und ein Glas Limonade 7 a Taschenmesser b Küchenmesser
c Brotmesser 8 a €2,60 b €4,80 c €3,60 d €2,60 e €3,30 f €2,40
g €3,70 h €2,30 i €6,50 j €5,90

## UNIT 16

Listening exercise 26 1 Wienerschnitzel, chips, lettuce 2 Chicken,
chips and tomato salad 3 Roast pork with mashed potatoes and
sour pickled cabbage 4 Trout, boiled potatoes and red cabbage
5 Pork fillet, rice and asparagus 6 Jägerschnitzel (escalope) with
noodles and beans 1 Magst du…?/Isst du gern…?/Trinkst du
gern…? a Fleisch b Fisch c Bier d Tee mit Milch e Tee mit Zitrone
f Kuchen 2 a Ist hier frei? b Was ist die Tagessuppe? c Haben Sie

Tomatensuppe? d Ich möchte ... e Nein. Das schmeckt mir nicht
f Ich nehme ... g mit ... h und zu trinken ... i Was empfehlen
Sie? j Ich nehme das k Ja, mit Sahne l Ja, bitte 3 a Do you want
something to drink with it? b Do you want a dessert? c Which
flavour? d Do you want ketchup? e Did you like it? f Together
or separately? Unit 12–16 Test yourself 1 false 2 true 3 Wo kann
ich hier Batterien kaufen? 4 Ich möchte eine dunkelblaue Hose aus
Baumwolle 5 fährt, nach 6 kommt, in, an 7 a 8 b 9 b 10 c

## UNIT 17

1 a Gehen Sie gern ins Kino? b Tanzen Sie gern c Gehen Sie gern
schwimmen? d Spielen Sie gern Karten? e Fahren Sie gern Rad?
f Sehen Sie gern fern? 2 a Spielst du gern Squash? b Spielst du gern
Fußball? c Läufst du gern Ski? d Spielst du gern Tennis? e Fährst du
gern Rad? f Spielst du gern Schach? 3 a Ich spiele gern Tennis b Ich
spiele gern Fußball c Ich fahre gern Rad d Ich gehe gern klettern
e Ich spiele gern Karten f Ich spiele gern Golf

Listening exercise 27

| | Like | Dislike |
|---|---|---|
| **1** | swimming | dancing |
| **2** | tennis/badminton | table tennis |
| **3** | walking | jogging |
| **4** | swimming/reading | football |
| **5** | football | |
| **6** | skiing/bike | |

4 a Morgen Vormittag spiele ich Tennis. Kommen Sie mit?
b Morgen Abend gehen wir schwimmen. Kommen Sie mit?
c Heute Abend spielen wir Karten. Haben Sie Lust Karten zu
spielen? d Heute Nachmittag gehen wir angeln. Kommen Sie mit?
e Heute Abend gehen wir in ein Nachtlokal. Kommen Sie mit?
f Samstagnachmittag gehen wir zum Fußball. g Kommen Sie mit?
h Das Spiel beginnt um ... i Haben Sie Lust danach Tennis zu
spielen? 5 a Ja, gerne. Um wie viel Uhr? b Wo treffen wir uns?
c Nein. Ich habe keine Lust. Ich spiele lieber Tennis d Um wie viel
Uhr? e Wo treffen wir uns? f Gerne. Ich bin noch nie Ski gefahren

g Um wie viel Uhr? h Wann kommen wir zurück? i Gut. Ich freue
mich schon darauf 6 golf-minigolf, sand yachting, table tennis,
volleyball, chess, bowling, fishing, surfing, woodland fitness circuit,
cycling, swimming, tennis, sailing 7 a i / iv / v / vii / ix b ii / iii / vi /
viii / x Listening exercise 28 1 playing cards 2 cycling 3 watching
TV 4 reading books 5 jogging 6 swimming 7 skiing 8 cinema
8 a Schneemann b Schneeball c Schneeballschlacht d Schneeflocken
e Schneeglöckchen f Schneeketten g Schneebrille h Schneeraupe
i Schneesturm

## UNIT 18

Listening exercise 29 1 fill up with super plus 2 20 litres of diesel
3 check the tyre pressures 4 Do you take credit cards? 5 clean
the windscreen 6 Where is the cash desk? 1 Können Sie …? i den
Reifendruck prüfen ii die Windschutzscheibe putzen iii den Ölstand
prüfen 2 a iii b v c i d vi e ii f iv 3 Ich bin auf … a der A4 zwischen
Köln und Aachen Richtung Aachen b der A1 in der Nähe von
Solingen Richtung Dortmund c der A5, in der Nähe von Offenburg
Richtung Basel d der A8 in der Nähe von Augsburg Richtung
München e der B10 in der Nähe von Geislingen, zwischen Stuttgart
und Ulm, Richtung Ulm Listening exercise 30 near Hannover,
near Munich and near Berlin 4 a near Friedberg b because of
an accident c at Augsburg d the B2 5 a What is wrong? b What
sort of car you have c Where you are d The make of your car e
If you are a member of an automobile club Listening exercise 31
1 breakdown 2 broken windscreen 3 run out of petrol 4 puncture
5 no water and overheating 6 won't start 7 Light not working;
can you change the bulb? 6 a Wo kann ich parken? b Wie komme
ich zum Bahnhof? c Wo kann ich hier parken? Der Parkplatz ist
voll d Wo ist die Tiefgarage? e Ist es teuer? f Und nach 8.00 Uhr?
g Haben Sie Kleingeld? h zwei fünfzig Cent Münzen 7 a lorries
b cars

## UNIT 19

1 a Ich habe eine Erkältung b Ich fühle mich nicht wohl c Haben
Sie etwas gegen einen Sonnenbrand? d Wie oft soll ich sie

einnehmen? e Ich habe Husten f Ich habe Zahnschmerzen Listening
exercise 32 1 headache 2 flu 3 temperature and sore throat 4 cold2
a Ich fühle mich nicht wohl b Ich habe Fieber, Kopfschmerzen und
Halsschmerzen c Haben Sie etwas gegen Kopfschmerzen? 3 a iii b
ii c vi d v e iv f i 4 a 8.30–1 and 2.15–6 b 8.30–1 and 2.15–4 c no
6 a Gibt es eine Apotheke in der Nähe? b Wann ist sie offen? c Bis
wann? 7 a Monday to Friday 8.45 to 18.30 and on Saturday 8.45
till 1pm except on the first Saturday of the month when it stays
open till 6pm b Works holiday from 14 to 28 July

## UNIT 20

1 a iii b v c i d ii e iv Listening exercise 33 1 send a photo 2 read
e-mails 3 save a document 4 book a flight 5 send an email 6 surf
the internet 7 look up train times 8 download a town plan

## UNIT 21

1 vacancies; full; accommodation listing 2 1/m, 2/f, 3/b, 4/k, 5/a,
6/g, 7/p, 8/d, 9/c, 10/e, 11/h, 12/n, 13/j, 14/i, 15/o, 16/l 3 i e, ii a,
iii h, iv g, v c, vi b, vii d, viii f 4 a Wie komme ich am besten zur
Messe? b Welche Buslinie? c Wie oft fährt sie? d Welche U-Bahn?
e Muss ich umsteigen? f Wie oft fährt sie? g Vielen Dank h eine
Ein-trittskarte i Einkäufer j … 5 a Wir brauchen einen Schlüssel
für den Stand b einundzwanzig c Wir haben keinen Strom d Wo
bekommt man Aschenbecher? e Wo bekommt man Wasser 6 a no
cycling b do not enter the building site c do not walk on the grass
d beware of traffic from the right e no smoking, f use the opposite
pavement g beware of level crossing h no entry Listening exercise
34 1 in the office on the 7th floor 2 in the restaurant here on the
2nd floor 3 snack bars everywhere, one in each exhibition hall 4 in
the corner: men on left, women on right 5 in the entrance hall
6 a viii b iv c v d vii e i f ii g iii h vi i ix Unit 17–21 Test yourself
1 3 2 there are a variety of ways 3 sometimes changes the word
that comes after it 4–5 Sie 6–7 end of the sentence 8 splits and the
prefix goes to the end of a sentence 9 past tense 10 gehen for going
on foot, fahren for going on transport

# Grammar summary

## NOUNS AND ARTICLES ('THE' AND 'A')

In German all nouns are masculine, feminine or neuter. The words for *the* and *a* change according to the gender of the noun.

**The definite article ('the')**

The word for *the* with masculine words is **der** (der Mann)
feminine **die** (die Frau)
neuter **das** (das Buch)

**The indefinite article ('a')**

The word for *a* with masculine words is **ein** (ein Mann)
feminine **eine** (eine Frau)
neuter **ein** (ein Buch)

For more details see Unit 8.

### Kein ('not a')

This is a negative form of the indefinite article which we do not have in English.

**Masc:** **Ich habe keinen Stuhl.** *I haven't a chair.*
**Fem:** **Ich habe keine Zeit.** *I haven't time.*
**Neut:** **ich habe kein Auto.** *I haven't a car.*

### Plurals

For information about the plural forms see Unit 12.

### Masculine nouns

The masculine forms **der/ein/kein** change to **den/einen/keinen** when they are used with the object of the sentence.

**Der** Hund    *but* Ich habe **einen** Hund. (*I have a dog*)
**Ein** Teller    *but* Ich brauche **einen** Teller. (*I need a plate*)
**Kein** Mantel    *but* Sie hat keinen **Mantel**. (*She hasn't a coat*)

For some examples see Unit 13 and Unit 15.

256

## NOUNS AND TRIGGER WORDS (PREPOSITIONS)

Some words (e.g. **mit**, *with*; **zu**, to) act as trigger words and change **der** to **dem**, **die** to **der**, **das** to **dem**, and **die** (plural) to **den**. For more information see Unit 8, Unit 9 and Unit 17.

These words are always trigger words:

| | | | |
|---|---|---|---|
| **aus** | *from/out of* | **aus dem Schrank** | *from the cupboard* |
| **bei** | *at/near* | **bei der Post** | *at the post office* |
| **gegenüber** | *opposite* | **gegenüber dem Café** | *opposite the café* |
| **mit** | *with* | **mit dem Bus** | *with/by bus* |
| **nach** | *after* | **nach der Pause** | *after the break* |
| **zu** | *to* | **zu der Bank** | *to the bank* |

These words are usually trigger words:

| | | | |
|---|---|---|---|
| **an** | *on* | **an der Hauptstraße** | *on the main street* |
| **auf** | *on* | **auf dem Tisch** | *on the table* |
| **in** | *in* | **im Kaufhaus** | *in the store* |

### PERSONAL PRONOUNS

| Singular | | Plural | |
|---|---|---|---|
| **ich** | *I* | **wir** | *we* |
| **du** | *you* | **ihr** | *you* |
| **er** | *he* | **sie** | *they* |
| **sie** | *she* | **Sie** | *you (polite form)* |
| **es** | *it* | | |

| Other forms | | | | | |
|---|---|---|---|---|---|
| Singular | | | | Plural | |
| **mich** | *me* | **mir** | *to me* | **uns** | *us/to us* |
| **dich** | *you* | **dir** | *to you* | **euch** | *you/to you* |
| **ihn** | *him* | **ihm** | *to him* | **sie** | *them* |
| **sie** | *her* | **ihr** | *to her* | **Sie** | *you* |
| **es** | *it* | **ihm** | *to it* | **ihnen** | *to them* |
| | | | | **Ihnen** | *to you* |

For more information about the different words for you see Unit 4.

## Table of irregular verbs

| Infinitive | He/she | Past (imp.) | Past (perf.) | English |
|---|---|---|---|---|
| *an/rufen | ruft/an | rief/an | habe angerufen | *to ring up* |
| *auf/stehen | steht/auf | stand/auf | bin aufgestanden | *to get up* |
| *-bleiben | bleibt | blieb | bin geblieben | *to stay/remain* |
| essen | isst | aß | habe gegessen | *to eat* |
| *-fahren | fährt | fuhr | bin gefahren | *to go/drive* |
| *-fliegen | fliegt | flog | bin geflogen | *to fly* |
| (*)geben | gibt | gab | habe gegeben | *to give* |
| *gehen | geht | ging | bin gegangen | *to go/walk* |
| haben | hat | hatte | habe gehabt | *to have* |
| *kommen | kommt | kam | bin gekommen | *to come* |
| *laufen | läuft | lief | bin gelaufen | *to run* |
| lesen | liest | las | habe gelesen | *to read* |
| nehmen | nimmt | nahm | habe genommen | *to take* |
| schlafen | schläft | schlief | habe geschlafen | *to sleep* |
| schreiben | schreibt | schrieb | habe geschrieben | *to write* |
| *schwimmen | schwimmt | schwamm | bin geschwommen | *to swim* |
| sehen | sieht | sah | habe gesehen | *to see* |
| sein | ist | war | bin gewesen | *to be* |
| sprechen | spricht | sprach | habe gesprochen | *to speak* |
| tragen | trägt | trug | habe getragen | *to wear/carry* |
| trinken | trinkt | trank | habe getrunken | *to drink* |
| verlieren | verliert | verlor | habe verloren | *to lose* |
| wissen | weiß | wusste | habe gewusst | *to know* |
| ziehen | zieht | zog | habe gezogen | *to pull* |

... and two regular ones

| machen | macht | machte | habe gemacht | *to make* |
|---|---|---|---|---|
| spielen | spielt | spielte | habe gespielt | *to play* |

For more information about verbs see Unit 11, and about separable verbs see Unit 17.

# English–German vocabulary

* this word is sometimes a trigger word

** this word is always a trigger word

Numbers are unit references

*after* **nach\*\*, 7**
*(this) afternoon* **(heute) Nachmittag, 17**
*also* **auch**
*always* **immer**
*(I) am* **(ich) bin, 11**
*and* **und**
*are* **sind, 11**
*between* **zwischen\***

*big* **groß**
*Bill, please* **Zahlen, bitte, 16**

*Can you?* **Kannst du?/Können Sie?**
*cheap* **billig**
*child* **das Kind**
*colour* **die Farbe, 13**

*daughter* **die Tochter**
*day* **der Tag**
*difficult/hard* **schwer/schwierig**
*to do* **machen**

*(this) evening* **(heute) Abend**
*every day* **jeden Tag**
*Excuse me* **Entschuldigen Sie, bitte**

*expensive* **teuer**

*far* **weit**
*fast* **schnell**
*for* **für**
*I am looking forward to it* **Ich freue mich darauf**
*friend* **der Freund/die Freundin**
*in front of* **vor\***

*girl* **das Mädchen**
*to go (on foot)* **gehen;** *to go (travel)* **fahren**
*good* **gut**

*(he) has* **(er) hat, 11**
*to have* **haben, 11**
*(I) have* **(ich) habe;** *Have you ...?* **Haben Sie ...?;** *I haven't a ...* **Ich habe kein/e/en...**
*he* **er**
*her* **ihr/e**
*him* **ihn**
*his* **sein/e**
*(in the) holidays* **(in den) Ferien**
*How?* **Wie?;** *How many?* **Wie viele?**

I *ich*
in *in\*, 17*
is *ist*

to live *wohnen*

May I? *Darf ich?*
me *mich*
to meet *treffen*
Mr *Herr*
Mrs *Frau*
my *mein/e*

near *neben\**
new *neu*
nice *schön*
no *nein*

on *an\*/auf\*, 7, 9, 17*
old *alt*
opposite *gegenüber, 9*

Pardon? *Wie bitte?*
please *bitte*
possible *möglich*

quite *ganz*

it's raining *es regnet*
room *das Zimmer*

she *sie*

short *kurz*
slow *langsam*
small *klein*
sometimes *ab und zu/
   manchmal*
son *der Sohn*
I'm sorry *Es tut mir Leid*

thank you *danke/vielen
   Dank*
their *ihr/e*
there is/there are *es gibt*
they/them *sie/sie*
tired *müde*
to *zu\*\*, 7, 9, 17*
today *heute*
tomorrow *morgen*
too *zu*

until *bis*

I was *ich war*
week *die Woche*
with *mit\*, 9*
without *ohne*
I would like *ich möchte*
to write *schreiben*

yes *ja*
yesterday *gestern*
young *jung*
you, *4*

# German–English vocabulary

* this word is sometimes a trigger word
** this is always a trigger word (der → dem/das → dem/die → der)
Numbers are unit references

Remember:
**der** tells you a word is a masculine word;
**die** tells you a word is a feminine word;
**das** tells you a word is a neuter word.

**der Abend** *evening*
**abends** *in the evening*
**alt** *old*
**am ... (an + dem)** *on the..., 7, 17*
**an\*** *on, 10*
**an/rufen** *to call, phone;* **ich rufe
... an** *I'll ring ..., 9*
**der Anzug** *suit*
**die Anschrift** *address, 5*
**auch** *also*
**auf\*** *on:* **auf der rechten/linken
Seite** *on the right/left side, 9;*
**auf Wiedersehen** *goodbye*
**aus\*\*** *from/out of*
**die Auskunft** *information*
**das Ausland** *abroad*
**die Aussicht** *view*
**der Ausweis** *identity card, 5*
**die Autobahn** *motorway*

**das Bad** *bath*
**der Bahnhof** *station*
**bei\*\*** *at/near, 18*
**der Beruf** *job*
**besetzt** *engaged*
**besuchen** *to visit;* **ich besuche**
*I visit*
**die Bibliothek** *library, 8*
**der Biergarten** *beer garden, 8*
**billig** *cheap*
**ich bin** *I am, 11*
**der Bindestrich** *hyphen, 4*
**bitte** *please;* **Wie bitte?** *Pardon?*
**Bitte schön** *Here you are*
**bleiben** *to stay or remain;* **ich
bleibe** *I stay*
**brauchen** *to need;* **ich brauche**
*I need*
**der Brief** *letter*

**die Briefmarke** postage stamp
**die Brücke** bridge, 8
**der Buchstabe** letter (of the alphabet)
**die Bushaltestelle** bus stop

**der Campingplatz** campsite
**da** there
**Damen** ladies
**Danke/Dankeschön** thank you
**dann** then
**das tut mir Leid** I'm sorry
**der Dom** cathedral, 8
**das Doppelbett** double bed
**das Doppelzimmer** double room, 6
**dort drüben** over there, 8
**die Dose** tin/can, 15
**drücken** to press/push; **ich drücke** I press
**dunkel** dark
**durch** through
**dürfen** to be allowed to; **ich darf** I may
**die Dusche** shower

**die Einladung** invitation, 10
**das Einzelzimmer** single room, 6
**der Empfangstisch** reception desk
**Entschuldigen Sie, bitte** Excuse me, please
**er** he
**erst/e** the first; **am ersten** on the first
**es** it; **Es geht mir gut** I am well
**essen** to eat
**etwas** some

**fahren** to drive; **ich fahre** I drive
**der Fahrstuhl** lift
**die Familie** family
**die Farbe** colour
**die Feiertage** holidays, 10
**das Fenster** window
**der Fernseher** television
**die Flasche** bottle
**der Flughafen** airport, 14
**die Frau** woman/wife/Mrs
**das Fräulein** young lady/Miss
**frei** free
**das Freibad** open-air swimming pool, 8
**Ich freue mich …** I am looking forward …
**das Frühstück** breakfast
**für** for
**zu Fuß** on foot, 9

**ganz** quite
**der Geburtstag** birthday
**gegenüber** opposite, 9
**gehen** to go; **ich gehe** I go; **Geht das?** Is that all right?; **Es geht** It's all right
**genau** exactly
**geradeaus** straight ahead, 9
**gern/e** willingly/with pleasure, 10, 16
**das Geschenk** present
**geschlossen** closed, 19
**gestern** yesterday
**gesund** healthy
**gleich** immediately/straight away
**groß** big
**die Größe** size
**gut** good/well

**haben** *to have, 11:* **Haben Sie…?** *Have you …?*
**halb** *half, 7*
**Haupt-** *main;* **Hauptbahnhof** *main station*
**heiß** *hot*
**heißen** *to be called;* **ich heiße** *I am called*
**der Herr** *man/Mr/husband;* **die Herren** *men*
**heute** *today, 17*
**hier** *here*
**holen** *to fetch;* **ich hole** *I fetch, 11, 17*

**ich** *I*
**immer** *always*
**inbegriffen** *included*
**das Inland** *inland*

**ja** *yes;* **jawohl** *yes indeed*
**die Jugendherberge** *youth hostel*

**kalt** *cold*
**kaputt** *broken*
**kaufen** *to buy;* **ich kaufe** *I buy*
**kein/e** *not a*
**Ich habe kein/e/en …** *I haven't a …*
**der Kellner** *waiter*
**das Kino** *cinema, 8*
**die Kirche** *church, 8*
**klein** *small*
**die Kneipe** *pub, 8*
**kommen** *to come;* **ich komme** *I come*
**Kopfschmerzen** *(pl.) headache, 20*
**krank** *ill, 20*

**das Krankenhaus** *hospital, 8*

**langsam** *slow;* **lamgsamer** *slower*
**laut** *loud/noisy*
**ledig** *unmarried, 5*
**leider** *unfortunately*
**lieber** *rather;* **ich trinke lieber Tee** *I would prefer tea*
**links** *left*

**machen** *to make;* **ich mache** *I make, 11*
**der Mann** *husband*
**die Milch** *milk*
**mit\*\*** *with, 9*
**ich möchte** *I would like, 6*
**morgen** *tomorrow, 17*
**müde** *tired*

**nach\*\*** *after/past, 7*
**nächst/e** *next, 14*
**die Nacht** *night*
**nehmen** *to take;* **ich nehme** *I take, 13*
**nicht** *not*
**noch** *still/yet/more*
**nur** *only*

**oder** *or*
**ohne** *without*
**Ostern** *Easter, 10*

**die Polizei** *police*
**die Postleitzahl** *postcode, 5*
**prima!** *great!, 10*

**die Quittung** *receipt*

**das Rathaus** *town hall, 8*
**rechts** *right*
**die Reise** *journey*
**die Rolltreppe** *escalator*
**rot** *red*

**das Schloss** *castle*
**der Schlüssel** *key*
**schnell** *quick/fast*
**schwimmen** *to swim;* **ich schwimme** *I swim*
**sehen** *to see;* **ich sehe** *I see*
**sehr** *very*
**seit\*\*** *since*
**sie** *she/they;* **Sie** *you, 11*
**sind** *are;* **sein** *to be;* **Sind Sie …?** *Are you …?, 11*
**spielen** *to play;* **ich spiele** *I play*
**sprechen** *to speak,* **ich spreche** *I speak*
**die Straße** *street, 8*
**das Stück** *piece*
**süß** *sweet*

**die Tankstelle** *petrol station, 18*
**die Telefonauskunft** *directory inquiries*
**teuer** *expensive*
**treffen** *to meet;* **Treffen wir uns?** *Shall we meet?, 7*
**trinken** *to drink;* **ich trinke** *I drink*
**trocken** *dry*
**Tschüs/Tschüss** *bye*

**die Uhr** *clock, 7*
**um** *at/around, 7*

**verboten** *forbidden*
**verheiratet** *married*

**verlieren** *to lose;* **verloren** *lost*
**verstehen** *to understand;* **ich verstehe** *I understand*
**viel/e** *many;* **vielen Dank** *many thanks*
**Viertel** *quarter, 7*
**von\*\*** *of/from, 10*
**vor\*** *before/to, 7*
**die Vorwahl** *(telephone) code, 5*

**wählen** *to dial/to choose, 5*
**Wann?** *When?*
**Was?** *What?;* **Was für …?** *What kind of …?*
**der Wecker** *alarm clock, 7*
**weiß** *white*
**ich weiß** *I know*
**Weihnachten** *Christmas*
**weit** *far*
**Welche/r?** *Which?*
**Wer?** *Who?*
**Wie?** *How?;* **Wie bitte?** *Pardon?;* **Wie viele?** *How many?*
**Wiederholen Sie, bitte** *Please repeat*
**Wo?** *Where?*
**die Woche** *week, 10*
**wohnen** *to live;* **ich wohne** *I live*

**zahlen** *to pay;* **Zahlen, bitte!** *Bill please!, 16*
**die Zeit** *time*
**ziemlich** *rather*
**das Zimmer** *room*
**zu\*\*** *to, 9, 17; zu too, 6*
**der Zucker** *sugar*
**zuerst** *at first*
**der Zug** *train;* **mit dem Zug** *by train*
**zwischen** *between, 18*